CLARENDON LIBRARY OF LOGIC AND PHILOSOPHY

General Editor: L. Jonathan Cohen

KNOWLEDGE

KNOWLEDGE

KEITH LEHRER

University of Arizona

CLARENDON PRESS · OXFORD

1974

Oxford University Press, Ely House, London W.1

GLASGOW   NEW YORK   TORONTO   MELBOURNE   WELLINGTON
CAPE TOWN   IBADAN   NAIROBI   DAR ES SALAAM   LUSAKA   ADDIS ABABA
DELHI   BOMBAY   CALCUTTA   MADRAS   KARACHI   LAHORE   DACCA
KUALA LUMPUR   SINGAPORE   HONG KONG   TOKYO

ISBN 0 19 824406 1

© *Oxford University Press 1974*

Printed in Great Britain by
Butler and Tanner Ltd, Frome and London

To
Adrienne

Preface

THIS book contains ten chapters which lead to the articulation and defence of a theory of knowledge and justification. I do not attempt to base knowledge either on a foundation, on fundamental first principles, or even on scientific materialism. Knowledge, on my analysis, is based on belief, something quite subjective. Hence, the final three chapters of the book, in which my account is laid down, may, if read by themselves, appear somewhat extraordinary. I have progressed gradually in the book from doctrines which, though they may well be disputed, are not unfamiliar, to some that are more esoteric. The reader who finds the earlier chapters insufficiently provocative may wish to skip to the later ones for novelty. On the other hand, the reader who begins near the end to see what the author has up his pages, may, if what he reads seems outrageous, care to return to the beginning to learn by what reasoning the author reached his conclusions. I have supplied a table of contents adequate to reveal to epistemologists, and perhaps others of more general interests as well, what they are likely to find therein. Moreover, in the earlier chapters, very little prior background in philosophy is assumed. Though I have attempted to transcend current theories, I have also attempted to provide enough background material to make the contents of the book accessible to students of philosophy and scholars in other fields.

For anything that is of value in this book, I am indebted to my teachers, most of all to R. M. Chisholm with whom I disagree but whose influence is everywhere present. It is his philosophy with which I have argued most and which I frequently undertake to refute. Whether the refutation is successful and whether the doctrine I defend is an opposing theory or a modification of Chisholm's epistemology, I leave it to the reader to decide. The other teacher to whom I am most indebted is W. F. Sellars. In many ways, some of them rather indirect, I have depended on his writings and less formal communication. It is from Gilbert Harman and Edmund Gettier, Jr., that I have otherwise learned the most and to whom I am grateful for enlightening discussions and correspondence. I should also like to mention Risto Hilpinen, Jaakko Hintikka, Isaac Levi, Carl Hempel, and W. V. O. Quine, as philosophers who have shaped the development of my thought and writing. To my most gifted students, especially Marshall Swain, Thomas Paxson, Jr., and James Van Cleve, as well as my colleagues, Henry Kyburg, Jr., Rolf Eberle, John Pollock, and S. Milton Jones, I am deeply indebted for ideas, criticism, and erudition. I am also indebted to Richard Ketchum, Nicholas Smith and Natalie Tarbet for reading, commenting on, and editing parts of the manuscript.

There are others to whom I am indebted. Most of all, perhaps, I am indebted to my wife, who not only put up graciously with five years of anguished composition, but also discussed epistemology with me, applying her well-trained and perceptive mind to a subject that interested her rather little. Terence Ackerman helped me prepare the footnotes. Ruth Spall, Karen DeVisser, and Roslyn Creson assisted me by typing the manuscript. With the exception of the last three, who occasionally introduced some modifications into the manuscript, none of those I mentioned is responsible for what I have said. I doubt that any of them would agree with the conclusions I have reached.

Finally, I should like to express my appreciation to the American Council of Learned Societies, the National Science Foundation, the Center for Advanced Study in the Behavioural Sciences, and the University of Rochester for their financial support of my research.

K. L.

Acknowledgements

THE author expresses his appreciation to the editors and publishers who permitted him to reprint material from the following articles written by the author.

"Belief and Knowledge", from the *Philosophical Review* (1968), 491–9, by permission of the editors.

"Believing that One Knows", from *Synthese*, xxi (1970), 133–40, by permission of D. Reidel Publishing Company, Dordrecht-Holland; Boston, U.S.A.

Contents

What is Knowledge?

ONLY man knows what is true or false, or so he says. Some men have denied that we know what is true or what is false, and they have remained sceptics. Scepticism must have a hearing, but we shall begin our study with the opposite assumption: we assume that men have knowledge. But what is knowledge?

Three Senses of 'Know'

We may begin to answer the preceding question by noticing the ambiguity of the word 'know'. Consider the following sentences:

I know the way to Lugano
I know the expansion of *pi* to six decimal places
I know how to play the guitar
I know the city
I know John
I know about Alphonso and Elicia
I know that the neutrino has a rest mass of 0
I know that what you say is true
I know the sentence number (3) on page 29 is true
I know the sentence 'Some mushrooms are poisonous' is true.

These are but a small sample of different uses of the word 'know'. We can easily see that the meaning of the word differs in some of these sentences. If we are interested in finding out what a man has when he has knowledge, we must first sort out the different senses of the word 'know'. Then we may ask our question again, once it has been disambiguated.

In one sense, 'to know' means to have some special form of competence. Thus, to know the guitar or to know the multiplication tables up to ten is to be competent to play the guitar or to recall certain products of any two numbers not exceeding ten. If a man is said to know *how* to do something, it is this competence sense of 'know' that is usually involved. If I say I know the way to Lugano I mean that I have attained the special kind of competence needed either to get to Lugano or to direct someone there. If I say that I know the expansion of *pi* to six decimal places, I mean that I have the special competence required to recall or to recite the number *pi* expanded to six decimal places.[1]

Another sense of 'know' is that in which the word means to be acquainted with. When I say that I know John, I mean I am acquainted with John. The sentence 'I know the city' is more difficult to disambiguate. It might mean simply that I am acquainted with the city, and hence have the acquaintance sense of 'know', or it might mean that I have the special form of competence needed to find my way around the city, geographically and/or socially. If I say that I know the city, I might mean that I know it in both the competence and acquaintance senses of 'know'. This example illustrates the important fact that the senses of 'know' we are distinguishing are not exclusive; thus, the term 'know' may be used in more than one of these senses in a single utterance.[2]

The third sense of 'know' is that in which 'to know' means to apprehend that something is information. If I know that the neutrino has a rest mass of 0, then I apprehend that something is information, namely, that the neutrino has a rest mass of 0. The last three sentences on the list all involve this *information* sense of the word 'know'. It is often affirmed that to know something in the other senses of 'know' entails knowledge in the information sense of 'know'. I must have some information about Lugano if I know the way to Lugano; about the expansion of *pi* if I know the expansion of *pi* to six decimal places; about the city if I know the city; about the guitar if I know how to play the guitar, and so forth. Thus, the information

---

[1] See John Hartland-Swann, *An Analysis of Knowing* (Allen and Unwin, London, 1958), chapter 4, 'Knowing *How* and Knowing *That*', 56–66; and Gilbert Ryle, 'Knowing How and Knowing That', *Proceedings of the Aristotelian Society*, xlvi, (1945–6), 1–16.

[2] Russell used the expression 'knowledge by acquaintance', but in a somewhat more technical sense. See his 'Knowledge by Acquaintance and Knowledge by Description', *Proc. Aris. Soc.* xi (1910–11), 108–28, and reprinted with some alterations as chapter 5 in *The Problems of Philosophy* (Oxford University Press, London, 1959), 46–59.

sense of the word 'know' is often implicated in the other senses of the word.

In our study, we shall be concerned with knowledge in the information sense. It is precisely this sense that is fundamental to human cognition and required both for theoretical speculation and practical investigation. Some philosophers have denied the existence of such knowledge and also that such knowledge is essential to both theory and practice.[3] We shall consider this viewpoint when we turn to our investigation of scepticism. We may assume, however, that such knowledge has played a fundamental role in both theory and practice even if, with some subtle sceptical strategies, this could be avoided.

Analysis and Meaning

The foregoing discussion was designed to isolate that sense of the word 'know' used to characterize the kind of knowledge that is to be the subject of our study. However, to indicate the information sense of the word 'know' as being the one in question, and to say what that sense is, is quite different from giving an analysis of the kind of knowledge we have picked out. To isolate a sense of a word and to communicate that sense to others, it is only necessary to select some other words having roughly the same meaning as the word in question which will serve to distinguish and communicate that sense of the word. If I tell a person that 'muzhik' means 'Russian peasant', I can communicate the same information by saying that 'muzhik' means the same as 'Russian peasant'. Here we supply a synonym, or an approximately synonymous term, to say what a term means, but to do this is not to analyse anything.

Many philosophers have identified the task of analysing what a word means with that of analysing what it denotes.[4] Thus, for example, some philosophers have supposed that to analyse the meaning of the word 'good' would be to analyse the

---

[3] For recent defences of such scepticism see Keith Lehrer, 'Why Not Scepticism?' *Philosophical Forum*, ii (1971), 283–98, and Peter Unger, 'A Defense of Scepticism', *Philosophical Review*, lxxx (1971), 198–219. For a history of scepticism, see Richard Popkin's *A History of Scepticism from Erasmus to Descartes* (Van Gorcum, Assen, Netherlands, 1960).

[4] The most illustrious is G. E. Moore in *Principia Ethica* (Cambridge University Press, London, 1903). See chapter 1, sections 6–8.

kind of goodness denoted by the term used in that sense. Much of this is confusing, and much of the confusion is generated by the term 'analysis' itself.

On Analysis

The first matter to be clarified concerns the question of what constitutes an analysis of something. An analysis is always relative to some objective. It does not make any sense simply to demand the analysis of goodness, knowledge, beauty, or truth, without some indication of what purpose such an analysis is supposed to achieve. To demand the analysis of knowledge without specifying further what you hope to accomplish with it is like demanding blueprints without saying what you hope to build. Thus, before asking for an analysis of either knowledge or of the meaning of the word 'know', one must be able to explain what goals one hopes to achieve with such an analysis, or else one cannot sensibly expect an answer.

Usually, the objectives that guide an analysis are not made explicit in philosophy, and this is most unfortunate. Much of the dialogues between Socrates and his students reveals very clearly that those who replied did not understand what Socrates was after when he asked such questions as, 'What is justice?' Only when Socrates stopped to explain what sort of answer he was seeking did he obtain the sort of answers that were relevant. There is no better lesson in the importance of clearly formulating one's objectives before asking 'What is . . . ?', than the misunderstanding that occurs in some of the dialogues of Socrates.

With these remarks in mind, let us consider the distinction between analysing the meaning of the term 'know' in the information sense of that term and analysing the kind of knowledge denoted. A man who is seeking an analysis of the meaning of that term may have some theory of meaning in which part of a complete theory would involve a theoretical explication of the meaning of that term. For example, one might have a theory of meaning designed to assign semantic interpretations to strings of words in order to explain how a speaker communicates with a listener, how a listener understands what is uttered by a speaker, and how a speaker understands his own words. An analysis of the meaning intended to fulfil the objectives of such a theory belongs to a theory of semantics.[5]

Semantics and Philosophical Analysis

Many philosophers have been interested in the task of analysing the meaning of the word 'know' and some have argued that such a project should supplant the job of analysing knowledge.[6] Indeed, many would argue that there is no need for philosophical analysis remaining once we have a satisfactory analysis of the meaning of the term 'know'. This restrictive conception of philosophical analysis is sustained by a dilemma. Either a theory of knowledge is a theory about the meaning of the word 'know' and semantically related epistemic terms, or it is a theory about how people come to know what they do. The latter is not part of philosophy at all, but rather that part of pyschology called learning theory. It follows that if a theory of knowledge is part of philosophy, then it is theory of knowledge about the meaning of the word 'know'. That is the argument, and it is one that would reduce the theory of knowledge to a theory of semantics.

It is not difficult to slip between the horns of the dilemma. A theory of knowledge need not be a theory about the meaning of epistemic words any more than it need be a theory about how people come to know what they do. Instead, it may be one explaining what conditions must be satisfied and how they may be satisfied in order for a person to know something. When we specify those conditions and explain how they are satisfied, then we shall have a theory of knowledge. An analogy should be helpful at this point. Suppose a man says that there are only two kinds of theories about physical mass. Either a theory of

---

[5] Recent treatises of importance on semantics include L. Jonathan Cohen's *The Diversity of Meaning* (Methuen, London, 1962), Robert Fogelin's *Evidence and Meaning* (Routledge and Kegan Paul, London, 1967), Jerrold Katz's *Semantic Theory* (Harper and Row, New York, 1972), and Paul Ziff's *Semantic Analysis* (Cornell University Press, Ithaca, N. Y., 1960). For an anthology see *Theory of Meaning*, ed. Adrienne and Keith Lehrer (Prentice Hall, Englewood Cliffs, N.J., 1970).

[6] For example, see A. J. Ayer's *The Foundation of Empirical Knowledge* (St Martin's Press, New York, 1955) and *The Problem of Knowledge* (Penguin, Harmondsworth, Middlesex, 1957).

matter is a theory about the meaning of 'mass' and semantically related physical terms, or it is a theory about how something comes to have mass. This dichotomy would be rejected on the grounds that it leaves out the critical question of what mass is, or to put it another way, it leaves out the question of what conditions must be satisfied for something to have a given mass.

A theoretician in physics might be concerned with precisely the question of what conditions are necessary and sufficient for an object to have mass, or more precisely, to have a mass of n, where 'n' is a variable that would be replaced by a number. Similarly, a philosopher might be concerned with precisely the question of what conditions are necessary and sufficient for a man to have knowledge, or, more precisely, to know that p or that S is true, where 'p' is a variable that would be replaced by a declarative sentence and 'S' by the name of a sentence.

Again, philosophers who are the followers of Wittgenstein have objected to the attempt to formulate such conditions on the grounds that the meaning of 'know' and other such terms have certain semantic peculiarities ensuring that no set of conditions is necessary and sufficient for the application of the term.[7] The cases to which the term applies, according to such philosophers, have only a family resemblance to each other, and that is why it is impossible to give an analysis of the desired kind. This argument is defective, however. First, it is extremely difficult to see how, from the fact that the objects to which a term applies have only a family resemblance to each other, it could be thought to follow that there are no necessary and sufficient conditions for the application of the term. Obviously, a necessary and sufficient condition for the application of the expression 'S knows that p' is precisely the condition of S knowing that p. This could be made less trivial with little difficulty. The objection conceals the confused idea that a set of conditions necessary and sufficient for the application of a term constitutes a kind of recipe for applying terms which would enable us to decide quite mechanically whether the term applies in each instance. However, we may, without taking any position on the question of whether such a recipe can be found for applying the term 'know', state flatly that this is not the purpose of our theory of knowledge or the analysis of knowledge incorporated therein. Our interests lie elsewhere.

The Form and Objectives of an Analysis of Knowledge

We shall then approach the question 'What is Knowledge?' with the objectives of formulating necessary and sufficient conditions for a man having knowledge (in the information sense of the term 'know') and of explaining how those conditions may be satisfied. Our project is contiguous with scientific investigations having analogous objectives. Thus, we contend that the distinction between philosophy and theoretical science is a bogus distinction whether viewed historically or systematically.[8] Historically, it is clear that the special sciences break off from philosophy when some theory emerges that deals with a circumscribed subject in a precise and satisfactory manner. Philosophy remains the residual pot of unsolved intellectual problems. To date, theories of knowledge have remained in the pot. It is not claimed that the current study or other recent research has brought us to the point where the theory of knowledge should be poured out into a special science, but it may be hoped that we are approaching closer to that goal than some suspect and others fear.

A formulation of an analysis of knowledge may be expressed by an equivalence. Again, the analogy with mass is helpful. An analysis of mass may be given in an equivalence of the following form:

O has a mass of n if and only if . . .

where the blank to the right of the equivalence is filled with a sentence describing a set of necessary and sufficient conditions. Similarly, an analysis of knowledge may be given in an equivalence of one of the following two forms:

S knows that p if and only if . . .

or

S knows that Q is true if and only if . . .

[8] The attack on this distinction is, most recently and impressively, due to W. V. O. Quine's discussion in his article, 'Two Dogmas of Empiricism', *Philosophical Review*, lx (1951), 20–43. The theme is further developed in Quine's later works, e.g. in 'Epistemology Naturalized' in *Ontological Relativity and Other Essays* (Columbia University Press, New York, 1969).

where the blank to the right of the equivalence is filled with a sentence describing a set of necessary and sufficient conditions. When considering candidates for such sets of conditions, two qualifications are critical. First, there must be no experiment, of fact or thought, which would falsify the resulting equivalence. To say that there is no experiment of thought to falsify the equivalence means there is no example one can think of that is a logical possibility and is consistent with other postulates of the theory under consideration which would yield the result that one side of the equivalence is satisfied and the other is not. In short, there must be no counterexample.

In our investigation we shall begin without making any assumptions concerning the postulates of our theory of knowledge and thus consider any logically possible case as a potential counterexample. This procedure could have the result of making our analysis more restrictive than it needs to be because certain cases that are logically possible might be ruled out by postulates that are formulated subsequently in the development of our theory of knowledge. In our exposition we shall omit the consideration of examples which could be ruled out by principles to be introduced subsequently.

In addition to being immune from counterexamples, such an equivalence will only be a suitable analysis if it facilitates reaching our epistemic objectives. Thus, though some analyses are definitely mistaken because we can find acceptable counterexamples, there are other equivalences which fail to constitute satisfactory analyses because they are unenlightening. The equivalence we would obtain, by writing the same thing in the blank space to the right that is already written to the left of the 'if and only if', though immune from counterexamples, would completely fail to explain or inform. We are beginning with the analysis of knowledge rather than with a discussion of how the conditions of knowledge are satisfied. The explanatory role of our analysis will be illustrated throughout the remainder of our study.

Some initial clarification of the projected role of such an analysis may, however, provide at least basic guidance. We shall be concerned with an analysis that will be useful for explaining how knowledge claims may be justified. Thus, if a man claims to know that p, he may be asked either how he knows or why he thinks that *p*. For example, if I claim to know that all the Perch in the Genesee River will be killed by a pollutant that raises the temperature of the water two degrees, someone might ask me how I know that or why I think it is true. Such questions and the answers provided are the basis for critical discussion and confrontation in cognitive inquiry. The replies to such queries show us whether or not the conditions for knowledge have been satisfied. Consequently, an analysis of knowledge intended to facilitate explanation of how the conditions of knowledge are satisfied will be most fruitful if the conditions contained in the analysis enable us to explicate the way in which knowledge claims may be justified.

The Analysis of Knowledge

With these preliminary remarks to guide us, we shall now offer an analysis of knowledge. Each condition proposed will be the subject of a subsequent chapter. Moreover, in the case of some controversial conditions, we shall not undertake a detailed defence in the present chapter. Our intention here is only to provide the analysis with some intuitive justification which will subsequently be developed and defended.

A Truth Condition

The first condition of knowledge is that of truth. When a man is asked to justify his claim to knowledge, he must explain why he thinks what he says is true. Thus, if I claim to know that the next man to be elected President of the United States will have assets of at least one-half of a million dollars, and I am asked to justify that claim, I must offer my reasons for thinking that this claim is true. Moreover, if my claim is false, that is, if the next man to be elected President of the United States does, in fact, have assets of less than half of a million dollars, then my knowledge claim was incorrect. I did not know what I said I did. Thus, we shall accept the following conditionals:

(iT) If S knows that p, then it is true that p

and

(iiT) If S knows that the sentence Q is true, then Q is true.

It is essential to clarify these two conditionals each of which expresses a necessary condition of knowledge. Both say that if a man knows something then it is true, but what a man is said to know in the conditional is different in each case.

Consider the difference between my saying that I know that Andorra is a small nation in the Pyrenees, and my saying that I know that the sentence 'Andorra is a small nation in the Pyrenees' is true. At first these two sentences might seem to be the same, but it is well to note some simple differences. First, when I say that I know that Andorra is in the Pyrenees, though I utter the words 'Andorra is in the Pyrenees', I need not have uttered those words, or any English words, to say that I know that Andorra is in the Pyrenees. I might have made the same claim in French or some other language. The crucial fact is that, though I utter the sentence 'Andorra is in the Pyrenees' in claiming to know that Andorra is in the Pyrenees, I say nothing whatever about that sentence. I do not even say that the sentence exists. I merely use the sentence to say that I know that Andorra is in the Pyrenees. Thus, it is consistent with what I claim that there should be no such sentence at all, though, in fact, my speech shows that there obviously is such a sentence. In sentences having the form of the antecedent of (iT), nothing is said about any sentence. It is not claimed that any sentence is true or even that any exists.

The most perplexing feature of the foregoing remarks is the contention that if I say I know that Andorra is in the Pyrenees, I have not said any sentence is true. It might be objected that according to (iT) I have said that it is true that Andorra is in the Pyrenees. Though I have used the sentence 'Andorra is in the Pyrenees' to say that it is true that Andorra is in the Pyrenees, I have said nothing about that sentence. An analogy involving names is helpful in this instance. If I use a man's name to say something about a man, for example, if I say that Alphonso is a homosexual, I have not said anything about the name 'Alphonso'. I have, instead, used that name to say something about the person. On the other hand, when I say that I know that the sentence 'Andorra is in the Pyrenees' is true, I have obviously said something about that sentence, for example, that there is such a sentence and that the sentence is true. Thus, when we consider the consequent of (iiT), we see that when I say I know that the sentence 'Andorra is in the Pyrenees' is true, a necessary condition of my knowing what I say I know is the truth of the sentence 'Andorra is in the Pyrenees'. In this case, then, unlike the first, I have said that a sentence is true. This contrasts with the first case where I do not say that any sentence is true but rather use a sentence to state what is true.

These distinctions, which will be elaborated further in the next chapter, have led philosophers to distinguish between what they call the *absolute conception of truth* embedded in a sentence of the form

It is true that the snow is white

and the *semantic conception of truth* embedded in sentences of the form

The sentence 'the snow is white' is true.[9]

The first is called the absolute conception because there is no reference to a language, or to any part of language, and, thus, this conception of truth is not in any way relative to a language or to the meaning of any terms in a language. As Arthur Pap has stressed, it is true that the snow is white even if there is no language anywhere to describe that fact.[10] The colour of the snow and the snow itself are what they are quite independently of any description anyone might care to give of the snow and its colour. On the other hand, the semantic conception is so called because the truth of a sentence depends not only upon the facts but upon what the sentence means, upon the semantics of the sentence. Whether the sentence 'Snow is white' is true depends not only upon the snow and its colour but upon the meaning of the sentence and the words contained therein. Though much more sophisticated semantic interpretations of the sentence might be offered, the truth of the sentence depends most simply on the sentence meaning that snow is white.

[9] See Alfred Tarski's 'The Semantic Conception of Truth' in *Readings in Philosophical Analysis*, ed. Herbert Feigl and Wilfrid Sellars (Appleton-Century-Crofts, New York, 1949).

[10] See Arthur Pap's article, 'Note on the "Semantic" and the "Absolute" Concept of Truth', in *New Readings in Philosophical Analysis*, ed. Herbert Feigl, Wilfrid Sellars, and Keith Lehrer (Appleton-Century-Crofts, New York, 1972), 208–14. Hereafter, this anthology is referred to simply as *New Readings*.

One final point may be anticipated before proceeding to consideration of the second condition of knowledge. We shall in the next chapter argue that the condition (iiT) may be reduced to a condition that is equivalent to (iT). Hence, we shall in the remaining discussion concern ourselves only with the problem of formulating conditions of S knowing that p. Thus, we shall drop the semantic conception of truth from our discussion at this point and justify this deletion later.

A Belief Condition

The second condition of knowledge is belief. If I deceitfully claim to know that Jan married Jay on 31 December, 1969, when I do not believe it, then I do not know Jan married Jay on that date even if, contrary to what I believe, they were married then. Indeed, it matters little what other conditions are satisfied. If I do not believe that p, then I do not know that p. Thus, the following conditional expresses a condition of knowledge:

(iB) If S knows that p, then S believes that p.

There are problems concerning the implications of this condition, because the term 'believe', like 'know', has more than one sense. The fundamental ambiguity of the term which affects our analysis concerns the strength of conviction implied by saying that a person believes something. Some philosophers have insisted that a man may know something is true even though he lacks conviction of its truth, while others, in diametric opposition, have contended that a man only knows something is true when he is sure, or certain, of the truth of what he believes. Thus, certain philosophers have denied condition (iB) on the grounds that a man may know something to be true that he does not believe at all,[11] and others have maintained that for a man to know something to be true he must believe it to be true with considerable certainty.[12]

Our position is that conviction is required: a man must be

---

[11] Colin Radford, 'Knowledge—By Examples', *Analysis*, xxvii (1966), 1–11.
[12] See G. E. Moore's *Philosophical Papers* (Allen and Unwin, London, 1959), 'Certainty', 226–51; and A. J. Ayer's *The Problem of Knowledge*, chapter 1, section (iii), pp. 14–26.

convinced if he knows something to be true. On the other hand, we see no reason to require that the conviction approach certainty. So long as the man believes that p is true in the sense of being genuinely convinced of the truth of p, he may be said to know that p, provided the other conditions of knowledge are met. This question will be examined in more detail in a later chapter where the opposing arguments will be examined.

A Justification Condition

The third condition affirms the need for justification, and thus requires explication of the manner in which our claims to knowledge are justified. Moreover, while we allowed that a man need not be completely certain of p in order to know that p, we shall insist that a man must be completely justified in his belief that p in order to be said to know that p. Our condition may be formulated as follows:

> (iJ) If S knows that p, then S is completely justified
> in believing that p.[13]

The locution 'S is completely justified in believing that p' will be used in a somewhat technical way, and so we offer some clarification of what is meant.

In colloquial usage, a speaker may say that another is completely justified in believing that p because the speaker has strong evidence that p. There may be no implication that the other has such evidence. For example, if someone says 'Alexander believes his wife is unfaithful', and I reply 'He is completely justified', I may be implying only that I have evidence of her infidelity, never mind how I acquired it, without any implication that Alexander has such evidence. Thus, I could expand the previous utterance and say instead, 'He is completely justified as it happens, but really has no evidence of her infidelity —she is too clever.' This use of the expression 'completely justified' is not acceptable in (iJ). When we say that S is completely justified, we shall mean that if his belief is based on

---

[13] Ayer in *The Problem of Knowledge*, 31–5, formulates the condition as the right to be sure. Chisholm formulates it as having adequate evidence in *Perceiving: A Philosophical Study* (Cornell University Press, Ithaca, N.Y., 1957), 5 and 17, and as something being evident for a man in *Theory of Knowledge* (Prentice Hall, Englewood Cliffs, N.J., 1966), 18–23.

evidence, then he is completely justified by the evidence he has in believing that *p*. Thus, that I am completely justified in believing that *p*, by the evidence I have, does not by itself warrant my saying another is completely justified in his belief that *p*. He too must have evidence which completely justifies his belief before he is, in the required sense, completely justified in believing that *p*.

The moral of the preceding remarks is that our answer to the question of when a belief is completely justified will not be enslaved to ordinary thought and speech. For the sake of theoretical advantage, we shall delete unwanted implications and allow expedient expansion within the theory of justification we articulate below.

Justification and Basic Beliefs

There are, however, two possible ways in which a man may be completely justified in believing something. First, he may be completely justified in believing that *p* because he has some evidence which completely justifies him in believing that *p*. This is perhaps the most familiar way in which a man may be completely justified in his belief. The concept of being justified by the evidence requires further elaboration, but, before turning to this matter, we must notice one other possibility. Some philosophers, Thomas Reid for example, have maintained that a man may be completely justified in believing something without need of evidence or other justificatory support for the belief.[14]

The beliefs alleged to be so justified are of a special kind, for example, fundamental beliefs of common sense concerning memory or perception. They are considered to be the *basic* beliefs constituting the evidence in terms of which all other beliefs are justified. It is, however, altogether controversial whether there are or need to be any basic beliefs. On the whole, empiricist philosophers affirm the existence of some such beliefs by maintaining all justification would be impossible without them. They aver that unless there are some basic beliefs to

[14] Thomas Reid, *Essays on the Intellectual Powers of the Mind*, from *The Philosophical Works of Thomas Reid*, ed. Sir William Hamilton (James Thin, London, 1895), particularly Essay VI, 'Of Judgment', sections 4–6.

which we may appeal in justification, we shall lack a necessary starting-point for justification. In the absence of basic beliefs the whole edifice of justification would collapse for want of a foundation.

Other philosophers, who defend coherence theories of justification, have argued that there need not be any basic beliefs, that all beliefs may be justified by their relation to others, and that there is nothing untoward in such mutual support.[15] Justification is like a house of cards: the edifice of justification stands because of the way in which the parts fit and support each other. We shall not attempt to adjudicate between such theories at this point, for it is a matter that will require extensive examination, but it is important to leave open the possibility of basic beliefs.

Some philosophers hold basic beliefs to be essential to an analysis of knowledge containing condition (iJ).[16] Their reasoning is that unless there are such basic beliefs, condition (iJ) will lead either to a circularity or to a regress. If non-basic beliefs are completely justified by evidence, then, it is argued, they must be justified by some knowledge; and nothing counts as evidence unless it is known to be true. Hence, if we agree that a condition of a man knowing that p is his being completely justified by his evidence, then we are requiring that he be completely justified by something that he knows. If his evidence for p is q, then he must know that q. It follows that, in the absence of basic beliefs completely justified without evidence, we should, in the attempt to justify a claim to knowledge, always appeal to other knowledge claims which in turn must be justified by appeal to still others, and so forth. This means that such justification must either never end and hence lead to a pernicious regress, or it must run in a circle and hence force us to assume the very claim we seek to justify.

Such arguments are more directly concerned with theories

---

[15] Gilbert Harman defends such a theory. See his article, 'Knowledge, Inference, and Explanation' in *New Readings*, 357–68.

[16] Most recently, Anthony Quinton holds this position in his book, *The Nature of Things* (Routledge and Kegan Paul, Boston, 1973), 119. See also Arthur C. Danto's *An Analytical Theory of Knowledge* (Cambridge University Press, London, 1968), 27–8, and C. I. Lewis's *An Analysis of Knowledge and Valuation* (Open Court, LaSalle, Ill., 1946), 186. However, philosophers too numerous to cite have held this position which was clearly formulated both by Plato and Aristotle.

of justification than with the analysis of knowledge, and we shall reconsider them when we discuss those theories. Nevertheless, it is important to refute the foregoing argument in order to show that condition (iJ) does not commit us to the doctrine of basic beliefs. Let us undertake the refutation. First, justification need not proceed until all claims to knowledge employed in the justification are themselves justified. If we consider justification in a social context, the justification of knowledge claims need proceed only as long as some claim to knowledge is disputed. Thus, if we suppose that justification is a response to a query or demand, then there is no reason to suppose that the argument need proceed beyond the point at which agreement is reached. Hence, even if all completely justified beliefs are justified by evidence, not all claims to knowledge, employed to defend some other such claims, need themselves be justified. They only need to be justified when they engender disputation.

There is yet a more decisive refutation than the preceding. It undermines the attempt to produce a regress or circularity by repudiating the initial assumption of the argument, to wit, that for something to be evidence it must be known to be true. Why need we know that p is true before we may appeal to it as evidence? In practice we surely appeal to anything as evidence that we are completely justified in believing, and such appeals are deemed legitimate. Let us only require a man to be completely justified in believing that q before he may justify his belief that p by appeal to the evidence that q. Then any semblance of circularity in the analysis of knowledge vanishes. Moreover, any attempt to obtain a regress of justification could be met by arguing that some beliefs are completely justified because of the way they cohere with a system of beliefs rather than by appeal to evidence or other forms of argumentation.

It follows, then, that if we agree that it is logically consistent with condition (iJ) to deny the existence of basic beliefs, just as it is logically consistent with it to affirm the existence of basic beliefs, we may conclude that an analysis of knowledge containing condition (iJ) neither precludes nor entails the existence of such beliefs. Thus, we leave the problem of basic beliefs to be resolved by a theory of justification. Such theories are of fundamental importance; indeed, they are of greater importance than the analysis of knowledge itself. These theories explain what completely justifies a belief and hence when we are justified in claiming to know. It is, therefore, entirely appropriate that our analysis of knowledge should leave the question of basic beliefs to be answered by a theory of justification.

We shall argue that complete justification is a matter of coherence within a system of beliefs. Most philosophers have thought that knowledge claims, when completely justified, were justified on the basis of some objective method of assessing such claims. Some thought the test was that of experience, others of reason, and there have been mixed methodologies as well. All have assumed that beliefs must be checked in some objective manner. They have repudiated with epistemic horror the idea that belief itself could be the last court of evidence. That a man believes something is considered far too subjective a datum to serve as a solid basis for justification. Even those philosophers who argue that some beliefs are self-justified sought some principle by means of which we can determine which beliefs are self-justified and which not. They too have held that we must somehow transcend the subjectivity of belief in order to demarcate the area of justified belief. This conception has become so ingrained philosophically as to impose itself on common sense. However, the assumption that there is some objective method, for distinguishing the honest coin of justified belief from the counterfeit of the unwarranted, shall not go unexamined. We shall study in some detail those theories that rest on this assumption, but, to warn the reader fairly, in advance, no such theory shall prevail once we have exhibited our mint for epistemic approval.

The theory of justification we shall ultimately defend may strike some as closely aligned with scepticism. We shall examine this charge, but even here it should be noted that our sympathies with the writings of the philosophical sceptics of the past are strong. Too often contemporary writers seek the most effective method for liquidating the sceptic without asking whether his teaching may not be of more importance than his mode of burial. Since the most brilliant philosophers of past and present have been sceptics of one form or another, it would behove those who study scepticism to consider whether these sceptics have some truth in their grasp. We claim they do. There is no exit from the circle of ones own beliefs from which one can sally forth to find some exquisite tool to measure the merits of what lies within the circle of subjectivity. Nor is there such a tool, as we shall show. But subjectivity when directed toward truth and away from error can provide the basis of demonstrably reasonable justification.

A Counterexample

Some philosophers have suggested that the conditions which are individually necessary for knowledge as formulated in (iT), (iB), and (iJ) are jointly sufficient for knowledge as well.[17] This would amount to affirming the following equivalence as an analysis of knowledge:

> S knows that p if and only if it is true that p, S believes that p, and S is completely justified in believing that p.

In short, knowledge is completely justified true belief. Nevertheless, this analysis has been disputed by Gettier and requires amendment.[18]

Gettier argues that a man might be completely justified in believing that F by his evidence, where F is some false statement, and deduce T from F, where T is some true statement. Having deduced T from F, which he was completely justified in believing, the man would then be completely justified in believing that T. Assuming that he believes that T, it would follow from the analysis considered that the man knows that T. He might, however, not know this at all, especially if T is a disjunction of two statements, the statement F and a true statement Q, and the man in question has no reason whatever for thinking that Q is true. In such a case, the belief that T will be true, but the only reason the man has for believing T to be true is the inference of T from F. Since F is false, it is a matter of luck that the man is correct in his belief that T.[19]

An example should help to illustrate the point. Suppose a teacher wonders whether any member of his class owns a Ferrari and, moreover, suppose that he has very strong evidence

[17] Ayer and Chisholm defend similar analyses in works cited above.
[18] Edmund Gettier, Jr., 'Is Justified True Belief Knowledge?', *Analysis*, xxiii (1963), 121–3. Bertrand Russell made a similar observation in *The Problems of Philosophy*, 132.
[19] Gettier, op. cit.

that one student, a Mr. Nogot, owns a Ferrari. Mr. Nogot says he does, drives one, has papers stating he does, and so forth. The teacher has no other evidence that anyone else in his class owns a Ferrari. From the premiss that Mr. Nogot owns a Ferrari, he draws the conclusion that at least one person in his class owns a Ferrari. The man might thus be as completely justified in believing this conclusion as he was in believing Mr. Nogot owns a Ferrari. Now imagine that, in fact, Mr. Nogot, evidence to the contrary notwithstanding, simply does not own the Ferrari. He was out to deceive his teacher and friends to improve his social status. However, another student in the class, a Mr. Havit, does own a Ferrari, though the teacher has no evidence or inkling of this. In that case, the teacher would be quite correct in his belief that at least one person in his class owns a Ferrari, only it would not be Mr. Nogot who he thinks owns one, but Mr. Havit instead. In this case, the teacher would have a completely justified true belief when he believes that at least one person in his class owns a Ferrari, but he could not be said to know that this is true because it is more due to good fortune than good justification that he is correct.[20]

Two philosophers, Irving Thalberg and Charles Pailthorp, have attempted to show that such examples as this are not counterexamples to the analysis of knowledge in question by arguing that a belief cannot be completely justified by being deduced from a false statement.[21] This line of argument fails for a number of reasons. First, the teacher in our example might infer that at least one person in his class owns a Ferrari directly from true statements about Mr. Nogot concerning the car he drives, and so forth, without accepting the false statement that Mr. Nogot owns a Ferrari. If the teacher is a clever man and is only interested in the question of whether there is at least one Ferrari owner among his students, he might reason that,

[20] This example and related ones are taken from Keith Lehrer, 'Knowledge, Truth, and Evidence', *Analysis*, xxv (1965), 168–75. This article and others on the same topic are included in *Knowing*, ed. Michael Roth and Leon Galis (Random House, New York, 1970).

[21] See the article by Charles Pailthorp, 'Knowledge as Justified True Belief', *Review of Metaphysics*, xxiii (1969), 25–47, and the reply by Keith Lehrer, 'The Fourth Condition of Knowledge: A Defense', ibid. xxiv (1970), 122–8. Also see Irving Thalberg's 'In Defense of Justified True Belief', *Journal of Philosophy*, xvi (1969), 794–803, and David Coder's reply in the same journal, lxvii (1970), 424–5.

though his only evidence of a Ferrari owner among his students is what he knows about Mr. Nogot and a certain car, there is at least the possibility that someone else owns one, and, hence, it is safer to accept the more general statement that at least one person in his class owns a Ferrari than the quite specific claim that Mr. Nogot owns one. Hence, without concluding that Mr. Nogot owns a Ferrari, the teacher in question concludes that at least one person in his class owns a Ferrari. This conclusion is derived from a set of perfectly true statements about Mr. Nogot and the consideration that someone else in class may, for all he knows, own a Ferrari. But even this clever reasoner does not know that there is a single Ferrari owner among his students. Thus, the counterexamples to the analysis do not essentially depend upon inference from a false statement.

There is, however, a second reason for rejecting the idea that such counterexamples may be met by arguing that inference from a false statement can never yield complete justification. Similar examples may be found that do not seem to involve any inference. An example taken from R. M. Chisolm illustrates this. Suppose a man looks into a field and spots what he takes to be sheep.[22] The object is not too distant and the man is one who knows a sheep when he sees one. In such a case it would be natural to regard the man as being completely justified in believing he sees a sheep in the field without any reasoning at all. Now imagine that the object he takes to be a sheep is not a sheep but a dog. Thus, he does not know that he sees a sheep. Imagine, however, that an object further in the distance which he also sees, but does not think is a sheep, happens in fact to be a sheep. So it is true that the man sees a sheep, and, moreover, he believes and is completely justified in believing that he sees a sheep. Of course, he still does not know that he sees a sheep because what he takes to be a sheep is not, and the sheep that he sees he does not take to be a sheep.

A Fourth Condition: Justification without Falsity

In two of the cases we have described, a man has completely justified true belief but lacks knowledge and does not infer what he thus believes from any false statement. There is some merit,

[22] R. M. Chisholm, *Theory of Knowledge*, 23, footnote 22.

however, in the idea that the falsity of some statement accounts for the lack of knowledge. Somehow it is the falsity of the two statements that Mr. Nogot owns a Ferrari and that what the man takes for a sheep is one which accounts for the problem. We may say that in the first case the justification that the teacher has for his belief that at least one person in his class owns a Ferrari depends on the false statement that Mr. Nogot owns a Ferrari even though that statement is not a premiss in any inference the man actually makes. We shall explore the kind of dependence involved subsequently, but here we may notice that the clever teacher would be unable to justify completely his belief that there is a Ferrari owner among his students were he to concede the falsity of the statement that Mr. Nogot owns a Ferrari. Similar remarks apply in the case of the sheep.

To render our analysis impervious to such counterexamples, we must add the condition that the complete justification that a man has for what he believes must not *depend* on any false statement—whether or not it is a premiss in inference. We may thus add the following condition to our analysis:

> (iD) If S knows that p, then S is completely justified in believing that p in some way that does not depend on any false statement.[23]

A Final Analysis of Knowledge

The preceding condition enables us to complete our analysis of knowledge. We shall adopt the following as an analysis of knowledge:

> (AK) S knows that p if and only if (i) it is true that p, (ii) S believes that p, (iii) S is completely justified in believing that p, and (iv) S is completely justified in believing that p in some way that does not depend on any false statement.

It is apparent that on one very natural interpretation of these conditions they are logically interdependent. Thus, for example,

[23] This proposal is similar to one made in the articles by Keith Lehrer cited above, and by others as well in the series of articles elicited by the Gettier article. See especially Gilbert Harman, 'The Inference to the Best Explanation', *Philosophical Review*, lxxiv (1965), 88–95.

it is natural to interpret condition (iii) in such a way as logically to entail condition (ii), that is, if a man is completely justified in believing that *p*, then this entails that he believes that *p*. Similarly, one might interpret (iv) in such a way as to entail (iii), that is, if a man is completely justified in believing that *p* in some way that does not entail any false statement, then this entails that he is completely justified in believing that *p*. Given these entailments, the analysis would be subject to reduction by the elimination of conditions (ii) and (iii), because condition (iv) would entail those two conditions. We would thereby reduce the analysis to conditions (i) and (iv).

The reduction of the analysis to conditions (i) and (iv) would simplify the analysis in terms of the number of conditions contained therein, but it would leave us with a very complicated condition (iv) having various logical consequences each of which would require separate treatment in an adequate theory of knowledge. Thus it will be useful to replace conditions (ii), (iii), and (iv) with logically independent conditions. We can do this quite easily. All that is required is that we make use of the logicians notion of a material implication. Logicians say that *p* materially implies *q* if and only if it is not the case that *p* is true and *q* is false. It is clear that this is a much weaker condition than entailment, for *p* entails *q* if and only if it is logically impossible that *p* is true and *q* is false.

We can make conditions (iii) logically independent of (ii) by turning it into a material conditional. Instead of (iii), we would have (iii') as follows:

> (iii') If *S* believes that *p*, then *S* is completely justified in believing that *p*.

It is clear that (iii') does not logically entail condition (ii), that is, *S* believes that *p*, because (iii') is logically consistent with the denial (ii), that is, it is not the case that *S* believes that *p*. To make it clear that (iii') does not require that '*S* believes that *p*' entails '*S* is completely justified in believing that *p*', we may rewrite (iii') making the material implication explicit as follows:

> (iii') If *S* believes that *p*, then this materially implies that *S* is completely justified in believing that *p*.

We may then reformulate (iv) so that it entails neither (ii) nor (iii) in a similar way as follows:

(iv′) If S believes that p and S is completely justified in believing that p, then this materially implies that S is completely justified in believing that p in some way that does not depend on any false statement.

If we then substitute (iii′) for (iii) and (iv′) for (iv) in the analysis of knowledge (AK), the fourth condition will clearly not entail either the second or third, and the third condition will clearly not entail the second. Thus, the earlier mentioned logical interdependencies will be eliminated. It is such an analysis of knowledge that we shall assume. Our next task is to examine each of these conditions of knowledge in order to formulate a theory of knowledge explaining how and why claims to knowledge are justified.

2

Truth and Knowledge

PERHAPS the greatest agreement among philosophers has concerned the relation of knowledge and truth. As we noted in the first chapter, the kind of knowledge we are concerned with is knowledge that something is true. It is natural to conclude that if a person knows something is true, then it must be true. Thus, if I know that the atom has been split, then it must be true that the atom has been split. Another way to put the matter is to say that if I know that the sentence 'The atom has been split' is true, then the sentence 'The atom has been split' is true. I cannot possibly know that any sentence is true unless that sentence is true. Hence truth is a condition of knowledge.

Knowledge and The Absolute Theory of Truth

We may formulate the preceding result in terms of the following two conditions:

(iT) If S knows that p, then it is true that p.

(iiT) If S knows that the sentence Q is true, then the sentence Q is true.

The first of these two conditions may be formulated without reference to truth because of the following condition, sometimes called the absolute theory of truth:

(AT) It is true that p if and only if p.[1]

This condition tells us that it is true that the atom has been split if and only if the atom has been split, which, though it hardly

[1] See the following articles for important discussions of the theory of truth: Rudolf Carnap, 'Meaning and Necessity', *New Readings*, 173–80; Arthur Pap, 'Note on the "Absolute" and the "semantic" Concept of Truth', *New Readings*, 208–14; P. F. Strawson, 'Truth' in *Philosophy and Analysis*, ed. Margaret Mac-Donald (Basil Blackwell, Oxford, 1966), 260–77; and Alfred Tarski, 'The Semantic Conception of Truth', *Readings in Philosophical Analysis*, ed. Feigl and Sellars, 52–84.

seems very informative, is a logical truth. Therefore, it follows that (iT) is logically equivalent to the following:

(iTa) If S knows that p, then p.

Thus, we may eliminate all reference to truth in (iT) without loss of logical content.

Truth and Levels of Language

In order to appreciate the difference between conditions (iT) and (iiT), it is essential to draw some distinctions that are fundamental to semantic theory. The basic distinction concerns different linguistic levels. For example, suppose someone says 'The atom has been split.' Such a person is speaking about an object, the atom, and, though he is using language, he is not speaking about language. This sentence may thus be said to be a sentence in the object language. If someone says of the sentence just uttered 'The sentence about the atom is true', he is speaking about the sentence and has moved to a second linguistic level. This level of language is called the metalanguage. If a man now says of what this man has said 'The sentence about the sentence about the atom is true', he has moved to a still higher linguistic level in that he is now speaking of a sentence that was about a sentence. Thus, he is speaking in the meta-metalanguage, or more simply, the second metalanguage.

This distinction between levels of language might seem somewhat artificial and unnecessary, but it has some rather general implications concerning the concept of truth. First of all, it allows us to avoid certain logical paradoxes involving the concepts of truth and falsity. The most familiar paradox is the following:

(S) This sentence is false.

It is reasonable to assume that (S) is either true or false. But if it is true, then, as it says, it is false. On the other hand, if the sentence is false, then, since it says it is false, it is true. Therefore, if the sentence is either true or false, then it is both true and false.

It is sometimes thought that such sentences simply have the defect of referring to themselves, and thus that we may avoid paradox by ruling that all sentences that refer to themselves are not well formed. This strategy would deal with sentence (S), but the paradox would recur in sentences that do not refer to themselves. Consider the following two sentences:

(A) Sentence (B) is true.
(B) Sentence (A) is false.

If one considers sentence (A) and supposes it is true or false, one reaches the conclusion that it is both true and false. If (A) is true, then (B) is true, and (B) says that (A) is false, so (A) is false. If (A) is false, then (B) is true because (B) says that (A) is false, so (A) is true. Hence, if (A) is either true or false, then it is both true and false. Moreover, sentence (A) does not refer to itself; it refers to sentence (B).

Both of the paradoxes cited may be avoided by carefully distinguishing between different levels of language and requiring that sentences at one level refer only to sentences of a lower level. Consider sentence (S). As a sentence of a certain level, it must be about sentences of a lower level, and thus, sentence (S) would have to belong to the metalanguage of level n and the sentence referred to by the word 'sentence' in (S) would have to be a sentence in metalanguage $n-1$, or if $n=1$, in the object language. Thus, sentence (S) would read as follows: This sentence of language level $n-1$ is false. But then the sentence becomes false because it says that the sentence is of language level $n-1$ when in fact it belongs to language level n. Let us reconsider sentence (A) and (B) once the language level is made explicit. Assume (A) is in language n. Thus, (A) reads as follows:

(A) Sentence (B) in language level $n-1$ is true.

Since sentence (B) is about sentence (A) in language level n, it is in language level $n+1$, and reads as follows:

(B) Sentence (A) in language level n is false.

It is now apparent, however, that sentence (A) is false because it says that sentence (B) is in language level $n-1$ when, in fact, sentence (B) is in language level $n+1$. Hence, specification of language levels will enable us to avoid paradox.

We may draw an important conclusion from these results concerning the concept of truth, namely, that a sentence is true or false in a certain language. For example, sentence (B) is false in language level n. Hereafter, instead of saying that a sentence is true, we shall say that it is true in L, and the language of the next higher level we shall, for convenience, call the metalanguage, of L.

Knowledge and the Semantic Theory of Truth

With these considerations in mind, we may now turn to a reconsideration of (iiT). It should now be rephrased in such a way as to make the reference to language levels explicit as follows:

> (iiT) If S knows that the sentence Q is true in language L, then the sentence Q is true in language L.

We found that by appealing to the absolute theory of truth we could eliminate reference to truth in (iT), and the question now arises as to whether we can formulate a theory of truth that will enable us to eliminate reference to truth in (iiT). Such a theory would be a semantic theory of truth.

Alfred Tarski has proposed as a *condition of adequacy* for a semantic theory or definition of truth that all equivalences of the form

> (CA) S is true in L if and only if p,

follow from the definition provided 'we substitute in place of the symbol 'p' in this schema any sentence, and in the place of 'S' any individual name of this sentence' in L.[2] If we replace 'p', for example by 'the atom has been split', and we replace 'S' by a name of that sentence, for example, ' "the atom has been split" ' we obtain the following equivalence:

> 'The atom has been split' is true in L if and only if the atom has been split.

The condition of adequacy, if satisfied, would allow us to eliminate one reference to truth in (iiT) by substituting according to (CA) as follows:

> (iiTa) If S knows that the sentence Q is true in L, then p;

[2] Alfred Tarski, 'The Concept of Truth in Formalized Languages', in *Logic, Semantics, and Metamathematics* (Clarendon Press, Oxford, 1969), 155–6. Also see Tarski, 'The Semantic Conception'.

provided that '*p*' is replaced by a sentence of *L*, and '*Q*' is replaced by some name of that sentence in the metalanguage of *L*. As a consequence we could obtain the following:

> If *S* knows that the sentence 'the atom has been split' is true in *L*, then the atom has been split.

Moreover, the condition suggests that we should be able to establish an important relation between the antecedents of (iT) and (iiT). It is as follows:

> If *S* knows that the sentence *Q* is true in *L*, then *S* knows that *p*;

provided that '*p*' is replaced by a sentence of *L*, and '*Q*' is replaced by a name of that sentence in the metalanguage of *L*. This result has the following consequence:

> If *S* knows that the sentence 'the atom has been split' is true in *L*, then *S* knows that the atom has been split.

Needless to say, the results of applying Tarski's condition are very plausible.

Objections to the Semantic Theory of Truth

We have seen that the condition of adequacy leads to some quite plausible results. The merits of it have been disputed however. It is not doubted that formal systems may be constructed in which a definition of truth is given from which it follows that the condition of adequacy is satisfied. Nor is it denied that such a definition would be fruitful. What is denied is that the condition is true by definition for parts of natural languages.

According to the condition any adequate definition of truth must have the following as a consequence provided that 'the atom has been split' is a sentence of *L*:

> (E) 'The atom has been split' is true in *L* if and only if the atom has been split.

We may here let '*L*' designate part of English. The equivalence (E) written above would follow from a definition of truth according to the condition of adequacy. Therefore, if the condition of adequacy is reasonable, then (E) should follow from a definition of truth and hence be true by definition.

In opposition, Arthur Pap has argued that (E) is not true by definition because it is not a logical truth.[3] He argues that the sentence

(Ei) 'The atom has been split' is true in English

has logical consequences that should not be logical consequences of

(Eii) The atom has been split

and concludes that (Ei) and (Eii) are not logically equivalent. For example, sentence (Ei) has as a logical consequence the following:

(Eicl) 'The atom has been split' is a sentence of English.

This sentence is not a logical consequence of (Eii) because it is logically possible that the atom should have been split even if 'the atom has been split' were not a sentence of English, indeed, even if there was no such language at all. A world in which the atom was split by men who spoke some language other than English and in which there was no such language as English is a logically possible world. Thus, it is logically possible that (Eii) should be true and (Ei) false, and hence the latter is not a logical consequence of the former.[4]

The preceding argument leaves open the question of whether (Eii) is a logical consequence of (Ei). This is a more plausible contention, but there is an argument against it as well. Suppose that the sentence 'the atom has been split' does not mean what it says, perhaps in the way in which a man writing a letter for a special purpose might write 'we hope to have the opportunity to serve you again' when it is quite clear from the context that what he means is just the opposite. If the sentence 'the atom has been split' does not mean that the atom has been split, then it might be that the sentence is true even though the atom has not been split. This would yield the result that (Ei) is true when (Eii) is false.[5]

This argument has been rejected by some philosophers on the grounds that the sentence (E) is itself in English and hence

---

[3] Arthur Pap, op. cit. [4] Ibid.
[5] This argument was suggested to me in conversation many years ago by R. C. Sleigh, Jr. I do not know whether he would any longer accept it.

whatever 'the atom has been split' means in English is what it means when it appears in the right hand side of 'if and only if' in (E). Such an objection misses the point. Suppose we translate (E) into another language, German for example. If we do so, we must not translate 'the atom has been split' as it occurs in quotation marks to the left of 'if and only if' in (E), because the sentence in quotation marks would no longer be a sentence in a language in which it is said to be true, namely, English. On the other hand, the occurrence of that sentence to the right of the 'if and only if' in (E) and not in quotation marks would properly be translated into German when we translate (E). Thus (Eii) would be translated

(EiiG) Man hat das Atom gespalt

while (EiG) would be translated

(EiG) 'The atom has been split' ist wahr auf Englisch.

But (EiG) does not logically imply that (EiiG) is a translation of (Eii) into German, though in fact it is. Since it is logically possible that 'the atom has been split' should not mean in English the same thing as 'Man hat das Atom gespalt' in German, it is logically possible (EiG) should be true when (EiiG) is false. Therefore, it is possible that the German translation of (Ei) would be false. But if one sentence logically implies a second, then a translation of the first must logically imply a translation of the second. Since the translation of (Eii) does not logically imply the translation of (Ei), it follows that (Eii) does not logically imply (Ei).[6]

A Modification of the Semantic Theory of Truth

The preceding objections to (E) suggest the following modification:

(EM) 'The atom has been split' is true in English and means in English that the atom has been split if and only if 'the atom has been split' is a sentence of English meaning that the atom has been split and the atom has been split.

[6] This argument is, of course, adopted from the translation argument of Alonzo, Church in 'On Carnap's Analysis of Statements of Assertion and Belief', *Analysis* x (1950), 97-9.

The foregoing suggests as a condition of adequacy of a semantic theory of truth for a natural language that all equivalences of the form

(CAm) S is true in L and S means in L that p if and only if S is a sentence in L meaning that p and p

follow from the theory provided, again, that we substitute for 'p' any sentence of L and for 'S' any name of this sentence in L.

The preceding condition of adequacy meets not only Pap's objection but some objections raised by Herbert Heidelberger as well.[7] Heidelberger has pointed out that if we allow sentences that are neither true nor false, such as 'Knock before entering', to be substituted for 'p' in (CA), then we obtain the following:

'Knock before entering' is true in English if and only if knock before entering.

The preceding sentence is not only ungrammatical and ill-formed, it illustrates quite clearly that what occurs to the right of the 'if and only if' is not logically equivalent to what occurs to the left of that expression. The latter is false because it is false that 'Knock before entering' is true in English, but the former, since it is a command, is neither true nor false.[8] This objection is met by (CAm) because, according to that schema, we would obtain the following when we replace 'p' by 'Knock before entering':

'Knock before entering' is true in English and 'Knock before entering' means in English that knock before entering if and only if 'knock before entering' is a sentence in English meaning that knock before entering and knock before entering.

In this formulation, the statements on both sides of 'if and only if' are sentences that are neither true nor false. The sentence to the left of the expression is neither true nor false because of that part of the sentence reading ' "knock before entering" means in English that knock before entering'. A sentence affirming that a sentence means *that knock before entering* is ungrammatical. Of

[7] Herbert Heidelberger, 'The Indispensibility of Truth', *American Philosophical Quarterly*, v (1968), 212–17.
[8] Ibid. 213–14.

course, the sentence to the left of 'if and only if' is ungrammatical for the same reason. Both sentences are ungrammatical and neither true nor false, because an imperative sentence fills the spot in a sentence that must be filled by a declarative sentence. In such contexts the word 'that' must be followed by a declarative sentence for the larger sentence in which it is contained to be grammatical and true or false.

Similar remarks apply to other of Heidelberger's objections to the condition based on (CA). For example, if we allow sentences that are neither true nor false to be substituted for 'p' in (CA), then, if S is such a sentence, we may conclude by substituting in (CA) that

(i) $\sim(S$ is true in $L)$

and

(ii) $\sim(\sim S$ is true in $L)$

where '$\sim$' is the sign for negation. But from a substitution instance of (CA) and (i) we may deduce

(ia) $\sim S$

while from another substitution instance of (CA) and (ii) we may deduce

(iia) S.

Heidelberger maintains that since we can deduce a contradiction, $\sim S$ and S, from a substitution instance of (CA), this condition must be rejected.[9]

One wishing to maintain (CA) could reply that the alleged contradiction, $\sim S$ and S, is not a contradiction on the grounds that this statement is neither true nor false because the conjuncts of which it is composed are neither true nor false. This reply does not, however, meet the objection in a satisfactory manner. Even if the conjunction is neither true nor false, it remains a consequence of (CA) that we may deduce a sentence which has the *form* of a contradiction by adding the premiss that there is a sentence S which is neither true nor false. And this is objectionable, for the premiss that a sentence is neither true nor false may be a factual premiss, one that as a matter of

[9] Herbert Heidelberger, 'The Indispensibility of Truth', *American Philosophical Quarterly*, v (1968), 213.

logic could be true or false. But the conclusion, $\sim S$ and S, that one may deduce from such a premiss together with (CA) is a conclusion, which as a matter of logic, could not possibly be true. Thus (CA) permits us to deduce a conclusion that could not possibly be true from a premiss that could be either true or false. Such a procedure is objectionable, as is a system in which a contradiction may be deduced from a contingent premiss.

Heidelberger's objection is only partially met by inserting (CAm) instead of (CA). As we have noted, a sentence such as 'Knock before entering', when placed after the words 'means that' in the contexts we have been considering, yields the result that the statements occurring on either side of 'if and only if' in the equivalence obtained from (CAm) are both ill-formed and hence that the equivalence is also ill-formed. This is not the end of the matter, however, for, according to P. F. Strawson, there are declarative sentences that are neither true nor false and these would yield a well-formed equivalence when used to replace 'p' in (CAm). Strawson contends that such a sentence as 'The present king of France is bald' is neither true nor false because the utterance of such a sentence presupposes that there is a present king of France and the falsity of this presupposition has the result that the sentence is neither true nor false.[10] This contention has been much disputed, and the most effective way to deal with the problem is to rule that such sentences are false, as Bertrand Russell has claimed.[11] Even if this involves some elements of stipulation, it enables us to obtain a gain in clarity and simplicity at no great loss. Moreover, Russell proposed an analysis of such sentences that would enable us to explain why such a sentence is false. The analysis of the sentence is such as logically to imply that there is one and only one person who is a king of France. With this issue decided, inserting (CAm) in the condition of adequacy meets the objections Heidelberger raised against using (CA).

Knowledge and the Elimination of Truth

With (CAm) inserted in the condition of adequacy for a semantic definition of truth, let us return to our consideration

[10] P. F. Strawson, 'On Referring', *New Readings*, 35–50.
[11] Bertrand Russell, 'Mr. Strawson on Referring', *New Readings*, 55–8.

of (iT), (iiT) and the relation between knowledge and truth. The preceding discussion does not raise any problem for the reduction of

(iT) If S knows that p, then it is true that p

to

(iTa) If S knows that p, then p

by appeal to the equivalence

It is true that p if and only if p

expressing the absolute theory of truth. When we employ the absolute concept of truth in contexts of the form 'It is true that . . .', the reference to truth may be eliminated in the formulation of the conditions of knowledge.

When we say, however, that some sentence is true in a language thus employing the semantic concept of truth, the reference to truth cannot be eliminated in so simple a manner. Consider the following condition:

(iiT) If S knows that the sentence Q is true in L, then the sentence Q is true in L.

We have already noticed that we cannot eliminate the reference to truth by appeal to (CA), because (CA) is defective. Condition (CA) yields the equivalence:

The sentence Q is true in L if and only if p

which should not follow from a definition of truth. For, as we have seen, that equivalence is not logical, that is, even when 'p' and 'Q' are replaced in the required manner, the sentence to the right of 'if and only if' will not logically imply the sentence to the left of that expression and the sentence to the left will not logically imply the one on the right. By the same considerations it follows that we cannot replace (iiT) with the very plausible

(iiTa) If S knows that the sentence Q is true in L, then p;

provided that 'p' is replaced by a sentence of L and 'Q' is replaced by some name of that sentence in the metalanguage of L. The reason for this is that even if 'Q' is replaced by a name of the sentence that replaced 'p', the sentence

S knows that the sentence Q is true in L

does not logically imply that the name that replaces 'Q' names the sentence that replaces 'p'. Therefore, it is logically possible that it should be false that p when S knows that the sentence Q is true, even though in fact this will not arise because of the manner in which 'Q' and 'p' are replaced. Since there is nothing in logic to prevent the situation of it being true that S knows that the sentence Q is true and false that p, the conditional in (iiTa) is not a logical implication.

There is, however, a modification of (iiTa) that is acceptable, namely, one in which we add a clause to the antecedent of the conditional formulating the relation between the name that replaced 'Q' and the sentence that replaces 'p'. It might be thought that this could be accomplished by simply modifying the conditional in (iiTa) as follows:

If S knows that the sentence Q is true in L *and* the sentence that replaces 'p' in L is named by the sentence that replaces 'Q' in the metalanguage of L, then p.

But this would be to mix language levels in precisely the way that leads to paradox. Suppose that the sentence is of level n. Since the replacements referred to are replacements in that sentence, it follows that the sentence is in the metalanguage of n and thus on the higher level $n + 1$. But this contradicts the supposition.

To avoid this difficulty, we may modify (iiTa) in a different way, namely, by adding that Q means that p in L to the antecedent of the conditional in question. We then get the following:

(iiTb) If S knows that the sentence Q is true in L *and* Q means in L that p, then p.

This condition is considerably simpler than (iiTa) and the meaning clause enables us to dispense with the proviso concerning replacement. It does, however, bring in the concept of meaning which some philosophers, Quine most especially, have found to be objectionable.[12] However, the study of

---

[12] See discussions by Quine on this matter, particularly, 'Two Dogmas of Empiricism', sections 1–4, and 'The Problem of Meaning in Linguistics', both in *From a Logical Point of View* (Harvard University Press, Cambridge, Mass., 1953), 20–46 and 47–64, respectively.

meaning in natural languages, though still in an explorative stage, holds promise of offering a satisfactory analysis of the concept.[13]

The Elimination of Truth

Let us review our progress. We have carried out this investigation to see if we could eliminate the reference to truth in the formulation of the truth condition of knowledge. Replacing (iT) with (iTa) achieves that objective with respect to formulating the truth condition of S knowing that p. The substitution of (iiTb) for (iiT) accomplishes something of the sort for eliminating reference to truth in formulating the condition of S knowing that Q is true in L. Here, however, the elimination necessitates the addition of a clause formulating what Q means, and the reference to truth remains ensconced in the locution 'S knows that the sentence Q is true in L.' Is there any way to eliminate the reference here?

The most tempting manoeuvre would be the following reduction:

S knows that Q is true in L if and only if S knows that p

provided that 'p' is replaced by a sentence of L and 'Q' is replaced by a name of that sentence in the metalanguage of L. But the difficulty is that this is defective. First, there is again the problem that even though the proviso is met it does not follow from S knowing that Q is true in L that this is so. This problem could perhaps be surmounted by conjoining to each side of the equivalence the sentence 'Q means that p in L.' That strategy, however, would fail to meet the objection lodged earlier, that though S might know that p and though Q might mean that p, S might not know that Q means that p; indeed, he might not know what Q means, and hence he would not know that Q is true. To avoid such problems we should have to add to each side of the equivalence that S knows that Q means that p.

If we adopt this strategy we obtain the following equivalence:

S knows that Q is true in L and that Q means that p in L if and only if S knows that p and that Q means that p in L.

[13] See books by Cohen, Fogelin, Katz, and Ziff cited in chapter 1, footnote 5.

From this equivalence we can replace (iiTb) with the following:

> (iiTc) If S knows that p and that Q means that p in L, then p.

On the other hand, it is perfectly clear that in (iiTc) the reference to S knowing that Q means that p in L is, with respect to the conditions of knowing, simply superfluous. For (iiTc) follows from

> (iTa) If S knows that p, then p.

Thus the preceding reduction proves that (iiT) reduces to (iTa). There is no reference to truth in (iT). Therefore, the reference to truth may be eliminated in the formulation of the truth condition of knowledge.

Truth, Knowledge, and Meaning

There is one remaining problem concerning knowledge and truth. We have dealt successfully with contexts in which a person is said to know that sentence Q is true in L provided the expression that replaces 'Q' means that p in L. There are, however, contexts in which the expression that replaces 'Q' does not mean that p. For example, consider the following sentence:

> (s) Cornman knows that statement number (3) on page 29 of *Philosophical Problems and Arguments* is true.

The sentence on page 29 is

> Some mushrooms are poisonous.

However, though the expression 'sentence number (3) on page 29 of *Philosophical Problems and Arguments*' refers to the sentence 'some mushrooms are poisonous', sentence (s) is not logically equivalent to

> (t) Cornman knows that the sentence 'some mushrooms are poisonous' is true

or to

> (u) Cornman knows that some mushrooms are poisonous.

The reason is that Cornman might know that the sentence

number (3) on page 29 is true even though he does not know what that sentence is and, moreover, does not know that some mushrooms are poisonous.[14] This could happen if Cornman remembered that his co-author listed a number of true statements on page 29, as examples of true *a posteriori* sentences, but has completely forgotten what the sentences are. In that case (s) would be true even though (t) and (u) might be false. So (s) is not logically equivalent to either (t) or (u).

Moreover, there is no obvious general formula for handling sentences like (s) in order to eliminate the reference to truth. We may, however, accomplish the elimination, for (s) is logically equivalent to the following:

> (s′) Cornman knows that there is a sentence S which is numbered (3) on page 29 of *Philosophical Problems and Arguments* and that there is a p such that S means that p (in L) and p.

Sentence (s′) is equivalent to (s) if and only if knowing that a sentence is true is logically equivalent to knowing that there is a p such that the sentence means that p and p. This equivalence of (s) and (s′) might be disputed by philosophers like W. V. O. Quine who would, we may conjecture, wish to deny that locutions like 'S means that p (in L)' should be allowed.[15] That notwithstanding, we have already rejected such restrictions on the use of the term 'means' for our purposes.

Though no general formula has been offered for eliminating reference to truth in contexts like (s), the general strategy for elimination is to replace an expression characterizing a sentence in question with an expression asserting that there is a sentence so characterized and to eliminate the reference to truth by adding that there is a p such that the sentence means that p and p. By so doing we can eliminate the reference to truth in such contexts.

Meanings, Propositions, and Truth

Before concluding our discussion of truth, it is important to consider some objections to our account. First, it may be pro-

[14] On this point compare Heidelberger, op. cit., and Strawson, 'Truth' in *Philosophy and Analysis*, ed. Margaret MacDonald, 260–77.
[15] Quine, op. cit.

posed that by introducing the term 'means' we commit ourselves to an ontology of propositions or abstract entities. We have, of course, avoided the use of the term 'proposition', or any synonym for that term, but this term is commonly used to characterize what a sentence means when it means that p. Thus, to say that a sentence means that p is, on this account, equivalent to saying that the sentence means the proposition that p. Such a commitment to propositions is, I think, very likely to lead to confusion.

There are two commonly held assumptions concerning propositions that lead to contradiction. The first is that, whenever a sentence S is true or false, then there is a proposition that p such that S means that p. The second is that propositions are themselves either true or false. For example, it might be said that the sentence 'some mushrooms are poisonous' means the proposition that some mushrooms are poisonous, and the proposition that some mushrooms are poisonous is true. However, this sort of theory runs into difficulty with respect to demonstrative pronouns. As Richard Cartwright has pointed out, if I utter the sentence 'This is a glass' on two separate occasions, once when I am referring to a glass and subsequently when I mistakenly believe that what I am referring to is a glass, the sentence uttered does not change meaning. Hence, the proposition that the sentence means is the same on both occasions of utterance. On the other hand, what I asserted when I first uttered the sentence was true and what I asserted subsequently false. Therefore, if the proposition meant by the sentence is what is asserted by uttering the sentence on both occasions, then the proposition would be both true and false. The proposition that this is a glass would be both true and false which is contradictory and absurd.[16]

Obviously a defender of propositions would wish to deny one or the other of the premises of the foregoing argument. Cartwright suggests, quite plausibly, that one should deny that the meaning of a sentence is the same thing as what is asserted by uttering the sentence.[17] What is asserted by uttering the sentence may differ from one occasion to the next even though the meaning of the sentence is unchanged. This results from

[16] Richard Cartwright, 'Propositions', in *Analytic Philosophy*, ed. Ronald Butler (Barnes and Noble, New York, 1962), 81–103, but particularly section 10, 92–5.
[17] Ibid. 92–5.

the fact that some term may be used to refer to different things without the meaning of that term undergoing any change. There is some connection between the meaning of a sentence and what is asserted by uttering it: what is asserted by uttering the sentence is partially determined by the meaning of the sentence uttered. What is asserted is also partially determined by what we refer to by certain terms, for example, demonstrative pronouns.

If it is thus deemed useful to introduce the notion of a proposition, there is no need to suppose that sentences mean propositions, and we shall not make such an assumption here. If the term proposition is used, it shall only be used to refer to what is asserted or what is believed. Moreover though we have used the locution 'S means that p', we need not commit ourselves to a theory concerning what meanings are. It is quite consistent with our account to argue that meanings are no more entities of the universe than are average men. Just as the average man is an arithmetical abstraction, so may the meanings of words be semantic abstractions. Thus, we have not committed ourselves to propositions at all, and we need not make any commitment concerning the ultimate character of meanings of sentences other than to deny that the meaning of a sentence is what is asserted by the utterance of that sentence.

Another problem, raised by Heidelberger, concerns the use of the variable 'p' as it occurs in truth-eliminating equivalences presented by other authors. He argues that the following sentence is incoherent:

There is a proposition p such that S means p and p.

Consider how we are to treat the variable 'p'. Were we to substitute for the variable 'p' the expression 'that snow is white', the name of that sentence for 'S', and drop the existential clause, we would obtain the following:

'Snow is white' means that the snow is white and that the snow is white.

This sentence is not well formed because of the last conjunct.[18] On the other hand, if we substitute for 'p' the sentence 'snow is white' we obtain the following:

'Snow is white' means snow is white and snow is white.

18 Heidelberger, op. cit. 216.

It is not so clear that anything is the matter with this sentence; Heidelberger does not discuss it, but one might object that strictly speaking, 'snow is white' means *that* snow is white and does not mean snow is white. Such a point would not be decisive in terms of ordinary English usage because such usage allows dropping the word 'that' in these contexts. However, our formulation of truth-eliminating equivalences makes no reference to propositions and enables us to avoid such disagreements. We drop the reference to propositions and insert the word 'that' after the words 'means'. We then obtain the following sentence:

There is a p such that S means *that* p and p.

Substituting 'snow is white' for 'p', the name of the sentence for 'S', and dropping the existential clause, we obtain:

'Snow is white' means that snow is white and snow is white.

This sentence is well formed.

The only objection left concerns our use of the locution 'there is a p such that . . . and p'. Heidelberger says that the last occurrence of 'p' is 'a stray variable, or a stray name if we make a substitution, with no predicate to attach to it'.[19] To see what he means, consider the locution 'there is an x such that x . . .'. Here the variable 'x' must have a predicate attached to it or we arrive at nonsense. Thus, the locution 'there is an x . . . and x' is nonsense because the name that replaces 'x' cannot stand by itself without a predicate attached, or so Heidelberger argues. However, we may have a rule in our metalanguage which tells us how variables are to be replaced in such a way that the resulting instantiations, obtained by dropping existential clauses and replacing as directed, are well formed. Such rules for the dropping of existential clauses 'there is an x such that . . .' or universal clauses 'for any x . . .', and the replacement of variables, are sufficient for logical manipulation and hence for determining the logical consequences or the logical content of the sentences containing the clauses and variables. Thus, use of the usual replacement procedures in the formulas we have employed for the elimination of the concept of truth yields

[19] Ibid. 216–17.

well-formed sentences. This is shown by the substitutions considered above.

Other Theories of Truth: The Correspondence Theory

Formal objections to our elimination of the concept of truth from the analysis having been met, let us consider more philosophical objections. One such objection is that schemas (AT) and (CAm), which we may refer to as the elimination theory of truth, do not accomplish what a satisfactory theory of truth must achieve. A satisfactory theory of truth is one that tells us *why* a true sentence is true. The elimination theory merely tells us when a sentence S is true —crudely, S is true if and only if p—but it does not tell us why sentence S is true.

This objection requires some clarification that may be obtained by considering two theories of truth intended to tell us why a true sentence is true. They are the correspondence and coherence theories. Let us first consider the correspondence theory. According to it, the answer to the question of why a true sentence is true may be put as follows: a sentence S is true if and only if sentence S corresponds to the facts. A true sentence is true because it corresponds to the facts.

One might ask, however, to what facts must S correspond in order to be true? One answer to this question is: the facts of observation.[20] The object of the correspondence theory of truth is to guarantee a connection between language and observable reality, and thus to anchor truth in a reality of observable fact.

To determine whether such a theory of truth offers us some information about truth beyond that of the elimination of theory, it is important to have a more precise formulation of the correspondence theory. First, the theory must be formulated in such a way as to enable us to explain in what way general sentences and theoretical sentences must correspond to the facts in order to be true. It is easy enough to suggest that a sentence like 'This is a table' must correspond to the observable fact that this is a table for it to be true. Problems arise, though, with such statements as 'All mules are sterile' and 'The neutrino

[20] See Wilfrid Sellars's article, 'Truth and "Correspondence" ', in *New Readings*, 214–31.

has a rest mass of O'. The generalization about mules is stronger than any set of facts about observed mules. Even if we include among the facts to which the generalization must correspond all observable facts about all mules, it remains logically possible that there are other such facts about mules which might be inconsistent with the generalization. Hence, if the truth of the generalization depends upon a set of facts, the set must include not only such facts as that mule one is sterile, mule two is sterile and so forth to the fact that mule n is sterile, but also the further fact that the n mules are *all* the mules. If the last fact is not contained, then it remains logically possible that the generalization both corresponds to the facts about the n mules in question but is false because the n mules are not all the mules that there are. However, once the general fact that the n mules are all the mules is allowed among the facts of observation, it is apparent that we might more simply explain to what fact the generalization 'all mules are sterile' must correspond by appeal to the following:

> 'All mules are sterile' is true and if and only if it corresponds to the fact that all mules are sterile.

Similar remarks apply to the sentence 'Neutrinos have a rest mass of O'. It is tempting to suppose that there are some facts of observation that verify this sentence and to which it corresponds if it is true, but investigations in the philosophy of science have shown this to be a highly oversimplified account. That sentence requires for verification not only experimental observations but other theoretical sentences connecting observation terms to terms of the theory, for example sentences telling us what the observable effects of neutrinos are like, as well as ones relating theoretical terms to each other.

To avoid such problems most simply, one might explain to what facts a true theoretical sentence must correspond as follows:

> 'Neutrinos have a rest mass of O' is true if and only if it corresponds to the fact that neutrinos have a rest mass of O.

In order to say to what facts our theoretical sentence must correspond in order to be true, we would have to include some theoretical facts or else leave open the possibility that the sentence both corresponds to the facts and is false.

The preceding considerations suggest that any adequate correspondence theory of truth will have all equivalences of the following form as consequences:

(CTT) S is true in L if and only if S in L corresponds to the fact that p;

provided that the variable 'p' is replaced by a sentence in L and 'S' is replaced by a name of that sentence in the meta-language of L. However, (CTT) leaves us with two unexplicated terms 'fact' and 'corresponds'. The first is easy to eliminate because the following equivalence holds:

It is fact that p if and only if p.

This equivalence is an exact analogue of the absolute theory of truth. The term 'corresponds' is supposed to name that relation between a sentence and fact which holds if and only if the sentence is true. Meaning is just such a relation. That is, the following equivalence of correspondence and meaning holds:

(ECM) S in L corresponds to the fact that p if and only if S means that p in L and p.

Given this equivalence, the correspondence theory of truth reduces to the following:

(CTR) S is true in L if and only if S means that p in L and p.

With the minor alteration of conjoining to the left-hand side of (CTR) 'S means that p in L' in order to make the equivalence defensible against earlier objections, (CTR) becomes (CAm)— the elimination theory! Thus the correspondence theory, rather than telling us something more than the elimination theory, reduces to it.

It should not be concluded from this that those philosophers who have defended the correspondence theory were either so wise as to have anticipated the elimination theory or so foolish as to have held the elimination theory while believing that they held something more. Neither would do justice to the substance or the confusion contained in the correspondence theory of truth. The thesis that underlies this particular theory of truth is not a theory of truth at all but one of verification. It is: what verifies a sentence is the facts and nothing but the facts. However, the term 'verify' conceals a fundamental ambiguity. One meaning of the term 'verify' is 'to make true'. In this sense of the term, we may agree that a true statement is one that is verified, that is, made true, by the facts, but this contention reduces to the elimination theory of truth. There is, however, another meaning of the term 'verify', namely, 'to *determine* the truth'. Here the word 'determine' is used epistemically to mean 'find out'. When one says that a true statement is verified by the facts, using the term 'verify' in this sense, one is saying that we *determine* the truth of a statement by appeal to the facts. This thesis is not one about truth, but about how we find out or come to know the truth. It is a theory of how we justify belief and claims to knowledge. When the correspondence theory of truth is understood as a geniune theory of truth, it reduces to the elimination theory, and when it does not reduce to such a theory, then it is not a geniune theory of truth at all, but a disguised theory of epistemic justification.

It should be noted that at least one philosopher, Wilfrid Sellars, has suggested that we may be able to equate truth with some form of *ideally* justified belief.[21] Perhaps such a theory can be sustained. It is not our intention to deny it. Such ideal justification should not, however, be confused with the actual complete justification that is a condition of knowledge. As we use the expression in our analysis, a man may be completely justified in believing something which is in fact false. We shall later argue that the actual justification we have for our beliefs provides no guarantee of truth. Hence, ideal justification that might be equated with truth differs from the actual justification we have for what we believe. The justification we seek to determine whether our beliefs are true must, therefore, be distinguished from any ideal justification identical with truth.

The Coherence Theory of Truth

Finally, then, let us consider the traditional rival of the correspondence theory of truth, the coherence theory. This

[21] Wilfrid Sellars, 'Are There Non-Deductive Logics?' in *Essays in Honor of Carl G. Hempel*, N. Rescher and other eds. (Reidel, Dordrecht-Holland, 1970), 96.

theory says that truth does not consist of correspondence with the facts but coherence among sentences.[22] The idea is that truth does not depend on a relation between language and reality but only upon the relation between sentences, bits of language. We might formulate the theory as follows:

> (CohTT) S is true in L if and only if S coheres with other sentences of L.

The most common objections to this theory concern the relation of coherence. It is objected that we have no proof that sets of sentences that cohere with each other will be consistent with other sets of sentences that cohere with each other, and, what is most fundamental, we have no assurance that there is one and only one set of sentences that cohere with each other. Of course, no such objection can be met until the relation of coherence is specified. Even without such a specification, we can show that either (CohTT), the coherence theory, reduces to (CAm), the elimination theory, or else the coherence theory must be rejected.

If any substitution instance of the following equivalence does not hold, then the coherence theory is incorrect:

> S coheres with other sentences of L if and only if S means that p in L and p;

provided the variable 'p' is replaced by some sentence of L and 'S' is replaced by a name of that sentence in the metalanguage of L. Such an equivalence must hold, because a sentence without meaning cannot be true, and if a sentence does mean something, that is, means that p, then the sentence is true if and only if p. It cannot be the case that the sentence is true when it is not case that p no matter how snugly the sentence coheres with other sentences.

An example makes this obvious. Suppose someone says that the sentence 'the total number of leptons in the universe remains constant' is true in L if and only if S coheres with other sentences of L. This sentence, since it is a highly theoretical contention, is an example that would seem most likely to fit the coherence theory. The truth of the sentence would seem to

---

[22] For a discussion of this theory, see Nicholas Rescher, *The Coherence Theory of Truth* (Clarendon Press, Oxford, 1973).

depend upon the way it coheres with other sentences of the language, namely, the postulates of particle physics. Notice, however, that the sentence 'the total number of leptons in the universe remains constant' means that the total number of leptons in the universe remains constant, and consequently, is true only if the number of leptons in the universe remains constant. Therefore, if the number of leptons in the universe does *not* remain constant, then the sentence 'the number of leptons in the universe remains constant' is *not* true no matter how well it coheres with other sentences of the language.

This proves that either the equivalence of '*S* coheres with other sentences' and '*S* means that *p* and *p*' must be accepted by a coherence theory or else the coherence theory will have the consequence that a true sentence, one that coheres with other sentences, could mean that *p* when it is not the case that *p*. This consequence is absurd; therefore, the equivalence in question must be conceded by the coherence theorist. Once that is conceded, it is obvious that the coherence theory reduces to the elimination theory in precisely the same manner as the correspondence theory reduces to the elimination theory.

The foregoing argument has the effect of showing that both the correspondence and the coherence theories of truth must either be rejected as inadequate or else they reduce to the elimination theory. Moreover, the philosophical motivation and confusion that makes the correspondence theory appealing is the same that makes the coherence theory seem plausible. Again, the coherence theory has often been a disguised form of a theory of how we *determine* that a sentence is true or *justify* the claim to know that it is true. The epistemological theory, which we shall investigate in a later chapter, maintains that claims to know that a sentence is true are justified, not by appeal to observation, but by appeal to other sentences with which the sentence in question coheres. As such, the coherence theory is not a theory of truth at all but a theory of justification. We shall revisit those theories of justification, but it is essential to notice that such theories are not theories of truth. They can only be masqueraded as theories of truth by affirming that a sentence is *verified* by cohering with other sentences, and thus play upon the ambiguity of 'verify' mentioned above.

Truth and Knowledge: An Objection

Before concluding our chapter on truth it is useful to mention one objection to having truth as a condition of knowing. Some are inclined to object on the grounds that we have no way of deciding whether the truth condition is satisfied until we know that it is, and therefore, making truth a condition of knowledge renders it impossible to decide whether we know anything. The answer is that such a condition of knowledge is not one that we must find to be satisfied *before* we find out that we know: it is rather part of an analysis of knowledge and hence a condition that must be satisfied when we know. This reply to the objection might seem to render the objection unworthy of consideration, but that is not so. In fact, the objection reveals a confusion which has had the most deleterious impact on epistemological theories.

A person, who objects in this way to truth as a condition of knowledge, is construing the analysis of knowledge as a recipe for ascertaining whether one knows. The analysis of knowledge is one thing, and the rules for deciding whether one knows are quite another. The latter are conditions of justification for knowledge claims. Once those conditions have been satisfied, a man has done all he can to find out that *p* or to justify his belief that *p*. He cannot, over and above this, check to see that all the conditions in the analysis are satisfied. There is nothing more he can do or needs to do to determine that the truth condition has been satisfied.

3

Belief and Knowledge

LET us now turn to a consideration of the second condition of knowledge contained in the following conditional:

(iB) If S knows that p, then S believes that p.

It is rather surprising that this condition has been a battleground of controversy. Ultimately, such controversy must be met by clarification of the concept of belief, but it will be useful to explore the objections to condition (iB) at the outset in order to appreciate the need for such clarification.

Two kinds of arguments have been employed in the effort to refute (iB). The first depends on certain facts of linguistic usage. For example, it makes sense and is sometimes quite correct to say 'I do not believe that; I know it', or 'He does not believe that; he knows it.' This kind of argument represents an attempt to show that it is inconsistent to say both that a person knows that p and that he believes that p and, consequently, that the former does not imply the latter.[1] The second form of argument is less ambitious and consists of offering a counter-example to (iB), the favoured kind being one in which a person gives correct answers to questions he is asked without believing that his answers are correct.

The Consistency of Knowledge and Belief

Let us consider the first form of argument. From the fact that it makes sense and is even correct to say 'I do not believe that;

---

[1] This kind of argument is more popular with philosophers than the literature of the field reveals, and it would be hard to say who first formulated it. The late Austin Duncan-Johes remarked, 'Yet obviously, if "I think P" is used in the colloquial way, as equivalent to "I am inclined to think P", it doesn't follow from "I know P" at all, but is consistent with it.' In a footnote on the same page he remarks in support that we say, 'I don't think, I know,'. These remarks appear in 'Further Questions about "Know" and "Think"', *Philosophy and Analysis*, ed. Margaret MacDonald, 97.

I know it' or 'He does not believe that; he knows it', it hardly
follows that the thesis (iB) is false. The reason it makes sense
to say these things is to be found in the study of rhetoric
rather than logic. It makes sense to say 'I do not believe that;
I know it', not because it is logically inconsistent to say that a
man believes what he knows, but rather because this is an
emphatic way of saying 'I do not only believe that: I know it.'
To say the latter, however, is quite consistent with conceding
that the person referred to does believe, though not only believe,
what he is said to know. Similar remarks apply to the locution
'He does not believe that; he knows it.' An exact analogy
to these cases is one in which it makes sense to say 'That is not
a house, it is a mansion,' and the reason it makes sense is not
that it is logically inconsistent to say that a house is a mansion
but that rather that this is an emphatic way of saying 'That is
not only a house, it is a mansion.' Indeed, that something is a
mansion entails that it is a house. Once the rhetoric of emphatic
utterance is understood, the logic is left untouched.

We may clarify this matter by distinguishing two kinds of
implication as H. P. Grice suggests.[2] When we say, 'I believe
that . . .' or 'He believes that . . .', we often imply that the
person referred to does not know what he is said to believe.
Nevertheless, we deny that there is always such an implication.
Where the speaker has made it clear that he does not mean to
imply that the person referred to lacks knowledge, which he may
do without thereby stipulating any special meaning for the
words uttered, there will be no such implication. For example, if
I say 'I am not saying whether he knows', and then add 'He
believes . . .', then by uttering the latter I have not implied
that the person referred to does not know what he is said to
believe. Indeed, when a man says, 'I believe . . .' or 'He
believes . . .' and there is the implication that the person
referred to lacks knowledge, this is solely because the speaker has
implied this. What he said does not have this implication.
What is said when a speaker says that a person believes something will be perfectly consistent with what is said when a

[2] H. P. Grice, 'The Causal Theory of Perception', *Perceiving, Sensing, and Knowing*,
ed. R. Swartz (Anchor, New York, 1965), 438–72, and originally printed in
Proc. Aris. Soc., supp. vol. xxxv (1961), 121–52. The distinction between what a
speaker implies and what is implied by what he says is formulated and elaborated
by Grice in Swartz, op. cit. 441–51.

speaker says that that person also knows it, even though a man who says the first thing often implies something not implied by what he says, to wit, that someone lacks knowledge.

The distinction between what a speaker implies when he utters certain words and what is implied by what the speaker said, is in need of some elucidation. Sometimes a person implies something because what he said implies it, and such cases present no difficulty. Confusion is apt to arise when a person implies something not implied by what he said, because in such cases one may mistake the activity of the speaker for the logic of what he says. In order not to confuse what a speaker implies with the implications of what he says, we may employ a simple test for determining whether an implication is an implication of what is said or merely of the man speaking. Suppose that certain words are uttered and there is the implications that p. To decide whether the implication that p is an implication of what is said when those words are uttered, ask whether it is logically consistent to say 'I am not saying whether p, but . . .', where the words originally uttered by the speaker are added at the end of this locution. If it is consistent to say this, then what is said when the words in question were first uttered does not imply that p. If what is said when those words are uttered implied that p, then it would be inconsistent to utter those words and at the same time to say that one is not saying that p. For example, what is said when one utters the words 'That is a triangle' implies 'That has three sides', and thus it would be inconsistent to say 'I am not saying whether it has three sides, but it is a triangle.'[3]

As we have noted, it is consistent to say 'I am not saying whether I know, but I do believe that . . .' or 'I am not saying whether he knows, but he does believe that . . .'. Therefore, by applying the test proposed above, we may conclude that when one says 'I believe that . . .' or 'He believes that . . .' and there is the implication that the person referred to does not know what he is said to believe, this is not an implication of what is said but is merely something implied by the speaker. The existence of such implications in no way undermines condition (iB) because that is a thesis about what is said and

[3] In Swartz, op. cit. 446, Grice proposes a cancellation test that closely resembles my own test.

the implications of what is said. It is equivalent to the thesis that what is said when it is said that a person knows that p is logically inconsistent with what is said when it is said that the person does not believe that p. That speakers sometimes imply that a person does not know what the speakers say the person believes is, therefore, quite irrelevant to condition (iB).

'I Know' as a Performative Utterance

A more sophisticated attack on (iB) resting upon considerations of linguistic usage is derived from the writings of J. L. Austin. In a quite famous passage Austin compared the locution, 'I promise', to the locution, 'I know'.[4] His basic contention is that uttering such words is the performance of a certain ritual which alters one's relations to others. As he puts it, when I say 'I promise', I have not merely told you what I intend to do, 'but by using this formula (performing this ritual), I have bound myself to others, and staked my reputation in a new way'.[5] Moreover, it is essential to notice that saying 'I promise' is not saying 'I have performed an especially striking feat of intending thus binding myself to others and staking my reputation in a new way.'[6] I have done that, but I have not said I have done it. Austin draws a comparison between saying 'I promise' and 'I know' in the following words. 'Similarly, saying, "I know" is taking a new plunge. But it is not saying, "I have performed a specially striking feat of cognition, superior, in the same scale as believing and being sure, even to being quite sure", for there is nothing in that scale superior to being quite sure. Just as promising is not something superior, in the same scale as hoping and intending, even to merely fully intending; for there *is* nothing in that scale superior to fully intending. When I say "I know!", I give others my word: I give others my authority for saying that "S is P".'[7]

The foregoing passage has been interpreted in support of denying condition (iB). Perhaps such interpretation results from Austin's later remark 'To suppose that "I know" is a descriptive phrase is only one example of the *descriptive fallacy*, so common

---

[4] J. L. Austin, 'Other Minds', in *Logic and Language*, second series, ed. A. G. N. Flew (Basil Blackwell, Oxford, 1959), 123–58.
[5] Ibid. 142–3.   [6] Ibid. 144.   [7] Ibid.

in philosophy. Even if some language is now purely descriptive, language was not in origin so, and much of it is still not so. Utterance of obvious ritual phrases, in the appropriate circumstances, is not *describing* the action we are doing, but *doing* it . . .'[8] Thus, the reasoning is that if we accept condition (iB) then we must admit that when a man says 'I know', he is describing his state as being one of belief. Since he is not describing himself at all, but is performing an epistemic ritual, according to Austin, he is not implying that he is in such a state of belief.

This argument might appear to run contrary to other things that Austin himself says. For he remarks 'When I say "*S* is *P*", I imply at least that I believe it, . . .'[9] Now, if a man says, 'I know that *S* is *P*', thus giving others his authority for saying that *S* is *P*, surely he has said that *S* is *P* and thus at least implied that he believes that *S* is *P*. It would seem to follow from Austin's own account that when a man says 'I know that *p*', he implies that he believes that *p*. As we have noted, however, from the fact that a man implies something when he speaks, it does not follow that what he implies is implied by what he has said. It is consistent with Austin's remarks to suppose that when a man says 'I know that *p*' he is performing a special ritual of giving others his word and has not said that he believes anything nor decribed his state of mind in any way at all.

But is Austin's argument any good? There is reason for rejecting it. Austin seems to have created a false dichotomy. A man may use words to perform a special ritual and *also* use them descriptively, both at the same time. A man who says to a waiter 'I would like some wine, Steinberger Beerenauslese 1959' has both performed the ritual act of ordering some wine, a very special wine at that, and also described himself as one who would like some of that wine. Here the descriptive use of words is perfectly compatible with the performative use. As R. M. Chisholm has said, to suppose that a performative use of words precludes a descriptive use might well be called the *performative fallacy*.[10]

Is one who argues that 'I know' is not descriptive because it is performative guilty of such a fallacy? It would seem so, for,

---

[8] Ibid. 146–7.   [9] Ibid. 143.
[10] R. M. Chisholm, *Theory of Knowledge*, 17.

even if Austin is correct in declaring that when I say, 'I know that S is P', I give others my authority for saying that S is P, the performance of this act is perfectly consistent with describing oneself as believing with complete justification that S is P. Indeed, the assumption that I am so describing myself when I say 'I know that S is P', helps to explain the way in which I give my authority for saying that S is P by saying 'I know that S is P'. I give my authority by affirming my belief and complete justification for believing that S is P. Indeed, if what I have said when I say 'I know that S is P' did not imply that I believed that S is P or that I was completely justified in such a belief, and therefore was perfectly consistent with my neither believing nor being justified in believing that S is P, then why in the world should saying 'I know that S is P' be taken as giving my authority for saying that S is P? It might more reasonably be taken as an expression of opinionless agnosticism.

The two preceding appeals to linguistic usage are closely allied and embody a similar misunderstanding. In both cases some aspect of the linguistic usage of the words 'know' and 'believe' is taken as evidence against condition (iB) which affirms that if one knows that p, then one believes that p. None the less, both arguments fail because the feature of usage, in one case special emphasis, in the other a special performance, does not yield the desired conclusion. This happens because it is consistent with these features of usage to suppose that a man who says he knows that p has said something that implies that he believes that p.

To reinforce our position, we may take note of an argument by D. M. Armstrong. He points out that a man who says 'I know that p' may express certainty that p. It is, moreover, just this kind of expression of certainty that gives others the right to take me as giving my authority for saying that p.[11] The performance of giving one's authority is accomplished precisely by expressing certainty in this way. If, however, a man expresses certainty by saying 'I know that p', this surely implies that he believes that p. Hence, the first-person use of 'know' ultimately is the one in which the implication of belief is most clear.

The preceding discussion fixed upon the first-person use of

[11] David Armstrong, 'Does Knowledge Entail Belief?', *Proc. Aris. Soc.* lxx (1969–70), 21–36.

the words 'know' and 'believe' because this use of the words has some special features. Austin insists that his analysis applies only to the first-person usage, and it must be added that the implication of certainty is unique to the first-person use of 'know'.[12] When I say 'I know that the wine was not what I ordered', I am expressing certainty, but when I say of another 'He knows that the wine was not what I ordered', I am not saying that he is certain. I am saying that he knows and hence that he believes that the wine was not what I ordered, but I do not say he is certain of it. The first-person implication of certainty may well be construed as an implication of the speaker rather than of what he said, and thus cannot be made the basis of an argument to demonstrate the truth of (iB). It only shows that those features of first-person use of the term to which philosophers appeal in order to refute (iB) are completely consistent with the truth of (iB).

Knowing but Believing one does not

Let us now consider the second form of argument directed against (iB), the attempt to produce a counterexample. The best instance of such an argument I have found is in an article by Colin Radford, who has carefully constructed an example which it seems correct to describe as a case in which a man knows something he does not believe.[13] The example concerns a man, Jean, who protests quite sincerely that he does not know any English history, but when quizzed is able to answer some history questions correctly, for example, ones concerning the dates of the death of Elizabeth and James I. Jean also makes some mistakes—indeed, he misses more often than he hits the mark— and he cannot tell when he is right and when wrong. Jean thinks he is guessing all along. Because he thinks he is guessing, he is not inclined to believe his answers are correct. Nevertheless, Radford contends that we should say that Jean knows some

[12] Austin, op. cit. 143, footnote 1.

[13] Much of Radford's attack in the article 'Knowledge—By Examples', *Analysis*, xxvii (1966), 1–11, is directed against the thesis that a person knows that *p* only if he is sure or feels sure that *p*. The examinee example was considered by A. D. Woozley, 'Knowing and Not Knowing', *Proc. Aris. Soc.* liii (1953), 151–72, and by L. Jonathan Cohen, 'Claims to Knowledge', *Proc. Aris. Soc.*, supp. vol. xxxvi (1962), 33–50.

history. For example, Jean gives the correct answer to the question concerning the year of Elizabeth's death, and so he knows the answer: that Elizabeth died in 1603. Radford bolsters this contention by asking us to suppose that Jean has previously learned these dates and, consequently, that the reason he gives correct answers is that he remembers them.

Must we concede that Jean knows that Elizabeth died in 1603 even though he does not believe (or disbelieve) that this is so?[14] We may resist the inclination to do so, if any exists, by arguing that Jean does not know that Elizabeth died in 1603. The crucial premiss of such a counterargument is that, though he knows some correct answers, he does not know that these answers are correct. This is shown by the fact that he has no idea which of his answers are correct, and would be unable to tell the correct answers from the incorrect ones. Thus, though Jean answers the question concerning the death of Elizabeth correctly, he does not know that his answer is correct. But what does he need to know in order to know that his answer, that Elizabeth died in 1603, is correct? To know it is correct, all he needs to know is that Elizabeth did, in fact, die in 1603. If he knew that she died in 1603, then he would also know that his answer is correct, but he does not know his answer is correct. Therefore, Jean does not know that Elizabeth died in 1603.

We have, from one example, elicited contradictory conclusions. Let us look at the arguments side by side. Put schematically, Radford's argument is as follows:

(1) Jean knows the correct answer to the question.
(2) The correct answer to the question is that Elizabeth died in 1603.
(3) If Jean knows the correct answer and the correct answer is that Elizabeth died in 1603, then Jean knows that Elizabeth died in 1603.
(4) Jean knows that Elizabeth died in 1603.

The opposing argument is as follows:

(1) Jean does not know that his answer is correct.
(2) Jean's answer is that Elizabeth died in 1603.

[14] The argument that follows as well as other material in this chapter is taken from an earlier article by the author, 'Belief and Knowledge', *Philosophical Review*, lxxviii (1968), 491–9.

(3) If Jean does not know that his answer is correct and Jean's answer is that Elizabeth died in 1603, then Jean does not know that Elizabeth died in 1603.

(4) Jean does not know that Elizabeth died in 1603.

The two arguments are equally persuasive, and, moreover, there is no equivocation in the word 'know' in the conclusions of these arguments to lessen the force of the contradiction. With such contradictory conclusions cogently defended, must we concede that the concept of knowledge is contradictory? Is knowledge impossible?

Fortunately, there is no need to concede the impossibility of knowledge. Instead, we may reject premiss (3) of Radford's argument. We may say that Jean knows the correct answer, that Elizabeth died in 1603, but deny that Jean knows that Elizabeth died in 1603. To see why, consider an example in which a man knows the correct answer to a question about the date of Elizabeth's death even though he is guessing and thus does not know that she died in 1603. Imagine another man, George, who is on a quiz programme and is asked the date of Elizabeth's death. He answers: '1603'. You, not having heard the answer, ask me, 'Did George know the correct answer?' To this question I could reply in the affirmative. Moreover, it might not matter whether I thought George was guessing or not. When the quizmaster says 'George, if you know the answer to the question I am about to ask, you will win that 1973 Ford', he does not intend to withhold the Ford if George guesses correctly. On the contrary, in this context to give the correct answer is to know the correct answer. When you asked, 'Did George know the correct answer?' I could have answered 'Yes, but I think it was just a lucky guess.' There is no question of whether George knows the correct answer once he gives it. He knew. Away he drives.

Thus George, like Jean, knows the correct answer, that Elizabeth died in 1603. George knew just as Jean did, even though George was guessing. Though we concede that George knew the correct answer, we should want to insist that he did not know that Elizabeth died in 1603. A lucky guess that p is not a case of knowing that p. The preceding argument shows that there are contexts in which it would be acceptable to say that a man knows the correct answer, which is that p, but would be clearly false to say the man knows that p.

A Proof that Knowledge Implies Belief

On the basis of these considerations we can prove that any case in which a man does not believe that p is also a case in which he does not know that p. Moreover, we shall base this conclusion on a premiss Radford himself defends. Radford, while asserting that Jean knows that Elizabeth died in 1603, concedes that it would be in some way improper for Jean, who thinks he is guessing, to say that he knows that Elizabeth died in 1603. He maintains its impropriety is due to the fact that Jean does not believe that he knows that Elizabeth died in 1603. As to why Jean does not believe that he knows this fact, Radford says that it is a necessary condition of a man believing that he knows that p that the man believes that p. And that is the premiss on which we may build an argument.

The preceding premiss may be reformulated as follows. If a man does not believe that p, then he does not believe that he knows that p. I think it is quite obvious, as Radford admits, that this is true, but we need one additional premiss.[15] If a man does not believe that he knows that p, then, even though he correctly says that p and knows he has said that p, he does not know that he correctly says that p. The reason for accepting this premiss is simply that if a man does not believe that he knows that p, then, even if he correctly says that p and knows he has said it— in a quiz, for example—he should, if he is honest, not say he knows that his answer is correct. If we ask such a man 'Do you know whether the answer you have given is correct?' the only right answer is 'No'. To these two premises we may add an assumption employed earlier, to wit, that if, even though a man correctly says that p and knows he has said that p, he does not know he correctly says that p, then he does not know that p. This assumption rests on the fact that if a man correctly says that p and knows that he has said that p, then all he needs to know in order to know that he correctly says that p is simply to know that p.

From the preceding premisses we may conclude that if a

[15] Radford, op. cit. 10–11.

person does not believe that p, then he does not know that p.
Formally, the argument is as follows:

(1) If S does not believe that p, then S does not believe that he knows that p.

(2) If S does not believe that he knows that p, then, even though S correctly says that p and knows that he has said that p, S does not know that he correctly says that p.

(3) If, even though S correctly says that p and knows he has said that p, S does not know that he correctly says that p, then S does not know that p.

(4) If S does not believe that p, then S does not know that p.

Conclusion (4) follows from the preceding premises by element-ary logic and, of course, it is equivalent to our original thesis. Informally, the argument is as follows. Suppose a man—for example, Jean—does not believe that Elizabeth died in 1603. In that case he obviously would not believe that he knew that Elizabeth died in 1603. Imagine that Jean happens to say, perhaps in response to a question, that Elizabeth died in 1603. Since Jean does not believe that he knows that she died in 1603, then, as he himself must admit, Jean does not know that he is correct about the date of Elizabeth's death. If, however, he does not know that he is correct about this, then he does not know that Elizabeth died in 1603, for that is all he would need to know in order to know that he is correct. Thus, if Jean, or anyone else, does not believe that Elizabeth died in 1603, then he does not know that she died in 1603. Therefore, if a person does not believe that p, then he does not know that p; and, equivalently, but less negatively, if a person knows that p, then he believes that p. This proves (iB).

An Objection: Remembrance without Belief

Radford has objected to the preceding argument on the grounds that the question has been begged against him.[16] He contends that his example shows precisely that one can know

[16] Colin Radford, "'Analysing' 'Know(s) That'", *Philosophical Quarterly*, xx (1970), 228–9.

the correct answer to a question (and not just guess) and yet not know the answer is correct. In support of this he appeals to the consideration that one may remember that p, and hence know that p from memory, when one does not know that one knows that p, believe that one knows that p, or even believe that p. Indeed, the example concerning Jean, as spelled out in detail, is one in which he has previously learned that Elizabeth died in 1603, though he has forgotten having learning it, and thus gives the right answer because he remembers what he once learned. He remembers even though he does not know or believe himself to have done so, and consequently believes he is guessing. Since Jean is remembering, he knows that p, even though he does not believe he knows, thinks he is guessing, and does not believe that p.

There is another quite similar sort of example that should be considered at this juncture, for, like Radford's, it is persuasive, and the reply to both examples is quite similar. Another philosopher, E. J. Lemmon, presented the following as an example to show that a man may know that p but not know that he knows that p.[17] A man, Alan say, who some time ago learned about the number pi when he studied geometry, is asked 'What is the expansion of pi to four decimal places?' Alan replies 'I don't know', and his answer is quite sincere. After a moment, he suddenly remembers, and says 'Yes I do, it is 3·1416.' Lemmon contends that at the time at which the man said, 'I don't know', he did in fact know, as is shown by his subsequent remark. So, when Alan said he did not know, he did know, but he did not know that he knew. He only knew that he knew once he remembered the expansion of pi. This example, though directed against the thesis that if a man knows that p, then he knows that he knows that p, might equally well be employed against the argument offered in defence of (iB). This follows because premisses (2) and (3) of that argument entail that if a man knows that p, then he believes that he knows that p. It could thus be contended that Alan, when he says he does not know, does not believe that he knows though in fact he does. Consequently, premisses (2) and (3) could not both be true.

---

[17] E. J. Lemmon, 'If I Know, Do I Know that I Know?', in *Epistemology: New Essays in the Theory of Knowledge*, ed. A. Stroll (Harper and Row, New York, 1967), 54–83, but particularly 63.

This example can be made to bear even more directly on (iB) by slight amendment. Suppose we have another man, Steven, and we ask him. 'Is 3·1416 the expansion of *pi* to four decimal places?' Steven, who studied mathematics a good time ago and is not much interested in our question anyway, might, without much reflection and with some irritation, reply 'I don't know.' Like Alan, Steven immediately recalls his mathematics, quickly adds. 'Oh yes, I do know, *pi* is 3·1416 when expanded to four decimal places, and it is 3·1415926536 when expanded to ten', and looks quite smug. In this example, it could be contended that the man did know that 3·1416 is the expansion of *pi* to four decimal places when he said he did not know, as his immediately subsequent feat of memory showed. He did not believe he knew, however, nor did he believe 3·1416 to be the expansion of *pi* to four decimal places when first he spoke. Thus, we seem here to have a counter-example both to a consequence of premises (2) and (3) in our proof, to wit, that if a man knows that *p*, then he believes he knows that *p*, and also to (iB), to wit, that if a man knows that *p*, then he believes that *p*.

Borderline Cases of Knowledge

What are we to say to these arguments against our proof of (iB) and (iB) itself? The most direct reply is one conceded by Radford. At one point, Radford admits that his examples are borderline cases of knowledge.[18] This is precisely the case, but what is a borderline case? To say that a case is borderline means there are quite conclusive considerations in favour of applying the term, and equally conclusive considerations in favour of not applying it. For example, if we see something that is very similar in colour to many red things, so much so that this is quite conclusive reason for saying that the object is red; but at the same time it is very similar to things that are orange and not red, so much so that is quite conclusive reason for saying that the thing is not red, then we have a borderline case of something red. Such cases abound. For most terms of everyday speech, we can expect to find that the term applies without doubt or controversy in a large number of cases, and that it also clearly

18 Radford, 'Knowledge—By Examples', p. 4, footnote 1.

fails to apply in many cases, but in between these cases there are examples of things where it is not evident whether or not the term applies no matter how much one knows about the example. Here we are very likely to conclude that the case is borderline. Debate on whether the term applies in such cases can produce arguments and profound speculation, but no one can win because the case is precisely one in which the application of the term is not fixed. As S. Körner has suggested, such terms are inherently inexact, and, therefore, the decision to apply or not to apply the term in borderline cases is a matter of choice.[19]

If we wish to defend (iB) by maintaining that the cases of Jean, Alan, and Steven are all borderline for the application of the word 'know', two tasks remain. First, we must show that the cases are genuinely borderline, and, second, we must justify our choice of applying epistemic terms in the manner required for the truth of (iB) and the soundness of our proof of (iB).

Some argument for the conclusion that Jean's is a borderline case of knowledge has already been given in the earlier presentation of two persuasive arguments, one yielding the conclusion that Jean does not know that Elizabeth died in 1603, and the other the exact opposite. Similar argument may be offered in the cases of Alan and Steven. Since each sincerely reports and believes that he does not know, neither knows that the correct answer to the question is 3·1416 at the time of his report. In order to know that 3·1416 is the correct answer, however, all that either man would have to know is that 3·1416 is the expansion of pi to four decimal places. Hence, neither man knows that 3·1416 is the expansion of pi to four decimal places when he says he does not know. This argument is in direct opposition to Lemmon's which was that, since Steven and Alan have not learned the answer to the question between the time of their first and second remarks, each must have known all along that 3·1416 was the expansion of pi to four decimal places. Hence again there are equally persuasive arguments for contradictory conclusions.

The arguments could be countered. To refute the argument

[19] Stephan Körner, *Experience and Theory* (Routledge and Kegan Paul, London, 1966), 19–47.

supporting the conclusion that they do know, one could say, with Radford, that a man may know the correct answer, namely, that p, and know that p, even though he does not know that the answer is correct. And to refute the argument supporting the conclusion that Alan and Steven do not know, one could reply that a man may come to know something without learning anything new, in just the way Alan and Steven came to know the expansion of pi after correctly reporting that they did not know, namely, by remembering it. Such arguments and counterarguments concerning these examples cannot settle the matter precisely because the examples are borderline cases. It is precisely like arguing whether something is red when it is as close to red as it is to orange. And no argument can settle that.

Knowledge and Conviction

Moreover, it is perfectly clear what makes these cases borderline. A perfectly straightforward case of believing or knowing that p must be one in which a man is convinced of the truth of p and is prepared to say so. When such conviction is lacking, then a man may sincerely deny that he believes or knows that p, and there will be good reason for agreeing with him. If there is also good reason for saying that he does believe or know that p in such a case, as there may well be, then there will be good reason for each of the contradictory conclusions, i.e. he believes that p, he does not, and he knows that p, he does not. Thus, it is precisely the absence of such conviction that p and the attendant lack of readiness to report that p, or that one knows that p, which makes these cases borderline.

We shall eventually defend choosing to regard those cases, in which such conviction that p is lacking, as being cases of neither knowing nor believing. Hence Jean, Steven, and Alan are all to be taken at their word when they say that they do not know. Before defending this ruling, we should notice that we beg no question. As we shall now show, whether or not one assumes that a conviction that p and the attendant readiness to report that p are conditions of knowledge and belief, condition (iB), and the premises used in support of it, all turn out to be true, *provided* that one either adds or deletes the requirement of conscious conviction from *all* uses of the terms 'believe' and 'know'.[20]

First let us suppose that a conviction that *p* and readiness to report that *p* in appropriate circumstances are conditions of believing that *p* as well as knowing that *p*. In that case, we find in both the Radford and the Lemmon example that the supposed knower is ignorant. The man in each example who is alleged to have knowledge that *p*, is neither convinced that *p* nor ready to assert that *p* at the time in question. Of course, the man in Lemmon's example ultimately asserts that *p*, but he lacks the readiness to assert that *p* at the time he is first questioned. This example helps to illustrate the sort of circumstance I wish to specify by the word 'appropriate'. There is a readiness to assert that *p* in appropriate circumstances only if an answer that *p* is forthcoming in response to an understood question that one desires (without conflict) to answer correctly. Neither of these counterexamples succeeds, therefore, on this supposition.

Now let us consider the opposite assumption, namely, that neither a conviction that *p* nor a readiness to assert that *p* are conditions of knowledge or belief. This is the assumption that the two examples depend upon, for both Lemmon and Radford assume that a man knows something which he is neither convinced of nor ready to assert. The man in Radford's example does answer that Elizabeth died in 1603, but without the conviction that characterizes assertion.

If, however, such lack of conviction and readiness to report are compatible with knowledge and belief, then both Radford and Lemmon fail to prove their point in another way. Radford assumes that the man does not believe that *p* because he says he is guessing. This does not follow on the current assumption. We have assumed that a man can know or believe that *p* even though he lacks conviction that *p* and a readiness to assert that *p*. That the man thinks he is guessing that *p* shows that he lacks such conviction and readiness to assert, but it fails to prove that he does not believe that *p*. Indeed, under the current assumption, a man may say in all sincerity that he neither believes nor disbelieves that *p*, even though he does in fact believe that *p*,

---

[20] The argument that follows is taken from an earlier article by the author 'Believing that One Knows', *Synthese*, xxi (1970), 133–40.

just as he may say that he does not know that p, even though in fact he does know that p.

The current line of argument is even more straightforward with respect to the Lemmon example. Lemmon assumes that a man can know that p at a time when he lacks conviction that p and is not then ready to assert that p. When it comes to knowing that one knows that p, the assumption is suddenly reversed, however. When the man says he does not know the expansion of pi to four decimal places, Lemmon takes this to show that, though the man knows that pi expanded to four decimal places is 3·1416, he does not know that he knows. The truth is that just as a man might be said to know that pi expanded to four decimal places is 3·1416 when he lacks conviction and a readiness to assert that pi expanded to four decimal places is 3·1416, so he might be said to know that he knows that pi expanded to four decimal places is 3·1416 when he lacks conviction and a readiness to report that he knows that pi expanded to four decimal places is 3·1416.

In short, both the Radford example and the Lemmon example fail for the same reason. The former wishes to show that there may be knowledge without belief and the latter that there may be knowledge without knowledge that one knows. Both take conviction and a readiness to report as a condition of the application of the epistemic term they wish to prove not to apply, while rejecting these as conditions of the epistemic term they wish to assume does apply. This is illegitimate precisely because these epistemic terms may all be used either as having such conditions as requirements of application or as not having them. When we consistently assume that such conditions are not required for the terms 'know' and 'believe', then the alleged counterexamples fail.

The crucial point may best be illustrated by considering the thesis: if a man knows, then he believes that he knows. If any of our theses are countered by the examples in question, this is the one that seems most directly affected. In both examples, the man says that he does not know when it is assumed that he does know. This is taken as showing that the man does not believe that he knows. The argument derives its persuasiveness from a presumed, though not explicit, connection between sincere affirmation and belief. The presumption is that if a man says in all sincerity that he does not believe something, then he does not believe the thing he says he does not believe. However, this presumption runs contrary to our assumption that knowledge and belief do not require conviction and a readiness to assert. Moreover, our assumption is perfectly consistent with one way in which the epistemic terms are used in careful and sophisticated ordinary usage. That a man sincerely says that he does not know that p does not prove that he does not believe that he knows that p. Indeed, there is nothing incongruous about the fact that a man might deny in all sincerity that he knows that p even though he knows that p, believes that p, believes that he knows that p, and knows that he knows that p.

If a man sincerely says that p, then, of course, he believes in some sense what he says. We may concede that there is both a sense in which he believes it and a sense in which he does not. The same can be said of knowledge. In the sense in which knowledge and belief require a conviction and a readiness to assert, the man who says in all sincerity that he does not know that p, neither knows that he knows nor believes that he knows that p; but in the sense in which knowledge and belief do not require these conditions, the same man may both know and believe that he knows that p. As long as these two different uses of 'belief' and 'know' are carefully distinguished, and the terms employed in thesis (iB) and the proof of (iB) are used in one way only, there are no counterexamples to them.

The Requirement of Conviction

In the preceding argument we have spoken of the two different senses of 'believe' and 'know' depending on whether there is the implication of a conviction that p on the part of the person said to know or believe that p. Some philosophers might object that the difference of implication is not due to an ambiguity in these words but to conflicting criteria for the application of each word in a single sense. Such disputes may be left to be settled within semantic theory. Our present task is to justify restricting the use of these terms in such a way that there is always the implication that the person said to believe or know has a conviction that p, even though we admit that the term is also commonly used in such a way as not to have this implication.

Radford suggests that one who argues in defence of (iB) as

we have is 'in the grip of a philosophical theory'. He also contends that a philosophical theory must not distort the phenomena, or if it does distort the phenomena, it is acceptable only if it is very fertile.[21] It should be noticed, however, that any coherent theory that does not lead to contradictory conclusions concerning the borderline cases we have been considering *must* 'distort' our inconsistent ordinary usage of the terms 'know' and 'believe'. For most purposes of everyday speech we can afford the semantic imperfection that yields the sort of contradictory conclusions we have derived from the study of Jean and company, but an acceptable *theory* must eliminate such imperfection for the sake of consistency.

We shall require that the epistemic terms in question carry the implication of conviction, for this will enable us to extricate our employment of the terms from the contradictions noted earlier. Such a requirement leads directly to the conclusion that Jean, Alan, and Steven do not know that p when they say they do not know, because they then lack conviction that p. By so doing, we are not dogmatically ruling out the possibility that some theory of knowledge might be constructed which would rule in the opposite direction, to wit, against the implication of such conviction. We should welcome the development of such a theory. However, as we affirmed earlier, our concern is to present a theory of knowledge and justification to explain how we are justified in our claims to knowledge. Since we are attempting to explain the justification of *claims* to knowledge, we are only concerned with knowledge in which a man would claim to know and thus claim justification for what he avers. Such cases are going to be ones in which the person in question is convinced that p and ready to report that p in the appropriate circumstances. To put the matter another way, when a man claims to know that p, he may be challenged to formulate why he believes that p. Our theoretical objective is to explain how such a challenge may be met. Again, such a claims require a subject with a conviction he is ready to express.

Finally, it is important to notice that not only are we concerned exclusively with those cases of knowing that p in which there is a conviction that p, but we shall also restrict our consideration to those cases of knowing that p in which the subject

21 Radford, "'Analysing' 'Know(s) That'", 228–9.

believes that he knows that *p*. It is only when a man believes, that is, is convinced, that he knows that *p*, that he may legitimately claim to know and thus be called upon to explain how he knows or why he believes that *p*. Hence, our earlier adoption of the assumption that if a man knows that *p*, then he believes that he knows that *p*. Only when a man is convinced and ready to report that he knows does the question of justification arise.

In defence of the foregoing restriction, it should be added that our decision to require the implication of conviction that *p* when a man believes or knows that *p*, and the conviction that he knows that *p* when he does know that *p*, is nothing arbitrary or idiosyncratic. It is warranted by the fact that our edifice of scientific knowledge and practical wisdom depends upon the social context in which criticism and defence determine which claims are to be employed as the postulates of scientific systems and the information for practical decisions. In such contexts, when a man thinks he is but guessing or when he admits ignorance, he is taken at his word; for, such a man is not willing to make the sort of epistemic commitments that would enable us to check his cognitive credentials. Of course, we may well be interested in his reasons, if he has any, for *conjecturing* what he does, but this is quite different from asking whether he is completely justified in his claim to knowledge. An affirmative answer to that question not only shows the man has knowledge, it also transfers that knowledge to those who understand the justification and apprehend its merit. Our theoretical concern with critical reasoning, and our attempt to explain how such reasoning succeeds, warrants our decision to rule that knowledge and belief must involve the forms of conviction cited above.

The foregoing results show that we might formulate (iB) to read as follows:

(iBC) If *S* knows that *p*, then *S* is convinced that *p*.

It is belief in the form of conviction that we require as a condition of knowledge. Moreover, we have employed two premisses in the proof of (iB) that yield:

(iBK) If *S* knows that *p*, then *S* is convinced that *S* knows that *p*.

Our justification for both (iBC) and (iBK) is based on the kind of theory of knowledge and justification we are seeking to construct, to wit, one which will explain how knowledge claims are justified. This completes our defence of (iB) interpreted as (iBC).

Knowledge without Conviction: Objections and Replies

Before concluding our chapter, it will be useful to comment on certain objections that have been raised, not against (iBC), but against (iBK). Strictly speaking we could ignore these objections and yet affirm (iBC), but since we have employed (iBK) in our proof of (iB), this would be inappropriate. Moreover, by considering the sort of objections raised against (iBK), we shall be able to clarify the difference between other approaches to the theory of knowledge and the one here pursued.

David Annis, following Arthur Danto, has argued that a man might know that something is true even though he does not believe he knows because the man lacks the concept of knowledge.[22] Thus, Annis argues that a person, for example a child, might have learned to tell that certain things are red, and to assert that they are red, even though he does not understand the word 'know' or any synonym. According to Annis, such a person would have the concept of a thing being red, and, therefore, know and believe that certain things are red, while at the same time lacking the concept of knowledge, and thus neither know nor believe that he knows anything. Hence he knows that p, but he does not believe he knows that p. This would refute (iBK).

The argument Annis presents is based on the assumption that a person can know something without having the concept of knowledge. It must be immediately conceded to Annis that a person can know something without understanding the word 'know' or any synonym. That does not settle the matter, however, for, even though a man does not understand the word 'know' or any synonym, he may yet have the concept of

[22] David Annis, 'A Note on Lehrer's Proof that Knowledge Entails Belief', *Analysis*, xxix (1968–9), 207–8; and Arthur C. Danto, 'On Knowing That We Know', in *Epistemology: New Essays in the Theory of Knowledge*, ed. A. Stroll, pp. 32–53, particularly section vi, pp. 49–53.

knowledge. To see that this is so, imagine a man who, though he does not understand the word 'red' or any synonym, but otherwise has a high degree of linguistic competence, learns a game in which landing on a red square is necessary to winning the game. Moreover, imagine that to win one must shout out 'Revolution!' when one lands on such a square. Now playing with the man in question might convince us beyond any doubt that he knows when he has landed on a red square. This conviction may be reinforced if the man tells us the winning square is different from another square, a green one, in the way in which a ripe tomato is different from one that has not yet begun to ripen. The fact that he has neither the word 'red' nor any synonym for that word in his understanding vocabulary surely fails to show that he lacks the concept of redness.

By the same reasoning, the fact that the boy in the Annis example does not understand the word 'know' or any synonym fails to show that he lacks the concept of knowledge. Suppose the boy says 'That is red', and, when confronted with opposition, insists doggedly that he is right, backing up his insistence with relevant argumentation, for example, comparison between the colour of the object in question and other objects conceded to be red. In this case, the boy is not just saying, 'That is red', he is claiming to know. It is quite clear that the boy thinks he knows, indeed, knows he knows, even if his vocabulary lacks the word 'know' or any synonym of that word. Whether or not he has the word, he believes he knows and in this sense has the concept of knowledge. Construed in this way, the case is not a counterexample to (iBK).

To obtain a counterexample, Annis must ask us to imagine that the boy who says 'That is red', is not claiming to know. The boy must therefore not be prepared to insist on what he says and defend it with cogent argumentation. Such insistence and defence would show that the boy thinks he knows. If, however, the boy does not exhibit such insistence and defence, but instead responds to questioning in a more uncertain and doubtful manner, then we have reason for concluding that he does not know that the object is red. His response places him in the same category with Jean who is similarly uncertain and doubtful. Even if what the boy has said is correct, the lack of conviction he exhibits gives us grounds for denying that he knows that what he says is correct. Assuming that the boy understands what he says, if he knows that the object is red, he would also know that what he said is correct. Therefore, our grounds for denying that the boy knows what he said is correct are also grounds for denying that he knows that the object is red. Construing the case in this way does not yield a counterexample to (iBK) either.

The upshot of the preceding arguments is a dilemma for Annis. Either the boy knows that what he says is correct, in which case he believes he knows the object is red and the counterexample fails for this reason; or the boy does not know that what he says is correct, in which case he does not know the object is red and the counterexample fails for that reason. We claim Annis cannot slip between the horns.

The preceding argument shows that we may throw the example Annis presents in the same barrel of borderline cases that already contains those of Jean, Alan, and Steven. However, the barrel is by now bulging a bit, and this may awaken some doubts about our decision to exclude such cases. To put all such doubts to rest, let us consider another objection which comes from the philosopher Annis follows, Arthur Danto.

We may adopt an argument from Danto, intended to be a counterargument against (iBK). Suppose we consider a man, who, unlike the person in Annis's example, has the concept of knowledge but, being a sceptic, denies that it applies.[23] Thus, in opposition to such a common-sense philosopher as Thomas Reid or G. E. Moore, this sceptic denies that he knows that he sees the hand before his very eyes. He believes and is convinced that he does *not* know that there is a hand before his eyes even though he holds his hand directly before himself. Moreover, he is not visually or mentally defective; on the contrary, he is a very clever defender of ignorance, one with whom we shall become much better acquainted in a later chapter. He might even go as far as to deny that anyone knows anything, but he need not be so extreme. Danto suggests that such a man obviously does know the very thing he sincerely denies he knows, to wit, that there is a hand before his eyes. So, according to Danto, this man knows that there is a hand before his eyes even though he does not believe he knows this, and, indeed, is convinced that he does not.

[23] Danto, op. cit.

Again we have an argument to show that the man does not know. For even when we ask him whether he knows that there is a hand before his eyes, he sincerely says that he does not know, and, therefore, does not know that it would be correct to say that there is a hand before his eyes. In order to know that it would be correct to say that there is a hand before his eyes, however, all that he would have to know is that there is a hand before his eyes. Since he does not know that it would be correct to say that, he does not know that there is a hand before his eyes. Hence, by this argument, we are again warranted in concluding that this example is at best a borderline case of knowledge, and, consequently, we may choose to conclude that it, along with the other alleged counterexamples, is not a case of knowledge.

Memory without Knowledge

At this point, we must honestly face the question, why do all these cases seem to be examples of knowledge to the philosophers in question? The answer is that we often ascribe knowledge to others in order to explain, in a common-sense manner, why they are correct. In each of the cases considered, someone is in a position to say something, either at the time he disavows knowledge or very shortly thereafter, which warrants our concluding that the man was in a position to give the right answer. It is not just a matter of luck that he can give a correct answer. On the contrary, it is because he acquired knowledge in the past that it is possible for him to come up with the correct answer now. If we suppose that the knowledge has vanished, then it seems difficult to explain how he can now be in a position to give the correct answer. For the purposes of explaining how he can now be in a position to give a correct answer, we conclude that the knowledge has not vanished. He still knows.

This very natural way of explaining correct answers is, however, highly defective, for something extremely important has disappeared in spite of such answers, namely, the conviction of knowledge and/or truth. In the absence of such conviction, there results a refusal to defend a claim to know and the lack of justificatory support. The difference between the man who, convinced he knows that p, is ready to defend the claim that he knows, and a man who does not know what knowledge is, or thinks he is just guessing that p, or who thinks there is no such thing as knowledge, is sufficiently great that we may justifiably mark the distinction by refusing to say that the latter knows that p. By doing so, we shall in *no* way prevent ourselves from explaining how a man can manage to give the correct answer, that p, without knowing that p.

The latter contention is supported by the application of another argument derived from Armstrong.[24] In a reply to Radford, he asks us to imagine a case in which a man, asked about the date of the death of Elizabeth, answers: 'Elizabeth died in 1306.' Now this answer, though incorrect, is sufficiently similar to the correct answer, 1603, so that we can see that it is not a mere matter of chance that he gave this answer. We cannot explain this man's answer by affirming that he knows that Elizabeth died in 1603, for, the numbers 6 and 3 having been transposed in his memory, he does not know that Elizabeth died in 1603. (To clarify this we may even imagine that when asked 'Are you sure it was not 1603', the man replies that he is sure it is 1306.) Just as it would be incorrect to explain why this man gives the answer he does by affirming that he knows the date of Elizabeth's death, so explaining why Jean and the others are able to give a correct answer, by affirming that they know, would be otiose. A theory of memory that explains how memory produces the results it does, whether correct or incorrect, does not require us to assume that a man knows his answer is correct whenever memory enables him to produce a correct answer. To do so would be to lump together the cases in which memory only functions well enough to yield a correct answer with those cases in which it produces conviction and justification.

Our contention is that sometimes memory is good enough to give us a correct answer when it is not good enough to give us knowledge that the answer is correct. When memory does not function well enough so that we know what we say is correct, then we are not in a position either to claim to know or to justify a claim to know. Thus, we wish to distinguish sharply between those cases in which memory serves us so well that we can both claim to know and are justified in that claim, from

24 Armstrong, op. cit.

those cases in which memory succeeds only well enough so what we say, however hesitantly, is nevertheless quite correct. That there is a distinction cannot be doubted, and, for purposes of constructing a theory to explain epistemic justification, we need only count as knowledge those cases in which a man is convinced that he knows and is ready to make a knowledge claim requiring justification. It is such cases that have top value in the epistemic marketplace of justificatory bartering, and all the rest may be discounted without incurring an explanatory deficit.

4

Justification and Knowledge:
The Foundation Theory (I)

In the first chapter, we gave the following as the third condition of knowledge:

> (iii) If S knows that p, then S is completely justified in believing that p.

This condition is the most important in the analysis of knowledge. Indeed, divergent epistemologies often diverge precisely on the question: what makes a belief completely justified? As we noted earlier, certain alleged theories of truth are often simply theories of justification. One such theory mentioned earlier was the correspondence theory, namely, that a statement is true if and only if it corresponds to the facts. We argued that, as theory of truth, this reduced to the elimination theory. We also noted, however, that it might be reinterpreted as a theory of how we *determine* the truth of a statement, and, as so construed, it would be a theory of justification. It would then affirm that we determine whether or not a statement is true by determining whether or not it corresponds to the facts.

The second theory of truth, which we also claimed reduced to the elimination theory, was the coherence theory. Again, we noted that this theory could be reinterpreted as a theory about how we determine the truth of a statement, and as so construed, it too would become a theory of justification. It would be one affirming that we determine whether or not a statement is true by determining whether it coheres with other statements belonging to some system.

Two Theories of Justification: Foundation and Coherence

These formulations are imprecise and in need of clarification. They suggest the basic division of theories of justification into two camps. The first assumes, with the correspondence theory, that there are certain *basic* facts, and that all beliefs that are justified are so by their relation to those facts. Beliefs concerning basic facts are basic beliefs. All other beliefs are justified in terms of basic beliefs. Such theories of knowledge and justification have come to be known as *foundation* theories because they fit the metaphor of knowledge as an edifice supported by a foundation of basic beliefs. Hereafter we shall refer to such theories as foundation theories.

The second kind of theory of knowledge eschews the idea that all justification depends on any set of basic beliefs and instead posits that the justification of beliefs depends only on relations between beliefs in some system of beliefs none of which is basic. The relation may be called a relation of *coherence*, but the mere introduction of that term is not intended to explicate the character of the justifying relation.

We shall attempt to explicate the character of both foundation theories and coherence theories of knowledge and justification. Ultimately, we shall decide between them. In this chapter and the next, we shall be primarily concerned with the foundation theory of justification, and in subsequent chapters we shall turn to the coherence theory.

The Foundation Theory

It is possible to give a more precise characterization of foundation theories by specifying the conditions that must be met for a belief to be basic. The first is that a basic statement must be self-justified and must not be justified by any non-basic belief. Second, a basic belief must either be irrefutable, or, if refutable at all, it must only be refutable by other basic beliefs. Third, beliefs must be such that all other beliefs that are justified or refuted are justified or refuted by basic beliefs. A theory of justification having these features is one in which there are basic beliefs which are self-justified and neither refutable nor justifiable by non-basic beliefs and which justify and refute all non-basic beliefs that are justified or refuted. These basic beliefs constitute the foundation of all justification.

Traditionally, the doctrine of empiricism has been associated with the foundation theory, for, according to empiricist theories of knowledge and justification, there are some empirical statements which constitute the content of basic beliefs. The belief that such statements are true is a self-justified belief which, if it can be refuted at all, can only be refuted by some other empirical statements. All beliefs that are justified are so because of the justification provided by the empirical statements in question. Thus, the beliefs that such empirical statements are true are basic. Exactly how the empirical statements are construed depends on the empiricist in question. However, the empirical statements which constitute the content of basic beliefs have always been statements to the effect that some item in sense experience has or lacks some quality or relationship discernible by means of the senses. Thus, the empirical statements are statements of observation.

Empiricists have disagreed about the *object* of sense experience. The item sensed may be conceived of as a physical thing, like a chair or a meter, or it may be construed as some more subjective entity, like an appearance or a sense datum. Moreover, they have disagreed about what makes such statements self-justified and about how basic beliefs justify other statements. They do agree that there are observation statements constituting the content of basic beliefs which justify all that is justified and refute all that is refuted.

Though empiricist epistemology is most commonly associated with a foundation theory, there is no logical restriction, or, for that matter, historical limitation, of foundation theories to empiricism. Rationalistic philosophies of knowledge, for example, that of Descartes, have been foundation theories. Such a rationalist maintains that a belief may be certified by reason as having characteristics that make it a basic belief. Reason is sufficient to determine that the belief is indubitable, or that it is a clear and distinct idea.

A strict rationalism would hold that basic beliefs, and the justification they provide for other beliefs, are certified by reason alone. Again, Descartes is often claimed to be such a rationalist. Historically, this position is probably mistaken. In a late section of the *Discourse on Method*, Descartes mentions how he had recourse to experiment to decide between competing hypotheses.[1] Thus, it is doubtful that Descartes was a strict rationalist. He seems to have agreed that at least upon some occasions justification is derived from sense experience. Similarly, a strict empiricism would hold that basic beliefs and the justification they provide for other beliefs are certified by experience alone. None the less, whatever the correct historical interpretation of these philosophers may be, almost none would contend that all justification is derived solely from reason or solely from experience. That a conclusion follows from premisses is ascertained by reason, and what the objects of sense experience are like is ascertained by experience. Of course, reason may play a role in the latter, and experience in the former, but it would generally be conceded that if all men were deprived of reason, then no one would be justified in believing any conclusion to be a logical consequence of a premiss, and if we were all deprived of our senses, then no one would be justified in believing there to be any objects of sense experience. These are obvious truths, mentioned only to illustrate how misguided it is to conceive of epistemology as the battleground between rationalism and empiricism.

The Foundation as a Guarantee of Truth

We are adopting an entirely different approach that cuts across traditional lines. Rationalists and empiricists often share a common conception which leads to a foundation theory and is perfectly easy to state. They conceive of justification as being *a guarantee of truth*. Empiricists think that experience can guarantee the truth of basic beliefs and rationalists think that reason is the guarantee of truth. Basic beliefs are basic because they cannot be false; their truth is guaranteed. With this initial guarantee of truth in basic beliefs, the next problem is how to extend this guarantee to other beliefs. The fundamental doctrine of foundation theories is that justification, whether it is the

[1] René Descartes, *Discourse on Method*, ed. Laurence LaFleur (Liberal Arts Press, New York, 1956), part vi, 'Some Prerequisites for Further Advances in the Study of Nature', 41–2.

self-justification of basic beliefs, or the derivative justification of non-basic beliefs, guarantees truth.[2]

Our earlier analysis of knowledge does, of course, explain why this doctrine should be held. Since one condition of knowledge is truth, it follows that no belief constitutes knowledge unless it is true. Thus, if our justification fails to guarantee the truth of what we believe, then it may leave us with a false belief. In that case, we lack knowledge. So justification sufficient to ensure us knowledge must guarantee the truth of what we believe.

There are many possible variations on the foundation theory. Some might formulate the doctrine in such a way that basic beliefs, though self-justified, might be refuted by non-basic beliefs. Or one might affirm that justification need not provide a guarantee of truth. If, however, either of these modifications are incorporated, we are forced to set aside a fundamental doctrine at the heart of the foundation theory. A central thesis of this theory is that beliefs which are justified by basic beliefs are safe from subsequent repudiation. If basic beliefs were refutable by non-basic ones, then all that was justified by basic beliefs might be undone if those basic beliefs themselves were refuted. In this case, we would be lacking a foundation for justification. Similarly, if the justification of basic beliefs did not guarantee their truth, then such beliefs would be open to refutation on the grounds that, though they are self-justified, they are in fact false. If there is nothing to ensure that such basic beliefs are true, then, *ipso facto*, there is nothing to ensure the truth of those beliefs they justify. Hence, they too are open to refutation.

Philosophers have claimed beliefs to be reasonable or evident without justification from other beliefs.[3] However, such views

---

[2] Panayot Butchvarov in *The Concept of Knowledge* (Northwestern University Press, Evanston, Ill., 1970), and Arthur C. Danto in *An Analytical Theory of Knowledge* (Cambridge University Press, London, 1968) have most recently expounded this view. See Butchvarov's discussion of the notion of sufficient evidence in his book, 49–50, and Danto's discussions of both direct knowledge, 26–49 and 147, and adequate evidence, 122, in his work. A. J. Ayer in *Foundations of Empirical Knowledge*, 78–84, proceeds from the same assumption and attempts to found justification on incorrigible statements.

[3] For example, see R. M. Chisholm's *Theory of Knowledge*, particularly chapter 2, 'The Directly Evident', and *Perceiving: A Philosophical Study*, particularly chapter 5, 'Justification and Perception'.

either reduce to the foundation theory we have formulated or they fall short of providing a foundation for justification. If such reasonable and evident beliefs are without any guarantee of truth, if such reasonableness and evidence provides no such guarantee, then, once again, the beliefs are subject to the epistemic indignity of being accused of error. Being without a guarantee of truth, they provide no foundation. They may be repudiated, along with all they justify, on the grounds that they are false. On the other hand, if the reasonableness and evidence of such beliefs guarantees their truth, then the theory reduces to the foundation theory articulated above. Thus, by examining the foundation theory as expressed, without pretending to have considered all conceivable modifications, we shall obtain a fair evaluation of the merits of this epistemology.

A foundation theory as so understood faces two problems. The first is to show that there are some basic beliefs which can guarantee their own truth. The second is to show how basic beliefs can guarantee the truth of other beliefs. The first of these problems will be the concern of the remainder of this chapter. Philosophers have maintained that some beliefs guarantee their own truth and are thus self-justified because they are incorrigible. We shall now examine the tenability of this thesis.

Incorrigible Belief

What is meant by saying that belief is incorrigible? Let us begin with the intuitive notion that an incorribible belief is one such that the man who has the belief cannot be mistaken in believing what he does. We are immediately faced with the tricky little word 'can', a semantic chameleon. What are we to understand it to mean? We may wisely begin with a technical notion which we can define with precision and then, should that prove insufficiently subtle, turn to some modification. We begin semantic operations with the notion of logical possibility.

The notion of logical possibility which is a candidate for the 'can' of incorrigibility is one that is predicated of statements rather than of bits of language. We sometimes speak of the logical impossibility of certain sentences, for example, we might say that the sentence 'John has a female brother' is logically impossible. However, when we say such things we are speaking elliptically. What is stated by the sentence is logically impossible. What the sentence 'John has a female brother' states is logically impossible. If one goes on to ask what the sentence states, we may say it states that John has a female brother. In a nutshell, it is logically impossible that something is the case.

Logical impossibility may, of course, be defined in terms of other logical notions, and these notions apply to chunks of language. We may say, for example, that it is logically impossible that John has a female brother if and only if the sentence 'John has a female brother' is a contradictory. We may then say that a sentence is contradictory if and only if it is analytically false. We thus come full tilt to the controversial notion of analyticity.

It is notoriously difficult to provide any satisfactory definition or criterion of analyticity or related notions. Some philosophers thus disregard the notion of analyticity as a philosophical relic of semantic battles lost long ago. This conclusion is premature. Some logical notion, whether that of contradictoriness, possibility, or impossibility, may be taken as basic and undefined. Once we concede that logical impossibility or some other logical notion must be taken as basic and undefined, we must also admit there are going to be cases in which it is difficult to ascertain whether what a sentence states is logically impossible. This is not because we are inept at logic or fail to understand the meaning of words, but rather, because the concept of logical impossibility is inexact and the distinction between logic and other areas of inquiry not clearly drawn. Nevertheless, there are many cases in which the application of the concept will be sufficiently precise for useful employment. The current case is one of these.

A Definition of Incorrigibility

Let us now define incorrigibility in terms of the concept of logical impossibility. We can say, roughly, that a belief is incorrigible if and only if it is logically impossible for the belief to be mistaken. More formally, the definition is as follows:

S has an incorrigible belief that p if and only if it is logically impossible that S believes that p and p is false.

Given this definition of incorrigibility, it follows immediately that if a person believes something and his belief is incorrigible, then what he believes is true. If it is impossible that he should believe that p and p should be false, then, given that he does believe that p, it follows that p is true. Hence, in one sense such beliefs guarantee their own truth.

Nevertheless, a problem arises when we consider whether incorrigible beliefs as so defined are self-justified or, indeed, justified at all, for it is logically impossible that any person should be mistaken in believing anything which is logically necessary. By saying that something is logically necessary I mean no more or less than that it is the denial of something logically impossible. Thus, it is logically impossible that 2 plus 7 does not equal 9, and hence logically necessary that 2 plus 7 equals 9. This means, however, that it is logically impossible that a man should believe that 2 plus 7 equals 9 and be mistaken in his belief. The reason is that it is logically impossible that 2 plus 7 should not equal 9.

A Counterexample

No matter how complicated or esoteric the arithmetical belief might be, it remains the case that if what is believed is logically necessary, then it is logically impossible that the belief should be false. Hence, the belief is incorrigible. For example, if a man believes that there is a one-to-one correspondence between the set of natural numbers and the set of even natural numbers, then he believes something that is logically necessary, and his belief is incorrigible. If, however, he believes this for some foolish reason, for example, he believes that after a certain point in the series of natural numbers there are no more odd ones, then we would conclude that, on the basis of his reasoning, he surely could have been mistaken and was quite unjustified in his belief. It was pretty much a matter of luck that what he believes was true, for he had no cogent reason for believing what he did. It is, of course, obvious that he did not know that what he believed was true because his belief was not at all justified.

In this example the man *could* have been mistaken, even though it was logically impossible that he should have been. Thus, there appears to be some important sense of the express-

ion 'could not have been mistaken' which our current specification of incorrigibility fails to capture. Moreover, this
demonstrates that the justification we have for believing certain
necessary truths in arithmetic, mathematics and logic is not
a simple consequence of the necessity of what is believed. A
man may believe something that is a necessary truth without
in any way knowing that his belief is true or even being justified
in his belief. This argument proves that the logical impossibility
of being mistaken does not suffice for justification when what is
believed in an arithmetical, mathematical, or logical truth.

It is important to understand exactly why the logical
impossibility of being mistaken does not produce justification
in such cases. The difficulty is that the logical impossibility
of being mistaken, and hence the incorrigibility of the belief, is a
logical consequence of what is believed, and has nothing to do
with the existence of the belief. If what is believed is logically
necessary, then it is logically impossible that it should be false.
When it is logically impossible that it is false that p, for any
condition C whatever, it is logically impossible that C should
hold and that p should be false. Thus, when it is logically
necessary that p, the logical impossibility of the conjunctive
statement that S believes that p and it is false that p is a direct
consequence of the logical impossibility of the falsity of p.
That S believes that p has nothing whatever to do with the
incorrigibility of his belief in these cases.[4]

An Amended Definition of Incorrigibility

This does not show that the notion of incorrigibility introduced
above must be completely abandoned. We may instead modify
the definition of incorrigibility by restricting it to statements that
are contingent. Contingent statements are ones that are neither
logically impossible nor logically necessary. We would then
obtain the following definition of incorrigibility:

> S has an incorrigible belief that p if and only if (i) it is
> contingent that p and (ii) it is logically impossible that S
> believes that p and it is false that p.

---

[4] Another method for dealing with these problems is presented by George
Nakhnikian in 'Incorrigibility', *Philosophical Quarterly*, xviii (1968), 207-15, but
Nakhnikian defines incorrigibility in terms of knowledge and this would be
unacceptable in the present context.

On this definition of incorrigibility, no belief is incorrigible when what is believed is logically necessary. Thus, if a person's belief is incorrigible in this sense, the incorrigibility of his belief will not be a simple consequence of the logical necessity of what he believes. On the contrary, what he believes must be contingent for his belief to be incorrigible, and hence, the incorrigibility of the belief will result from some logical connection between his having the belief and the truth of what is believed. It will not result simply from the logical necessity of what is believed.

Given that a belief is incorrigible in this sense, it is plausible to claim that the belief is self-justified because of the way in which it guarantees the truth of itself. The logical impossibility of the belief being false arises because the truth of what is believed is a logical consequence of the existence of the belief. More precisely, the statement that S believes that p has the truth of p as a deductive consequence, and the statement that S believes that p is essential to the deduction. Hence, the existence of the belief guarantees the truth of what is believed and the truth of the belief is not guaranteed by logic alone.

Even this definition of incorrigibility leaves us with a problem noted (in discussion) by Kenneth Konyndyk. Suppose that p is a deductive consequence of the statement that S believes p. Now, it is a general principle of deduction that if p is a deductive consequence of q, and t is a logical truth, then the conjunction of p and t is also a deductive consequence of q. This principle is but a corollary of the principle that a logical truth is a deductive consequence of every statement. Moreover, if p is a contingent statement, then so is the conjunction of p and t, where t is any logical truth whatever. Thus, if we suppose that there is some contingent statement which a man incorrigibly believes to be true, and if we suppose that every incorrigible belief is self-justified, then we arrive at the conclusion that if that man believes the conjunction of the contingent statement in question and any logical truth, no matter how foolish his reasons for believing the logical truth, then his belief in that conjunction is also incorrigible and self-justified. Consequently, we should have to say that he knew the conjunction to be true even though his reasons for believing one conjunct, the logical truth, failed to justify his believing it. A man does not, however, know a logical truth to be true simply because he happens to believe it in conjunction with some contingent statement that is incorrigible.

These reflections show that incorrigibility as defined is not sufficient justification of conjunctions or other logically complex statements. One way to avoid this problem is to restrict the definition of incorrigibility to statements that they are both con- tingent and non-complex, that is, atomic. However, the notion of atomicity, though it has a clear application within formal systems, lacks a comparably precise application within natural languages. Like the notion of an undefined or a logically primitive term, it has clear application in an artificial language where one may arbitrarily take any terms as primitive and any sentences as atomic. What is primitive and atomic in one system may be defined and complex in another. Such logical conceptions are thus always relative to a choice that we make in the construction of an artificial system. The contention of philosophers that some term is primitive, or that some sentence is atomic in a natural language remains obscure.

Moreover, the problem we have just uncovered shows rather clearly that incorrigibility is not a sufficient condition for self- justification, and, we shall accept that conclusion. It remains for us to consider whether incorrigibility is a necessary con- dition for self-justification. In short, even though not all incorrigible beliefs are self-justified, it remains possible that all self-justified beliefs are incorrigible, and moreover, are self- justified precisely because they are incorrigible. Thus, the notion of incorrigibility defined above will suffice for our purposes. The question that remains is whether there are incorrigible beliefs as so defined adequate to provide a founda- tion for the justification of all justified beliefs.

Alleged Examples of the Incorrigible

Many beliefs that a man has about himself are alleged to be incorrigible in this sense. The favourites are beliefs about subjective mental states of the moment, the idea being that a man cannot be mistaken about what is going on in his mind at the moment it is going on. Rather than beginning with a discus- sion of a belief about some mental or psychological state, though, let us go back to Descartes and consider the bare belief of man that he exists, whatever else might be true about him. Consider, for example, my belief that I exist.

My belief that I exist cannot, it is averred, conceivably be false. Yet when I say that I exist, my statement is perfectly contingent: it is not logically impossible that I should not exist. On the other hand, it does seem logically impossible that I should believe that I exist and yet not exist. If I do not exist, then how could I possibly believe that I do? The answer is that I could not. Thus, the notion of incorrigibility that we have defined is not empty.

Let us now consider a second example of incorrigible belief. If a man believes that he believes something, this logically implies that he believes something. The statement that I do not believe anything is logically contingent and non-contradictory, but it is logically impossible that I believe that I believe something and do not believe anything. Thus, the belief that one believes something is incorrigible.

The foregoing example must be distinguished from a closely related one. Once it is conceded that the belief that one believes something is incorrigible, it might be inferred that if a man believed that he believes that so and so, then his belief that he believes that so and so is incorrigible. I wish to deny this. A man might believe that he believes that so and so, in which case his belief that he believes something is incorrigible, but his belief that he believes that so and so is not. To be more precise, there is at least one sense of the term 'believe' in which a man may be mistaken about what he believes, namely, that sense in which belief involves conscious conviction. This fact is familiar from ordinary discourse, for a man is sometimes told that he does not believe what he honestly says he believes. He may be convinced that he is convinced of what he says, but subsequently realize he was not convinced of what he originally said.

To see that this is so, consider again the example that Lemmon used for other purposes.[5] We ask a man to tell us what he believes pi to be when rounded off to four decimal places and he, relying on memory, replies that pi is $3 \cdot 1417$. He immediately recalls that pi equals $3 \cdot 14159$, and corrects himself. Such a man might be said to have believed that he believed that

⁵ E. J. Lemmon, 'If I Know, Do I Know that I Know?' in *Epistemology: New Essays in the Theory of Knowledge*, ed. A. Stroll, 54–82.

pi is 3·1417 when first he answered, but then realized that he in fact did not believe that pi is 3·1417, but rather believed pi to be 3·1416. This example is but one of many in which a man can come to recognize that he does not believe what he says, and believes that he believes.

Someone may reply that the man who said what he believed and immediately changed his mind really *did* believe what he said he believed at the time he said so, but immediately afterwards did not believe what he said he believed. The man has made *some* mistake, however, and it is reasonable to conclude he was mistaken when he said that he believed that pi is 3·1417. He is mistaken in his saying that he had such a belief. The objection would have us accept the idea that when the man later says he does not believe pi is 3·1417, but rather 3·1416, this statement is incorrect because he did believe pi to be 3·1417 when he said so, even if he has now changed his mind. If, on the other hand, the man insists that he never believed pi to be 3·1417, though he admits unreflectively saying he believed pi to be 3·1417, the objection becomes untenable.

There is a final objection. It might be admitted that the man never did believe pi to be 3·1417, but also be contended that he did not believe that he believed pi to be 3·1417. If his saying that pi is 3·1417 does not show that he believed pi to be 3·1417, then why should his saying that he believes pi to be 3·1417 show that he believes that he believes pi to be 3·1417? This objection is crucial. The answer depends on what the man himself says. If he later admits to not having believed what he said when he said that he believed pi to be 3·1417, then it is most reasonable to accept the conclusion he did not believe that he believed it. None the less, it may also be that the man originally said 'I *believe* pi is 3·1417', and later said that, though he believed what he first said, he did not believe pi to be 3·1417. We may then conclude that the man believed that he believed pi to be 3·1417 but in fact did not believe pi to be 3·1417.

The Corrigibility of Thought

The preceding example opens the door to a demonstration that there are very few incorrigible beliefs about mental processes. One could offer similar arguments to show that it is logically possible for a person to be mistaken about what he hopes, fears, and wishes. Hopes, fears, and wishes are like convictions in that we sometimes realize that we did not hope, fear, or wish for what we believed we did. Such states are not, however, the best candidates for mental states about which we cannot be mistaken. Thinking is a better one.

We sometimes say of a person that he thinks that so and so when we are using the term 'think' to mean something very much like belief. That is not the sense of the term we shall consider now. Instead, consider that use of the term 'think' which is participial, for example, when we say 'John is thinking that Mary is a colonel.' Here we use the term to refer to some ongoing mental process. We shall now seek to determine whether a person can be mistaken in his beliefs about such occurrences.

Suppose I am thinking that Bacon is the author of *Hamlet*. Suppose secondly that I believe that Bacon is identical with Shakespeare, that is, that the man known to us as the author Shakespeare is none other than Bacon. However, though I believe this identity to hold, let us also imagine that this belief is not before my mind, I am not thinking of this identity at the time at which I am thinking that Bacon is the author of *Hamlet*. Now, suppose I am asked what I was thinking. I might conclude I was thinking that Shakespeare was the author of *Hamlet* because, believing that Bacon is Shakespeare, I also believe that thinking that Bacon is such and such is the same thing as thinking that Shakespeare is such and such. In short, I believe that thinking something of a subject is the same thing as thinking the same thing of anything identical to the subject. Am I correct?

The answer is no. The way to clarify this is to notice that sometimes when a man is thinking, he is talking to himself. Suppose my thinking, in this instance, consists of my talking to myself, of mulling things over in silent soliloquy. Let us be clear, however; there is no excuse for supposing that all thinking consists of such silent soliloquy. Sometimes it does not—for example, when a man goes to bed with an unsolved problem on his mind and suddenly awakens to discover that he has found the solution. This suggests the man is thinking while asleep, but there is no reason to suppose his thinking consisted of his making speeches to himself while asleep. Nevertheless, there are some cases in which thinking consists of talking to oneself, and by focusing on such cases we shall be able to reveal the way in which a man can be mistaken about what he is thinking. Suppose that when I was thinking that Bacon is the author of *Hamlet*, my thinking consisted of saying to myself: 'Bacon is the author of *Hamlet*.' Now, it is perfectly clear that to say 'Bacon is the author of *Hamlet*' is one thing, and to say 'Shakespeare is the author of *Hamlet*' is another. Thus, thinking that Bacon is the author of *Hamlet* is not necessarily the same thing as thinking that Shakespeare is the author of *Hamlet*, and we may, therefore, imagine I was not thinking the latter when I was thinking the former. Thus, when I reported that I was thinking that Shakespeare is the author of *Hamlet*, and believed what I said, I was quite mistaken. Hence, believing that one is thinking such and such does not logically imply that one is thinking that.[6]

There are several objections to this line of thought which must be met. The first is that even though my thinking that Bacon is the author of *Hamlet* might, in some way, consist of my saying 'Bacon is the author of *Hamlet*' to myself, it still does not follow that I was not thinking that Shakespeare is the author of *Hamlet* when saying to myself 'Bacon is the author of *Hamlet*'. Maybe I was thinking that Shakespeare is the author of *Hamlet*, but my so thinking did not consist of my saying 'Shakespeare is the author of *Hamlet*' to myself.

The reply to this objection is that there is no reason to say I was thinking Shakespeare was the author of *Hamlet* when I was saying something quite different to myself. My reason for saying I was thinking Shakespeare is the author of *Hamlet* is a faulty inference. From my belief that Bacon is Shakespeare I inferred that thinking Bacon is such and such is the same thing as thinking Shakespeare is such and such. The inference is as faulty as the inference from that belief to the conclusion that saying Bacon is such and such is the same thing as saying Shakespeare is such and such. This inference is incorrect, even if the two men are identical, because I did not *say* that they were identical. Hence, when I said Bacon was such and such I did not say that Shakespeare was such and such.

[6] Katherine Pyne Parsons in 'Mistaking Sensations', *Philosophical Review*, lxxix (1970), 201–13, raises some similar objections to the doctrine that statements about mental statements are incorrigible.

The argument just enunciated may be obscured by the consideration that if Bacon and Shakespeare are the same, then what I said of the one man is true if and only if what I said of the other is true. However, we can avoid this issue by assuming my belief that Bacon is Shakespeare to be false. Indeed, most scholars of Elizabethan literature would assume this. In that case, when I am saying that Shakespeare is the author of *Hamlet*, what I am saying is true, while, when I am saying that Bacon is the author of *Hamlet*, what I am saying is false. Hence saying the one thing cannot be identical with saying the other. The same is true of thinking. If, when I am thinking that Shakespeare is the author of *Hamlet*, what I am thinking is true, while, when I am thinking that Bacon is the author of *Hamlet*, what I am thinking is false—then my thinking the first cannot be identical with my thinking the second. Hence, if I believe that I am thinking Shakespeare is the author of *Hamlet* because I believe I am thinking Bacon is the author of *Hamlet*, as was the case in the example cited, the former belief may be mistaken, even though the latter is correct.

There is one hurdle left to leap. It could still be objected that I did not believe that I was thinking Shakespeare is the author of *Hamlet at the same time* I was thinking that Bacon is the author of *Hamlet*—I only believed the former subsequently when I responded to the query. Thus, when I am asked what I am thinking, I reply that I am thinking that Shakespeare is the author of *Hamlet* and at that time I do believe this. But this reply, according to the objection, refers to a time when the query was made, and there is no reason for concluding I believed I was thinking Shakespeare to be the author of *Hamlet* at any earlier time. I only held an erroneous belief about what I *was* thinking subsequent to the time I was doing the thinking, and this leaves unrefuted the claim that when I or anyone else has a belief about what is presently going on in his mind, his belief cannot possibly be false. Later through faulty memory or mistaken inference, the belief about what happened earlier may, of course, be in error.

This reply is met most directly by simply affirming that I may believe that I am thinking one thing while thinking another. The reason is that belief is not an action or even an occurrence. I can believe that I am thinking that Bacon is the author of *Hamlet* at the very time at which I am thinking that. My believing this is not some additional occurrence. It is something that can coexist with such a thought and yet be quite distinct from the thinking. I might have been thinking what I was without believing that what I was thinking was true. When a man talks to himself he need not believe what he says. If my belief that I am thinking that Bacon is the author of Hamlet can exist at the same time as my thinking that, then obviously my belief that I am thinking Shakespeare is the author of *Hamlet* can exist at the same time as my thinking Bacon is the author of *Hamlet*. Hence, the objection fails.

From the preceding argument we may conclude that a man can make all sorts of mistakes about what is presently going on in his mind. The preceding argument may be adopted to show that when a man believes that he is surmising that *p*, doubting that *p*, or pondering that *p*, he may be mistaken in his belief. It would be the most unforgivable pendantry to rerun the preceding argument for each of these states. Moreover, any state that involves conscious consideration of a statement is a state about which one can be mistaken. This should be clear from the preceding argument. Thus we have robbed consciousness of claims to incorrigible belief concerning even the present existence of states which have some statement as an object.

The Corrigibility of Beliefs about Sensations

The next issue to face is whether beliefs not having statements as objects are ever incorrigible. For example, let us consider beliefs about the sensations of sense experience. Following a philosophical tradition, we may refer to the objects of such experiences as sensations whether the experience is tactile, visual, auditory, and so forth. This use of the term 'sensation' has been thought to be pernicious, but the reasons for such misgivings are not germane to our discussion.

Armstrong's Argument

Armstrong has argued that reports about the sensations one is having are reports that can be mistaken even though no verbal slip or other verbal confusion is involved. It will be useful for our purposes to reformulate his thesis and arguments in terms of belief. The change is not fundamental. Armstrong argues that we might at some time have exceedingly good evidence both that a man was not lying or making a verbal error, and that he did not have the sensation he said he had. To this end, imagine that we have reached a level of neurological understanding beyond the present and have established that a man experiences a certain sensation when and only when in a certain brain state, call it state 143. Let us imagine that the sensation is a visual one, for example, that sort of visual experience that a normal man has when confronted with red objects in daylight. We may call this a sensation of red. Moreover, suppose we can give a man a drug which will make him truthful in a laboratory experiment. Now imagine we give a man such a drug, he reports a sensation of red, and we are able to observe that he is *not* in brain state 143. On the basis of the evidence that he is drugged, we conclude that he believes what he says. On the basis of the neurological evidence that he is not in brain state 143, we conclude that he is not having a sensation of red. This story, Armstrong would have us concede, is at least logically possible. If it is logically possible and involves no contradiction in conception, then it is logically possible that the man in question believes that he has a sensation of red when he does not have it.[7]

A Reply to Armstrong

The basic assumption of the example is that we could have evidence which shows a man believing he is having a sensation he is not having. If it is conceded that such evidence would render it highly probable that the man is not having the sensation without thereby rendering it at least as probable that he does not believe he is having the sensation, then the argument succeeds. We know it is a theorem of probability that if evidence renders a hypothesis highly probable then it renders any logical consequence of that hypothesis at least as probable. Let us abbreviate the hypothesis that the man is not having the sensation by 'NS', and the hypothesis that he does not believe he has

[7] David Armstrong, 'Is Introspective Knowledge Incorrigible?', *Philosophical Review*, lxxii (1963), 424.

the sensation by the letter 'NB', and the evidence Armstrong mentions by 'E'. Now suppose the evidence E renders NS highly probable, but does not render NB probable. This would show that believing one has a sensation does not logically imply having the sensation, because NS does not logically imply NB.

Nevertheless, the argument is defective. We all agree that an experimenter might have evidence which might *convince* him that it is highly probable that the man in the example believes he has a sensation but does not. It would *seem* to him that evidence E renders NS highly probable but fails to render NB equally probable. There are, however, *two* divergent explanations of our experimenter's attitude. One is that the evidence genuinely does render one hypothesis highly probable while failing to render the other as probable. The other explanation is that the evidence only seems not to render NB highly probable because the experimenter fails to realize that NS logically implies NB. Once the logical implication is recognized it becomes obvious that evidence does render NB highly probable. If a man does not recognize that one hypothesis logically implies a second, then evidence that favours the first hypothesis might not *seem* to favour the second, even though in fact it does.

Let us consider an example in which evidence renders one hypothesis highly probable, but does not seem to render highly probable a logical consequence of it. Imagine that I see a red die on my desk, and let us suppose my sensory evidence renders it highly probable that there is a red die there. This evidence then also renders it highly probable that there is a cube on my desk, since a die is by definition a cube. Now, suppose I do not know that it logically follows from the fact that something is a cube that it has twelve edges. In that case, though I maintain that my evidence renders it highly probable that there is a cube on my desk, I might deny that the evidence renders it highly probable that there is a twelve-edged solid object on my desk. Even so, the latter would be an error. The evidence that renders it highly probable that there is a cube on my desk must render it at least as probable that there is a solid object having twelve edges on my desk, for the former logically implies the latter.

Let us consider one further example. Suppose I am seated at my desk and witness the following scene. A man arrives and walks over to my car, takes out some tools with which he opens the door, then quickly enters it and runs off with the flashlight from my glove compartment. I conclude that a man has entered my car and taken my flashlight because I believe that I have seen this happen before my very eyes. Now imagine someone asserts that I am quite in error, that I did not see what I believed I saw, but rather that I was undergoing a hallucination. He grants that the flashlight is gone, but says I removed it earlier, being careful to conceal it where it would not be found, and, because of my demented state, completely forgot that this was so. Now, he might claim that the evidence I have could not refute his sceptical contentions, since I would believe and say just what I do if his account is correct. Thus, he might affirm that my thoughts and experiences do not render his hypothesis improbable and conclude that they do not render my hypothesis highly probable.

Such sceptical doubts have often worried philosophers more than they should. The correct reply is that evidence of my thoughts and experiences *does* render highly probable the hypothesis that I saw a man take my flashlight; and since this logically implies that I was not hallucinating, the evidence also renders highly probable the hypothesis that I was not hallucinating. Initially, my experiences and thoughts might seem to be irrelevant to the question of whether I was hallucinating, but this semblance vanishes when one discerns that the falsity of the hallucinatory hypothesis is logically implied by the hypothesis that I saw the man take the flashlight. Once this logical implication is noticed, one may conclude that the evidence renders the hallucinatory hypothesis highly improbable.

The application of these considerations to the issue at hand is to illustrate two different ways of explaining the reaction of our fictitious experimenter. One is to assume what the experimenter does. The other is to assume that the experimenter simply failed to notice that believing one has a sensation logically implies that one has it. On this assumption he has failed to notice that his evidence renders it highly improbable that the subject *believes* he has a sensation. This second explanation is consistent with the incorrigibility of beliefs about sensations.

These two ways, of explaining why the experimenter thinks what he does, are on exactly equal footing. We need some other argument to shake the dialectical ground beneath them.

Sensations and Incorrigibility: A Counterexample

Another argument is readily available. The argument is very similar to that by which we demonstrated the corrigibility of other beliefs. A man might believe that one sensation is the same as another when this belief is erroneous, and, consequently believe that he is having one sensation when he is having quite a different one. Let us consider an example of confusing two sensations, those of pain and itching. Imagine that a not very enlightened lady goes to her doctor to complain of a disagreeable sensation. Imagine that the sensation is sometimes distinctly one of pain and at other times distinctly one of itching. Moreover, suppose this person greatly admires her doctor and is inclined to believe what the doctor says even when his medical deliverances are somewhat preposterous. The lady is told by her doctor that it is not surprising that her sensation is sometimes one of pain and sometimes one of itching because *itches really are pains*. All itches, he says, are pains, though some are very mild. Such is the authority of the man, and such is the credibility of the lady, that his word is taken as a creed. From that moment on she never doubts that itches are pains, and, though they feel different, she firmly believes that she is in pain whenever she has the slightest itch. When she itches, therefore, she erroneously believes that she is in pain. Thus, believing that she is in pain does not logically imply that she is in pain.

It should be apparent that the lady in question might have been misled by her esteemed medical sage into believing that any sensation was another when in fact it was not. She might, without understanding how such things could possibly be true, believe that they are. It follows that it is logically possible that the lady may confuse almost any sensation with some other because she mistakenly believes that the one is the other and thus believes she is having the sensation when she is not. Hence, beliefs about sensations, like beliefs about thoughts, are corrigible. In general, very little that one believes about mental and psychological states of oneself is incorrigible. Error can, as a matter of logic, insert itself stealthily between belief and what is believed in this matter as in others.

We might note in passing that many beliefs about sensations are not simply beliefs about mental or psychological states. For example, if I believe that I have the pain from a wound in my leg, this is a belief, not only about pain, but about the etiology of the pain and about my leg. As such it is subject to all the epistemic hazards of beliefs about the etiology of sensations and the conditions of legs. Beliefs about the *location* of pain is a more difficult matter. It is clear that a man may feel a pain in one part of his body because another part of his body is undergoing some trauma, or even because he is undergoing some non-physical trauma. Here it seems reasonable to say the pain a man suffers must be where he feels it to be; but feeling is one thing and belief another. A man may, because of some peculiar beliefs, believe that he feels a pain in one part of his body when in fact he feels it elsewhere. In other words, a man may be mistaken about where the pain is.

Other Alleged Counterexamples

Other counterexamples to the thesis that beliefs about sensations are incorrigible concern people who are in a more or less aberrant state. Consider a man who believes he is about to undergo some painful experience, for example, that he is about to be touched by some very hot object, though in fact the object is cold to the touch. Because he expects to feel a burning sensation, he could believe that he was feeling such a sensation during the first moment or two when the cold object touched his flesh. This belief would then be false. The difficulty with such a counterexample is that it is problematic whether expecting to feel a burning sensation produces false beliefs or a burning sensation. The counterexample may be well taken, but it is hardly decisive.

Another kind of counterexample concerns those who are mentally aberrant and undergoing hallucination. For example, suppose that a very paranoid man complains that he is suffering excruciating pain because little green martians are cutting into his flesh. If he then goes on to tell us that the reason he shows no sign of being in pain (he does not grimace, wince, and so forth) is that he does not want to let the martians know they are succeeding in making him suffer, we might begin to think he believes he is in pain when he is not. The man might in fact not be undergoing any pain whatsoever even though he does genuinely believe that he is suffering. He might later, when the aberrance has vanished, report that this is what had happened. Some philosophers might doubt that the usual concepts of belief and sensation apply in such peculiar cases as this and others would have other doubts. Again, such examples, though not decisive from the standpoint of persuasion, may be genuine counterexamples. These two cases, like the one I set forth, stem from the same consideration, to wit, that a man may believe that he is having a sensation because of some erroneous conviction leading him to believe he is undergoing a sensation of a definite variety when this is not so.

Some Objections

It is essential that we consider counterarguments to the foregoing. Let us return to our gullible medical patient and her fanciful doctor. She believes that all itches are pains and hence when she itches she believes that she is in pain though she feels no pain. One objection is that the lady in question does not mean what the rest of us mean by the word 'pain'. Indeed, what she means by 'pain' is what the rest of us mean by 'pain or itch'. So when she says that she is in pain what she means is that either she is in pain or is itching. Consequently, her belief, which we have supposed to be false, would in fact be quite correct; but the words she uses to express those beliefs are not ones that would be customary.

This argument has an initial plausibility and a hard core of philosophical doctrine to support it. There is a philosophical tradition of treating systematic differences in what is said as differences in the meaning of words rather than as factual disagreements. Let us consider the matter of meaning. First, it is important to distinguish between what a person means and the meaning of the words a person utters. A person is asserting what he *means* when he utters words intending to say something true. The assertion and the meaning are the same in this case. When I say, 'The war is too long', I both assert and mean that the war is too long. What I mean by the words I utter may change, though words are the same, without there being any change in the meaning of the words uttered. For example, as Cartwright has shown, indexical words used to refer to times and places do not change meaning on the different occasions of utterance, but what is asserted or meant does change.[8] When I say 'Now is the time for protest', on 1 October 1967, I assert something different from what I assert when I speak those words on 1 October 1969. On both occasions I am asserting that a certain time is the time for protest, the time then referred to by the word 'now'. But the time referred to by the use of that word differs. I am asserting that a different time is the time for protest on each occasion.

Now let us consider whether the woman who says that she is in pain means that she is either in pain or itches. Does her use of the word 'pain' differ in meaning from its normal use? Unless it does, we should not conclude that she must mean something different when she says 'I am in pain' than would be customary. She may mean or assert exactly what the rest of us would ordinarily mean or assert by uttering those words. There is, we shall show, no justification for supposing the word 'pain' to have special meaning as she uses it.

To appreciate that the word 'pain' does not undergo a semantic transformation when it falls from her lips, let us consider her speech behaviour without supposing that we know why, when she itches, she says she is in pain. How should we explain it? We might initially imagine that she really does experience pain much more frequently than the rest of us, but once we notice that she does not exhibit the usual symptoms, we conclude that she is not subject to pain with any exceptional frequency. We conclude that either her use of the word 'pain' means something different from what it means to the rest of us, or else she very frequently believes that she is in pain when she is actually experiencing none. What is the correct explanation?

Consider the hypothesis that the meaning of the word is special. To check on it, we should investigate to determine whether there is anything special in the way that she learned

[8] Richard Cartwright, 'Propositions', cited in chapter 2, particularly section 10, pp. 92–5.

the word. We would then discover that her linguistic training is altogether jejune. Moreover, when we ask her to describe what pain is like, she describes it as throbbing, stabbing, and so forth, which seems appropriate. We then ask why she describes as pain certain states which lack these characteristics. We then are told that special intense cases of itching are painful, and agree. But why, we ask, does she call less intense and even very mild itches *pains*? We then learn that it is because of what the doctor has told her and her faith in his pronouncements. At this point, it is most reasonable to conclude that she has a very peculiar *belief* about pains, a belief she acquired in the way she affirms, and, consequently, there is neither need nor justification for assuming that as she uses the word 'pain' it means something special. We explain her speech behaviour in a completely satisfactory manner without postulating such a change.

We may imagine she is quite as puzzled as we as to why anyone should regard a mild itch as a pain, but she believes it is pain none the less. If we suppose that the word 'pain' has undergone a transformation of meaning in her vocabulary, then we mischievously deprive her of the linguistic means to describe her quite unusual belief. When she says that all itches are pains, she is making quite an extraordinary assertion, and this assertion is by no means reducible to the trivial claim that all itches are either pains or itches. The latter is all her assertion would come to if by 'pain' she meant 'either pain or itch'. Since her belief is preposterously false rather than trivially true, it must be that the word 'pain' has not been so transformed in meaning. When she says 'I am in pain', she means it.

To sum up the preceding discussion, a systematic difference in linguistic usage can result either from a change of meaning or from a change of belief. In some instances the simpler explanation is that there is a change of meaning, in others, a change of belief. In the example we have contrived, the more adequate explanation of the speech phenomenon is that there has been a change of belief: the woman has learned how to use the word 'pain' in the usual way to mean what is usually meant. When she begins to report pains that do not exist, this is due to the alteration of her beliefs by the doctor.

We may now conclude our remarks on the incorrigible. We

have found very few beliefs that are incorrigible in the relevant sense. The belief that I exist is incorrigible as is the belief that I believe, but any belief about what I think or believe about any sensation or feeling is corrigible and subject to correction. It is evident that from such a slim base as this we cannot justify all those beliefs, or even any large part of those beliefs, which we consider so well justified as to constitute knowledge.

5

Corrigible Justification :
The Foundation Theory (II)

THE preceding chapter has shown why a foundation theory of justification must subscribe to the doctrine that at least some basic beliefs are corrigible. There is reason to doubt the tenability of such a doctrine. A basic belief is one which guarantees its own truth, and it is problematic to suppose that a corrigible belief which can be false might nevertheless guarantee its own truth. Indeed, there is a traditional philosophical argument which, without formal representation, has led philosophers to conclude only incorrigible beliefs may guarantee their own truth.

The argument premisses that if a belief is corrigible, then it can be false, and proceeds to assume that if a belief can be false, then any justification of the belief guaranteeing its truth must be supplied by independent information. It is then concluded that if a belief is corrigible it must be justified by such information and, therefore, cannot be basic. If this argument is decisive, then either we must abandon the foundation theory or conclude we are ignorant of almost all we suppose we know.

Fortunately for the foundation theory, the foregoing argument is far from invulnerable. Thomas Reid long ago noted a primary perforation. The argument proceeds with the assumption that the justification of a belief which can be false must be obtained from an external source. Reid averred that some beliefs, for example perceptual beliefs concerning what we see immediately before us, are in no need of justification. Though they can be erroneous, Reid conceded, they nevertheless stand justified in themselves without need of independent corroboration, at least until some argument is brought forth to sustain the claim that such a belief is false. In short, such beliefs are self-justified because their justification is inherent. As Reid put it, they have a right of ancient possession, and, until this inherent right is successfully challenged, they remain justified without support from any other information at all.[1]

This line of thought may be recast in terms of the guarantee of truth that belongs to such beliefs. This guarantee is not anything derived from any independent source but is indigenous to the belief itself. We might, as Reid did, say that such beliefs are those of common sense. Whatever criterion one might employ to select corrigible beliefs which are nevertheless self-justified and basic, Reid has hit upon a critically important line of defence for the foundation theory. A simple analogy may illuminate the insight. If a company guarantees a product against defects in manufacture, this guarantee of soundness is not proof that the product is sound. Similarly, the guarantee of truth intrinsic to some beliefs is not proof that the belief is true. The manufactured items may be defective and the beliefs may be erroneous, but a reasonable man attaches some value to such guarantees none the less and relies upon them in forming his plans and shaping his convictions.

Thus, according to Reid, we may trust guarantees which are not infallible guides to success whether we seek a sound product of manufacture or a true belief of natural origin. Though we remain vigilant to detect errors, we may, in the customary affairs of life, rely upon the intrinsic guarantee of truth and the attendant justification that attaches as a birthright to various of our beliefs. They are completely justified in themselves without need of any independent information or justification. If this doctrine proves tenable, it could provide us with a set of basic but corrigible beliefs. The rights of birth and ancient possession have, however, been challenged in the political sphere, and we must bring them under close scrutiny here as well.

Complete Justification and Independent Information

Candidates for the status of self-justified beliefs whose justification does not depend on independent information are fre-

---

[1] Thomas Reid, *Essays on the Active Powers of the Mind*, from *The Philosophical Works of Thomas Reid*, ed. Sir William Hamilton (James Thin, London, 1895), 617.

quently perceptual. Let us consider some promising candidates and see if we can discover any worthy of the office. Suppose I believe I see a typewriter beneath my fingers. Now it might be supposed that, for my belief to be justified, I must have some independent information about what I see, namely, that a thing that looks like the thing beneath my fingers is a typewriter. If I did not have that information, then I would not be justified in believing I see a typewriter. In short, whenever I see a thing of a certain kind, my being justified in the belief that I am seeing a thing of that kind depends on independent information I have about how things of that kind look. This information justifies me in concluding that the thing I see is such an object.[2]

It is clear that a similar argument will confront us when we consider a simpler belief, for example, the belief that I see something red. It will be argued that, for me to determine that what I see is a red thing, I must have independent information about how red things look and, indeed, about how they look under various conditions. One might object to the argument that for a thing to be red is just for it to look red under standard conditions to normal observers, and thus it is not necessary to have *independent* information to determine that what one sees is red. It is only necessary to understand the meaning of the word 'red'. The reply to this objection is that a man needs to know more than that red things look red under standard conditions to normal observers to determine that what he sees is red: he must also know how to tell when conditions are standard and when an observer is normal. Thus, if something looks red to a person, he cannot justifiably conclude that it is red from the formula that red things look red in standard conditions to normal observers, he would also need to know that the conditions are standard and that he is normal. Independent information is, therefore, required for the justification of this perceptual belief, as well as the former. More generally, to justify such a belief requires the information that the conditions that surround a man and the state he is in are such that when something looks red in conditions of this sort to a person in his state, then it is red. Moreover, a man might justifiably believe he sees something

[2] This argument is derived from Chisholm in *Perceiving: A Philosophical Study*, chapter 5, 'Justification and Perception', 54–66.

red even though what he sees does not look red to him. He may have sufficient independent information for concluding that, though an object does not look red, when things look the way it does in the sort of conditions in which he finds himself, for example, when a coloured light is shining on the object, then the object is red.

The question to examine next is whether any more cautious perceptual belief has a justification that does not depend on independent information. A prime candidate is the belief that I see something, without specifying what sort of thing it is that I see. Here, one might think, is a belief which does not require any independent information for it to be justified. None the less, there is reason to doubt this if one construes the word 'something' in such a way as to imply that the object seen is some real thing and not, for example, something hallucinated. For once again, there is need of independent information that would enable the person in question to decide this is the case of seeing something, and not merely a case of hallucination or dreaming, or whatnot. Since a man may hallucinate, he cannot justifiably conclude he sees something as opposed to merely hallucinating unless he has information enabling him to distinguish hallucination from the real thing.

There are objections, rather standard ones, to the preceding line of thought. It might be objected, for example, that a man does not need to know anything about hallucination in order to believe justifiably that he sees something. A man who never had hallucinatory experiences, or any other experience leading him to believe he sees something when he does not, might believe with complete justification that he sees something even though he lacks any information about deceptive experience. If it be asked how he can be so justified in his belief even though he lacks the information to determine whether he is seeing rather than hallucinating, the answer is that such beliefs do not require the support of argument or independent information. They are justified until they are shown to be erroneous or unjustified. They are, as Reid suggested, innocent until proven guilty.[3]

There is a reply to the foregoing. Consider the examples of seeing a typewriter and seeing something red. In these cases,

[3] Thomas Reid, op. cit.

the need for independent information arose from the need to determine whether the circumstances in which a person finds himself are those in which a man may justifiably conclude that he is seeing a typewriter or seeing something red. However, this need also arises in the case of the simple belief that one sees something. Just as one needs some information to tell whether one is seeing a typewriter in the perceptual circumstances surrounding one, so one needs some information to tell whether one is seeing at all in one's circumstances.

The Inadequacy of Common Sense

No doubt, in everyday situations we uncritically allow that such beliefs are justified until they are shown to be unjustified, and no doubt in the case of the man who was innocent of hallucinating experience, we would *uncritically* allow that his perceptual belief was justified. Still, a little more critical circumspection shows that common sense should not be allowed to run unbridled in the epistemic field. All sorts of perceptual beliefs, the belief that one saw a bear-print for example, are considered justified when we have no great stake in the question of whether the belief is true or false. However, when a great deal (our personal safety for example) hinges on the matter of whether the person saw a bear-print or something else, then we become instantly more cautious and exacting. We require a man who knows a bear-print when he sees one. The same applies to the typewriter and the red thing. We are epistemically casual about the justifiability of a belief until something of practical importance or epistemic consequence rests on the question. Perceptual beliefs are considered innocent until proven guilty when we care not the least whether the belief is innocent or guilty. Once we do care, though, then we start to ask serious questions. The first we ask are aimed at establishing whether the belief is justified in terms of the information of the person who espouses the belief. We seek to determine if the person has information enabling him to decide whether he is seeing things of the sort he says he sees. Then the belief is neither innocent nor guilty by presumption. Whether it is justified or not depends on the adequacy of the information of the person involved.

The simple belief that one sees something raises similar problems. We concede a man innocent of hallucinatory and other misleading experience to be justified in believing he sees what he says he does when we could not care less whether he sees it or not. When we do care, however, we shall wish to ascertain whether he can distinguish seeing from other experiences of a quite different sort. If my life depends on whether he sees something, I shall be disconcerted, to say the least, when I find I am relying on a man who knows not the difference between seeing and experience of quite another sort. Being so disconcerted, I may wonder whether he even fully understands what it is to see something. I shall most likely conclude he does not. Lacking the information required to tell whether he is seeing something or not, his belief that he sees is surely not completely justified.

An Objection: Skill or Information?

It might be objected to the preceding that one does not require information to be justified in such a belief but rather a skill. To be able to tell whether one is seeing something or not is obviously essential to being justified in believing one is seeing something, but, it might be argued, the skill required need not involve the acquisition of information. One can have the ability to tell whether something is of a certain sort without need of information to make such determinations. Hilary Putnam contends that, though sensory experiences are needed for a man to know that he sees something, no premises describing such experiences are required to justify his belief.[4] Similarly, one might argue, a man need not have any independent information in order to respond to experience in such a way as to know that he is seeing something. It is sufficient to have learned to respond to such experience in the appropriate manner.

The foregoing objection must be met squarely. A man may learn to tell whether or not he is seeing something without appealing to any premises or making any conscious inferences. Gilbert Harman has suggested we might nevertheless construe

---

[4] Hilary Putnam, 'Minds and Machines', in *Dimensions of Mind*, ed. Sidney Hook (New York University Press, New York, 1960), 154–5.

such cases as examples of unconscious inference.[5] For the purposes of our epistemological analysis, however, we need not embrace or reject his theory. It is sufficient to notice that a man may be said to have information he cannot present verbally and to employ such information in various ways. For example, suppose I know the shortest route from Rochester to Buffalo, though I cannot tell you the number of the road. Moreover, imagine I am not very good at giving directions so I cannot tell someone how to get from Rochester to Buffalo. I do have the information I need to get from Rochester to Buffalo, however, though I am very poor at conveying this information to others. True, the primary manifestation of my having the required information is that I make the trip successfully. I have the skill needed to make the trip from Rochester to Buffalo, but the possession of that skill involves the ability to employ unarticulated information about the route. To consider another example, a man who types by touch might deny having any information concerning where the keys are placed. In fact, he has information, which he employs in an automatic and unthinking way, when he types. We may speculate on what way this information becomes effective in action, but these matters are best left to be settled by empirical psychology.

Any contingent belief whatever is open to similar argument concerning the need for independent information. Indeed, even the very subjective belief, that it seems to me that I am seeing something, is justified only if I have the information needed to tell whether it seems to me that I am seeing something; or whether I am having some quite different experience, for example, the experience of wondering whether I am seeing something. I may wonder whether I am seeing something when it does not especially seem to me that I am seeing something, and unless I have the information required to tell the difference, I am not completely justified in my belief. The most modest beliefs turn out to be ones requiring independent information for their justification. The preceding argument uncovers a ubiquitious need for independent information to justify belief, and in so doing it undermines the foundation theory.

[5] Gilbert Harman, 'How Belief is Based on Inference', *Journal of Philosophy*, lxi (1964), 353-9.

Chisholm and the Non-comparative Use of Words

The most important line of reply on behalf of the foundation theory is provided by Chisholm.[6] He distinguishes between the comparative and non-comparative uses of certain words. Ordinarily, when we apply a word, whether to our own states or to things, this application is based on a comparison we make. For example, if we say something appears red, we may be comparing the way this thing appears with the way other things appear. It is analytic in the comparative use of 'appears red' to say that red things appear red to normal observers in daylight. In the comparative use of words, Chisholm concedes the need for independent information to justify their application.

Chisholm, however, claims that words used non-comparatively may be applied without independent information. Words used non-comparatively may be homogenized producing a single term applying to the state of a man. As Chisholm suggests, we might speak adverbially and say that a man believes that he is being appeared-to-redly or, equivalently, that he is sensing-redly. The hyphenated term is intended to characterize the subjective state of the man in question without implying that some *thing* is appearing to him and without implying any comparison of this state to any other. Thus to say that one is sensing-redly does not entail that one is sensing the way normal observers sense in daylight when they are sensing a red object. It may, of course, be true that one is sensing in that way, but it is not an analytic consequence of the term 'sensing-redly' used non-comparatively.

There is an argument to show that there must be a non-comparative use of words. Such a use enables a man to describe what it is he experiences without comparing that experience to any other. To be able to describe a state in comparative terms, thus comparing it to other states, he must first be able to tell what the state is like in itself. Unless he can tell what his state is like in itself, he will be unable to compare it successfully to anything else. To be able to tell whether A is similar or

[6] R. M. Chisholm develops his doctrine concerning the non-comparative use of words in *Perceiving: A Philosophical Study*, chapter 4, 'Three Uses Appear Words', 50–3, and discusses it again in *Theory of Knowledge*, chapter 2, 'The Directly Evident', 34–7.

dissimilar to *B*, one must first know what *A* is like, or any such comparison will be unreliable. Therefore, there must be a way in which one can tell what something is like, for example, a state of oneself, without comparing it to anything else. The non-comparative use of words enables one to record these non-comparative determinations.[7]

(A number of philosophers, largely followers of Ludwig Wittgenstein, would deny the possibility of such non-comparative uses of words. The principle assumption of such philosophers is that language must have publicly accessible rules or criteria for the application of words. Such rules are essential for distinguishing between the correct and incorrect application of a word, as well as for distinguishing between applications that only seem to be correct and those that genuinely are correct.[8] Now from such assumptions it might well be concluded that words have only a comparative use. There could be no publicly accessible criteria, it might be argued, for the application of non-comparative terms. Such criteria for the application of a term would depend upon comparing one case to another in order to ascertain whether the term should be applied. This is a highly controversial line of reasoning because some would object that the rules for the application might be private rather than public. Others would object that rules for the application of words need not depend on comparing one thing to another.)

We agree with Chisholm that there is such a thing as a non-comparative use of words and ask whether this will sustain the thesis that beliefs expressed in non-comparative terms are completely justified without the need for independent information. For a man to be completely justified in believing that he is sensing in a certain way, that he is sensing-redly for example, he must have the information necessary to distinguish this manner of appearing from others. Perhaps, as Chisholm contends, the belief that one is appeared-to-redly does not entail any comparison of one's present state to any other. Nevertheless, it does entail that one's state is of a certain kind, and to be

[7] Chisholm offers such an argument in *Theory of Knowledge*, chapter 2, p. 36, footnote 20.

[8] See Ludwig Wittgenstein, *Philosophical Investigations*, trans. G. E. M. Anscombe (Macmillan, New York, 1958), particularly sections 256-8, 261, and 265.

completely justified in believing it to be of that kind, one must have the information needed to enable one to tell such a state from another. So we arrive at the conclusion reached earlier: to be completely justified in believing anything about a state or object or whatnot one always requires independent information.[9]

Semantics and Justification

The preceding reflections might seem to doom the foundation theory to epistemic oblivion. We have seen that the stockpile of incorrigible beliefs is epistemically inadequate to provide a justificatory foundation. We have now considered the possibility that some beliefs might be completely justified in themselves without the need for any independent information, and we have found this proposal wanting. The latter proposal may, however, be sustained with some modification. The effective modification is to claim that some beliefs are justified in themselves without need of any *evidential* justification. The independent information required for such beliefs to be justified, it may be argued, is not evidence used to justify the beliefs but *semantic* information required to understand the meaning of the statement believed to be true.

To return to our example taken from Chisholm, if I believe that I am sensing-redly, then before I can be said to be justified in believing this I must have the information enabling me to distinguish this state from others. Such information is required for me to understand what it means to say that I am sensing-redly. If I do not have the information enabling me so to distinguish that state from others, then I do not understand what it means to say that I am in that state. Thus, the information in question is semantic information in the sense that it is information required to understand what it means to say that one is in the state.

That semantic information is required, for a belief to be justified, is compatible with the claim that the belief is self-justified and guarantees its own truth. The semantic information is what makes the believed statement intelligible, and,

---

[9] This argument has been influenced by a similar argument in W. F. Sellars, 'Empiricism and the Philosophy of Mind', in his book *Science, Perception, and Reality* (Routledge and Kegan Paul, London, 1963), section 18, pp. 146-7.

hence, an understanding of that information is necessary for a person genuinely to have the belief. As an illustration, a person who does not understand what it means to say that something is red is one who also does not understand and hence could not genuinely believe that anything is red. Of course, this point must be formulated carefully. It is of course, not necessary for a person to understand what the English word 'red' means, or even to know that there is any such word, for him to believe that anything is red. Nevertheless, to be able to discriminate red from other colours, however impressive this capacity may be, is not the same thing as believing things are red in the sense under discussion here. Here we are restricting the term 'believe' to imply a conviction and readiness to affirm what is believed. It is belief in this sense that is germane to the justification of knowledge claims in the context of epistemic inquiry.

Since the information required by a person before a belief may be justified is sometimes nothing more than semantic information needed to understand the meaning of the statement believed to be true, the need for such information does not preclude the possibility of some beliefs being justified in themselves and guaranteeing their own truth. The semantic information is necessary for an understanding of the statement believed and hence for a person to have the belief in question. Once a person has the belief, however, this may suffice to guarantee the truth of the belief. Such beliefs would be basic in the requisite sense.

The preceding reflections, though admitted to rest on controversial assumptions, show how it is possible to defend a foundation theory, but this lean possibility wants sustenance. Once we abandon the incorrigible, the claim that any corrigible belief guarantees its own truth faces a difficult question. How does any corrigible belief guarantee its own truth? If this question is not satisfactorily answered, then the avowal of self-justification remains at the level of unreasoned assertion an dogmatism.

Meaning and Epistemic Principles

We shall now turn to a familiar answer to this fundamental question. Suppose it is affirmed that if a man believes he is sensing-redly (or in some other way described non-comparatively) then he is completely justified in his belief. What defence can be given of this epistemological principle telling us that beliefs of this sort are self-justified? One traditional answer, though not advanced by Chisholm, is to argue such principles are true by virtue of the meaning of words. Again, we are faced with a semantic solution to an epistemological problem. Is the solution effective?

When it is supposed that a principle of justification is true by virtue of the meaning of words, it is not claimed that they are analytic. We cannot substitute defining terms for defined ones in such a way that the result is a statement whose logical form shows it to be a truth of logic. A traditional example of a statement that is true by virtue of the meaning of words is 'All that is coloured is extended', but the statement is not analytic. Fundamental epistemological principles are candidates for similar status. Thus, just as we know that the class of coloured things is a class of extended things by a simple understanding of the meaning of words, so we can know that a certain class of beliefs is a class of self-justified beliefs in the same way. That is the thesis.

Some philosophers would regard the foregoing thesis as untenable on the grounds that all statements true by virtue of the meaning of words are analytic; but this is incorrect. The statement that if a person is taller than a second who in turn is taller than a third, then the first is taller than the third, cannot be shown to be true by appealing solely to logic and definitions, but it is necessarily true by virtue of the meaning of words. It cannot possibly be false.

There is an important point of disagreement in such matters which should be brought to the dialectical surface. Strictly speaking, it is always some *sentence* composed of words that is true by virtue of the meaning of those words rather than what is asserted by the utterance of such a sentence. Now an important question arises: is what is asserted necessarily true because the sentence is true by virtue of the meaning of words, or is the sentence true by virtue of the meaning of words because what is asserted is necessarily true?

Let us consider a concrete example. Consider the sentence 'If John is taller than Bill, then Bill is not as tall as John.' Now it is impossible that John should be taller than Bill and that Bill should be taller than John. Equivalently, it is necessarily true that if John is taller than Bill, then Bill is not taller than John. Suppose someone argued he could render this necessity no longer necessary and this impossibility no longer impossible by changing the meaning of words. He might say 'Let us mean by the word "taller" what we mean by the words "equal in height", and then meaning this by the word "taller" we will have arranged things so that it is not impossible that John should be taller than Bill and Bill taller than John.'

This merely confuses the issue. If by the words 'taller than' we choose to mean what we mean by the words 'equal in height', then if we say 'John is taller than Bill and Bill is taller than John', we would assert that John and Bill are equal in height. That is perfectly possible. Once we have made that change in the meaning of words, however, we would no longer be asserting that Bill is taller than John when we say 'Bill is taller than John.' We would be asserting something different. Hence, the change of meaning is quite irrelevant to the possibility or necessity of what we asserted by uttering those words before the change of meaning took place. One cannot render it true or even possible that John should be taller than Bill and Bill taller than John by altering the meaning of words. All one can do is alter what is asserted by uttering the sentence 'John is taller than Bill and Bill is taller than John.' This in no way affects the necessity or impossibility of what was asserted by the sentence before the meaning of words was changed.

We must meet an objection. It might be claimed that in the foregoing argument we have made our point only by refusing to use the words in question to mean what they mean once the change of meaning is stipulated. Thus, it might be charged that we continued to use the word 'taller than' as it was used before the stipulated change and that, had we not illicitly behaved in this manner, we would not even be able to formulate our thesis. When we said that it could not be true that John is taller than Bill and Bill is taller than John, we are obviously using the word 'taller than' with its original meaning rather than with its stipulated one.

The reply to this line of thought requires that we first admit to using terms in their original rather than stipulated sense, but then deny that it would be impossible to formulate the thesis in question without using terms in this way. If we agree to use 'taller than' to mean 'equal in height', this does not deprive us of our thesis, but only forces us to put the matter in other words. Now we would have to say that it is impossible that John exceeds Bill in height and that Bill exceeds John in height, which is what was asserted by the sentence 'John is taller than Bill and Bill is taller than John' before the change in meaning took place. Thus, we can say that what was originally asserted by the sentence is necessarily false. Moreover, what was asserted may be asserted in other words once the change in meaning deprives us of the usual words for asserting it. Consequently, the necessity or impossibility of what is asserted does not depend on the meaning of the words employed. The meaning of words determines *what* is asserted, but not the necessity or impossibility of what is asserted.

Meaning and Scepticism

Let us return to our fundamental question. Is there some way in which the meaning establishes the truth of epistemic principles? A sceptic might claim that none of them is true. He may share most of our beliefs, but he does not share our epistemic convictions concerning what is evident, certain, justified, and so forth. If our fundamental question is to be answered in the affirmative, then appeal to semantics, to the meaning of words, must suffice to refute the sceptic. Let us consider whether the meanings of words are sufficient to untie the sceptical knot.

Suppose a man always says he does not know what we say we do know. The sceptic could mean something quite different from what is ordinarily meant. The question is whether the sceptic *must* mean something different by epistemic terms simply because he speaks with a sceptical tongue. The answer to this question, happily for the sceptic, is that he need not mean anything different by these terms from the rest of us. The systematic difference in what he says from what the rest of us say may *suggest* he means something different, but we cannot force him to this position.

There are two ways to account for the fact that others regularly say different things from what we say in the same situations. One way is to suppose that the words they utter mean something quite different when uttered by them. The other is to suppose that the words mean nothing different, but the men differ in what they believe. When the sceptic utters epistemic words, we may either suppose that he means something different from the rest of us, or we may suppose that his beliefs differ from ours. How can we show which supposition is true?

John Lyons, following Jost Trier, has contended that we may explicate the meaning of words by means of the logical relations of the words to other words pertaining to the same subject. He calls a group of subject-related terms a 'semantic field'.[10] Whether we accept this as a method of semantic analysis or not, such considerations are evidence of what a person means by the words he uses. Thus a person who understands the logical relations among cooking words, construing those logical relations in the usual way, may reasonably be taken to understand the vocabulary of cooking words and to mean by those words what is ordinarily meant. If a man understands the semantic relations between such words as 'cook', 'fry', 'boil', 'broil', 'sauté', and so forth, then we would have evidence that he means what is usually meant by such words. Moreover, if he can provide plausible definitions as well, our evidence is so much the better.[11]

The foregoing remarks are somewhat oversimplified, for as Adrienne Lehrer has illustrated, there will be some differences in what each of us means by the terms we use.[12] None the less, a general core of agreement is reflected in the general pattern of semantic relations between terms within a field. Moreover, such evidence for determining what a person means by the words he utters illustrates additional considerations, relevant to deciding what a person means by the words he utters, other than considerations of how he applies terms. It is because semantic relations between terms are a determinant of meaning

[10] Jost Trier, *Der Deutsche Wortschatz im Sinnbezirk des Verstandes* (Carl Winter, Heidelberg, 1931); John Lyons, *Structural Semantics* (Basil Blackwell, Oxford, 1963). See chapter 4.

[11] Cf. Adrienne Lehrer, 'Semantic Cuisine', *Journal of Linguistics*, v (1969), 39–55.

[12] Adrienne Lehrer, 'Indeterminacy in Semantic Description', *Glossa*, iv (1970), 87–110.

that profound and systematic disagreement concerning application remains significant. If meaning was determined solely by
the way in which words were applied, then there would be no
possibility of systematic disagreement over facts and theories.
All such disagreements would vanish into semantics. They would
become nothing more than mere verbal disagreements resulting
from the one person meaning something different from another.

The meaning of words is not, however, determined solely by
the way they are applied any more than it is determined solely
by the semantic relations they have to other terms, even though
both of these ingredients are relevant to determinations of
meaning. When a man denies the statement 'If something is
frying, then it is cooking', then it is doubtful that he is using the
terms 'fry' and 'cook' to mean what is ordinarily meant.
Similarly, if he insists that something is cooking if and only if it
is frying, this is again evidence of deviance. In their customary
meaning, 'to fry' implies 'to cook' but not vice versa. Implication is a semantic relation, as are inconsistency and equivalence.
(Implication may be used to define the rest as may inconsistency.) Thus, the network of semantic relations is one determinant of the meaning of terms. We shall now appeal to this
determinant to answer the question of whether the sceptic must
be interpreted as meaning something special by epistemic
terms.

The sceptic can mean the same thing by his epistemic words
as we do. Terms like 'know', 'evident', 'justified', 'certain',
and so forth compose a semantic field. If a man understands
semantic relations between those terms to be what is customary, then we have evidence he means by those terms what we
ordinarily do. There is little doubt that the sceptic may employ
epistemic terms in such a way as to preserve the usual semantic
relations between those terms. He may agree that if we know
anything to be true, we are completely justified in believing it,
but deny that we know anything to be true. He may pass all
such tests concerning semantic relations among epistemic
words. He means what we mean.

Let us consider an objection to this argument formulated in
terms of colour words. Suppose a man semantically relates
colour words to each other as we do, but he applies each
colour word to the complementary colour to which it is usually

applied. This man, a colour-term invert, applies the term 'red' to green things and the term 'green' to red things. It must be admitted that this difference in application would force us to decide that he means something different by colour terms from the rest of us. Agreement in the construing of semantic relations among terms in a field is not sufficient for agreement of meaning.

This objection is important, but not decisive. First, it is not absolutely clear that the agreement can be sustained as other colour terms are added to the field. Such additions could reveal some latent differences in semantic relations. Notice that terms may be added to some semantic fields by ostension. For example, suppose the term 'heliotrope' is not yet included in the semantic field of colour terms. We find a sample, a flower, and lay it down that the colour term 'heliotrope' is to apply to things and only to things having the same colour as the sample. Suppose both we and the colour-term invert adopt this convention.

The term 'heliotrope' now belongs to our vocabulary and to that of the colour-term invert. Both of us have agreed to fix the meaning of that term by means of the colour sample. But semantic relations now diverge. We would affirm that every-thing heliotrope is purple, while the colour-term invert would deny this: he applies the term 'purple' only to the complement of purple. Differences of application resulting from a difference in meaning can be elicited by a semantic extension of the field in which new terms are introduced by ostension. We are not proposing that introduction of terms by ostension is a complete specification of the meaning; it is not. Meaning depends on the semantic relation of a term to others in the same field. Ostensive introduction of terms into already existent semantic fields may, however, enable us to relate the terms to others in the field almost automatically.

Epistemic terms in the vocabulary of a sceptic may have the same semantic relations as they have in ours. Could the process of ostension reveal an extended field of epistemic terms for the sceptic having different semantic relations than the extended field for the non-sceptic? Let us imagine that attempt to introduce an epistemic term by ostension. We indicate a belief and lay it down that the term 'agnoite' is to apply to beliefs and only to beliefs of the same epistemic sort as the sample belief. This would leave one without adequate understanding of the meaning of the term 'agnoite'. One could well remain unenlightened even after several examples had been produced. To clarify the meaning of the term 'agnoite' would most likely require the explanation that an agnoite belief is an ignorant belief. Moreover, the thus extended semantic field of the sceptic need not differ from our own. Once the sceptic understood that an agnoite belief was an ignorant belief, he could semantically relate the term 'agnoite' to other epistemic terms in the same way the rest of us do. The only difference in his employment of the term is that he will *apply* it to all beliefs.

The difference between the sceptic and the colour-term invert shows that the sceptical usage of epistemic terms should be explained as a difference of belief rather than as a difference of meaning. Let us compare the man who learns the meaning of the term 'heliotrope' by ostension to the sceptic who learns the meaning of the term 'agnoite'. Once the colour-term invert learns the meaning of 'heliotrope' by ostension, he has an extended semantic field whose terms differ in semantic relations from the terms belonging to the same extended field used by someone who attaches the customary meaning to colour words. This would be shown by his application of terms *and* by what he takes to be the semantic relations between terms. He does not apply 'purple' to purple things, and he denies that heliotrope things are purple. The best explanation of why he does these things leads to the conclusion that he means something different by the term 'purple' and other colour terms from the rest of us. But the sceptic is altogether different. When the sceptic learns the meaning of the term 'agnoite', this does not produce any deviation from the customary semantic relations among epistemic terms in the extended field. Since learning the meaning of other epistemic terms would not produce semantic deviation, some difference in belief rather than a difference in meaning explains the sceptical practice of denying what we assert about epistemological issues.

A summary of our argument may be useful. Two kinds of information are relevant to determining what a man means by the words he utters; information about how he applies the term and information about how he semantically relates the word to others in the same field. We then noted that two men might relate a word to others in the same way in a semantic field and yet not mean the same thing by the word. The example of colour terms illustrated this. We argued, however, that some extension of the semantic field would produce a difference in the way in which the two men would relate the word to others in the extended semantic field. Hence, if two men semantically relate a word in the same way, not only to terms actually in use but to terms in extended semantic fields as well, this is sufficient to show that they mean the same thing by the word in question. Finally, the sceptic may semantically relate the word 'know' to other epistemic words as others do, not only those actually in use but to epistemic terms in extended semantic fields as well. Therefore, the sceptic may mean what men ordinarily mean by the word 'know' and other epistemic terms.

We have examined the position that one cannot speak as a sceptic without meaning something different by the epistemic words one utters from what is ordinarily meant, and found it wanting. A sceptic might deny that any belief is completely justified and mean what is customarily meant by epistemic terms. One cannot, therefore, argue that any belief is basic and self-justified on the grounds that to deny this would necessitate attaching some novel meaning to epistemic terms. The foundation theory cannot be sustained by this line of argument.

Self-justification and Necessary Truth

There is a final line of defence for a philosopher wishing to argue that certain epistemic principles, ones affirming beliefs to be self-justified, are true by virtue of the meaning of words. He may affirm that what a sceptic says is necessarily false. Thus, for example, a foundation theorist may contend that if a man believes himself to be sensing-redly, then it follows from his so believing that he is *justified* in believing he is sensing-redly. Notice, we are not here reverting to the doctrine of incorrigibility. It is claimed here that it follows, from a man believing he is sensing-redly, that he is justified in his belief and not that this belief is true. Were the doctrine correct, a sceptic conceding someone believes he is sensing-redly but denying the person to be completely justified in so believing, would be espousing what is necessarily false.

The major difficulty with this position is that it is initially implausible and fundamentally dogmatic. The claims of the sceptic may seem odd. Nevertheless, there is little credibility in the idea that when the sceptic says a certain belief is not completely justified he is thereby saying something contradictory. Compare the sceptic's claim, that a person believes he is sensing-redly but is not completely justified in his belief, with the claim that there is a red object that is not coloured. The latter, if taken literally, is impossible. There is no logically possible way in which an object can be red but not coloured. The suggestion is logically incoherent. By contrast, the claim that a belief, any belief, is not completely justified, however contrary to our convictions, is logically coherent. We can understand how it is possible, for example, if there are no completely justified beliefs. The sceptic does not contradict himself. It would be plainly dogmatic and unwarranted to pin the label of inconsistency upon his pronouncements.

The sceptic could, furthermore, even accede to such semantic dogmatism and still defend himself with a minor readjustment. We initially imagined the sceptic admitting we believe such things as that we are sensing-redly, and then denying we are completely justified in our beliefs. Now, if we rule out this sceptical manoeuvre as a matter of the meaning of words, we rob the sceptic of his position through semantics. He can easily retaliate, however. Whereas he was formerly conciliatory with respect to the question of whether we believe ourselves to be in the states in question, he may now become more truculent. He may assert that we only *apparently* believe ourselves to be in those states, but actually do not believe it because we are not completely justified in believing ourselves to be in the states in question. In short, he may agree that certain beliefs, if they exist, are completely justified, but deny that such beliefs exist. They appear to exist, but appearances can be deceptive. Instead of believing that we are sensing-redly, for example, we are in a somewhat different state, one like that state but not entailing that anyone is completely justified in any belief. Though we are not here primarily concerned with scepticism, the perspective of the sceptic is important. It shows us that the appeal to the meaning of words to defend epistemic principles is philosophically otiose.

Consider a similar tactic a foundation theorist might employ in defence of such epistemic principles. When asked for defence, he might say that such principles, when believed, constitute basic beliefs. Hence, his justification for believing that a man who believes he is sensing-redly is completely justified is simply self-justification. The belief that the principle is true is basic. And, of course, when this claim is challenged, it may again be affirmed to be basic. It is clear this line of thought can be pressed into infinite service. It is equally obvious that such a line of defence is totally ineffective as it entirely begs the question in favour of the foundation theorist. The claim that epistemic principles are self-justified or true by virtue of the meaning of words simply lacks dialectical cogency.

How, then, might the claim be defended? The defence must take the form of showing the alleged basic beliefs to be self-justified in terms of the objective of such justification, namely, to guarantee the truth of the beliefs in question. The problem is to show that a man seeking to guarantee the truth of his beliefs could reasonably take some beliefs to be basic.

If it could be shown to be reasonable for a man, seeking a guaranteee of veracity in what he believes, to justify all his beliefs, in terms of certain ones which are not justified by any others, then it would be reasonable for him to lay down epistemic principles according to which the latter beliefs are self-justified. The question of whether there are such beliefs turns, however, on the question of what beliefs would be justified for a man striving for such a guarantee of truth. Consequently, we shall postpone our final judgement on the matter of whether any adequate defence of the doctrine of basic beliefs can be constructed until we have examined the status of non-basic beliefs.

6

Justification and Evidence:
The Foundation Theory (III)

IN this chapter we shall consider the problem of the justification of non-basic beliefs. Our special concern here is with such justification within the context of a foundation theory. For our immediate purposes we shall assume that we have a set of self-justified basic beliefs and consider how such beliefs might justify others. Moreover, we must keep in mind that it is a central tenet of the foundation theory that justification guarantees truth, and from this it follows that the self-justified basic beliefs which guarantee their own truth must, if they justify any non-basic belief, also guarantee the truth of such beliefs. We are thus seeking an account of justification of non-basic beliefs which guarantees the truth of non-basic beliefs.

How Justification is Based on Evidence

The project outlined above necessitates considering problems of justification that would arise for any theory of justification, so, before turning to the special issues arising within the foundation theory of justification, we must attempt to solve one general problem regarding justification. The solution will be neutral with respect to the debate between the foundation theory and an alternative to it. The problem concerns the way in which justification is based on evidence. If one statement or belief justifies another, then the former is evidence for the latter. Moreover, the justification, whatever its precise character, is based on the evidence. The problem is to say under what conditions a justification of a belief is based on evidence.

When a man's justification for his belief is based on evidence, then he believes what he does because of the evidence. This suggests a *causal* account of what is involved when the justification of a belief is based on evidence. The notion of a justification being based on evidence would then be explicated in causal terms. Following this proposal, a man's justification for his belief is based on certain evidence if and only if his belief is causally related in some specified way to the evidence. How to specify the exact way in which the belief must be causally related to the evidence would remain a problem on this approach, but it would be a problem of detail rather than of principle. All such theories must be rejected, however.[1]

Often the evidence on which a justification is based does causally explain the existence of the belief, and it may even be admitted that sometimes the belief is justified because of the way in which it is explained by the evidence. Nevertheless, it is also possible for a justified belief to be causally independent of the evidence in every way. Indeed, it may well be that the evidence in no way explains why the man holds the belief even though his justification for the belief is based on the evidence. The evidence that justifies a man's belief may be evidence he acquired because he already held the belief, rather than the other way round. Moreover, it might even be that he would no longer appreciate the evidence if the belief were to fade.

An example will illustrate. It is easy to imagine the case of someone who comes to believe something for the wrong reason, and consequently, cannot be said to be justified in his belief, but who, as a result of his belief, uncovers some evidence which completely justifies his belief. A lawyer who, because he has fallen in love with his client, believes she is innocent of a crime, though all the available evidence points to her guilt, might come to find conclusive evidence of her innocence that the rest of us fail to appreciate. He could not be said to know that she is innocent before he finds the evidence in question, even if *he* might say he knows, but once the lawyer finds the evidence and appeals to it to justify his belief, then he may correctly be said to know that she is innocent. In this example, the man did not originally come to believe that the woman was innocent

---

[1] Three important defences of the causal theory of knowing are Alvin Goldman's 'A Causal Theory of Knowing', *Journal of Philosophy*, lxiv (1967), 357–72. Gilbert Harman's 'Knowledge, Reasons, and Causes', *Journal of Philosophy*, lxvii (1970), 841–55, and Marshall Swain's 'Knowledge, Causality, and Justification', *Journal of Philosophy*, lxix (1972), 291–300.

because of the evidence he subsequently acquired, nor does that evidence in any way explain why he believes what he does. On the other hand, the evidence does completely justify his belief and explains how he knows that she is innocent.

There is a reply to this sort of example, supplied by Gilbert Harman, to the effect that the evidence which the lawyer subsequently acquired reinforces or supports his belief in such a way as to explain, at least conditionally, his belief. On the condition that the lawyer ceases to love his client and hence no longer believes in her innocence for that reason, the evidence would then sustain the belief. At the very least, the evidence partially explains why he believes in her innocence. Thus the evidence on which a justification is based either explains or at least partially explains the belief which it justifies.

The preceding argument may be met, however, by altering the example to insure that the evidence does not conditionally or partially explain why the man believes what he does. To this end, imagine a second lawyer who happens to be a gypsy with the gypsy's traditional reverence for reading the cards. He too has a client who appears guilty to the impartial observer. In fact, imagine that eight murders have been committed, all of them alike, carried out with the same sort of weapon under the same circumstances. There is no doubt about the fact that seven of these murders were committed by the client: that is conclusively established, and the eighth is like the other seven in every detail. The crimes are hideous, and it is assumed by all concerned including the lawyer that his client committed the eighth. However, one evening the lawyer is checking with the cards, reading them with gypsy skill and conviction, when the cards tell him that his client is innocent of the eighth murder though guilty of the others. He never doubts the cards. His conviction of innocence leads him to reconsider the evidence. He discovers a valid though complicated line of reasoning from the evidence to the conclusion that his client did not commit the eighth murder. Because the line of reasoning is complicated, others, impressed by the similarity of the crimes and eager to believe that the agent of them all has been apprehended, refuse to accept the lawyer's cogent reasoning. Nevertheless, he sincerely and correctly maintains that on the basis of evidence, he knows his client is innocent of the eighth murder. He freely admits, however, that the evidence which he claims shows that he knows his client to be innocent of that crime is not what convinced him of the innocence of his client, and, indeed, would not convince him now were he not already convinced by the cards. He agrees that it is extraordinarily difficult to be convinced by the evidence because of the emotional factors surrounding the crime. The evidence is quite conclusive, as shown by his complicated chain of reasoning, but even he would find himself unable to believe his client could be innocent of that eighth murder were it not for the fact that the cards told him it was so. It is what he read in the cards that completely convinced him his client was innocent of the eighth murder, and it is that which nurtures and supports his conviction. His conviction could not be increased by his consideration of the evidence because he was already completely convinced. On the other hand, were his faith in the cards to collapse, then emotional factors which influence others would sway him too. Therefore the evidence which completely justifies his belief does not explain why he believes as he does, his faith in the cards explains that, and the evidence in no way supports, reinforces, or conditionally or partially explains why he believes as he does. Since his belief is completely explained by his faith in cards, the evidence is irrelevant to explaining why he believes as he does. His belief is completely justified by the evidence, however: his faith in the cards is irrelevant to the justification of his belief.

The preceding discussion rests on a distinction between explaining why a man believes something, on the one hand, and explaining how he knows it on the other. When a man knows that his belief is true, the explanation of why he believes what he does may have something to do with his having the evidence he does, but it also may have nothing whatever to do with his having evidence. The explanation may rest on political, erotic, or other extraneous influences, but the explanation of how a man knows that his belief is true, when the justification of the belief is based on evidence, *must* be in terms of the evidence. It is how a man knows that is explained by evidence. Why he believes what he does may be explained by anything whatever. Therefore, a justification of a belief that is known to be true is based on certain evidence if and only if his having that evidence explains how he knows the belief is true.

The idea of evidence explaining how a man knows may be further clarified by recalling once again that our primary concern is to provide a theory to explain how knowledge claims are justified. It is the defence of knowledge claims which must be explicated by our theory. A knowledge claim is challenged by the question 'How do you know?' A justificatory reply to this challenge which appeals to evidence can constitute an explanation of how the person knows. It will do so if the reply is a correct one. Thus, we may say that a justification based on evidence explains how a man knows that p if and only if that justification would be a correct answer for the man to the question 'How do you know that p?' We have thus reduced the problem of specifying conditions under which a justification is based on evidence to the problem of explicating when a justification is a correct answer to the question 'How do you know?'[2]

Justification as a Logical Guarantee of Truth

According to the foundation theory, a correct answer to such a question must be one guaranteeing the truth of what a man has claimed to know. When the answer is a justification based on evidence, the justification must guarantee the truth of the non-basic belief so justified. Just as logical guarantees are sought for the truth of basic beliefs, so they are for non-basic beliefs. Hence, a justification based on evidence which logically entails the truth of the non-basic belief is our first candidate for the role of a guarantee of truth through evidential justification.

The attempt to formulate a theory of justification for non-basic beliefs has often lead to some sort of analytically reductive theory concerning those statements expressing non-basic beliefs. An analytically reductive theory affirms that statements containing terms of a specified class can be reduced by logical analysis to statements formulated in a more restricted vocabulary not containing the terms in question.

[2] This analysis was originally proposed in my 'How Reasons Give Us Knowledge, or, The Case of the Gypsy Lawyer', *Journal of Philosophy*, lxviii (1971), 311–13.

Phenomenalism, for example, affirms that statements containing physical-object terms can be reduced by logical analysis to statements formulated in a more restricted sense-data vocabulary not containing physical-object terms. Thus, phenomenalism, if correct, could provide the basis for a theory of justification avowing that some restricted class of sense-data statements, perhaps those reporting some past or present sense experience, express basic beliefs, while physical-object statements, and those statements to which they can be reduced by logical analysis, express non-basic beliefs.

Phenomenalism

There are a number of problems concerning phenomenalism that have led to its rejection. First, the language of sense-data is itself controversial. Sense-data language describes the appearances one senses, or the way in which one is appeared to, but it is also supposed to have other properties which are controversial. For example, Ayer suggested that some sense-data statements are incorrigible,[3] and we have considered the problems surrounding such a claim. Second, it is doubted by some philosophers that the required logical analysis of physical-object statements can be effected. For example, Chisholm has argued that no physical-object statement logically entails any sense-data statement.[4] This is so, he argued, because for any physical-object statement we consider, for example, that there is a doorknob before me, we can show that this does not logically entail any sense-data statement. For example, such sense-data statements as that I am sensing roundish, yellowish sense-data, or that if I were to sense certain kinesthetic sensations, I would sense hardish, coldish sense-data, are not entailed. We can prove this by framing a suitable hypothesis about the state of the observer. If we suppose that I am experiencing various hallucinations, which is logically possible, then, from the presence of the doorknob, nothing follows about what sense-data I am experiencing or would experience.

---

[3] See A. J. Ayer's defence of this thesis in *Foundations of Empirical Knowledge*, 78–84, and in *Philosophical Essays* (St. Martin's Press, New York, 1954), in the chapter entitled 'Basic Propositions', 105–24, but particularly 113ff.

[4] R. M. Chisholm, in the appendix to *Perceiving: A Philosophical Study*, 190–3.

Phenomenalism, however, though not commonly defended currently, is characteristic of analytically reductive theories. By examining it we can determine the relevance of such reductive theories to the foundation theory of justification. Though the term 'logical analysis' is used in a variety of meanings, we are concerned here with those analyses that satisfy the following condition: if L is a logical analysis of S, then L is logically equivalent to S. This condition is only a necessary condition of a logical analysis. The importance of the condition for a foundation theory of justification is that if L is logically equivalent to S, and if L is a conjunction of statements formulating basic beliefs, then the statement S is a logical consequence of the statements of basic beliefs making up the conjunction. As a result, the non-basic belief that S may be deductively justified by those basic beliefs. Since the justification would be deductive, the justification, assuming the truth of the basic belief to be guaranteed, would logically guarantee the truth of the non-basic belief. In terms of phenomenalism, those sense-data statements formulating basic beliefs, and also constituting the analysis of a physical-object statement, could deductively guarantee the truth of non-basic belief in the truth of the latter.

The appeal to an analytically reductive theory to support a foundation theory of justification of non-basic beliefs faces two serious problems. These can be illustrated by further consideration of phenomenalism. Suppose we have a physical-object statement, P, and we have a phenomenalistic analysis of P in sense-data terminology, where the analysis consists of a conjunction of sense-data statements S_1, S_2, and so forth through S_n. Let us for the sake of simplicity refer to the statements formulating basic beliefs as basic statements and those statements formulating non-basic beliefs as non-basic statements. Then we may ask a critical question about the set of statements S_1, S_2, and so forth to S_n. Are these statements basic or non-basic ones?

On any plausible analysis, a person is not completely justified in believing the entire set of sense-data statements as basic beliefs. That is, some of the statements S_1, S_2, and so forth to S_n will either be statements a person is *not* completely justified in believing, or they will be non-basic. Suppose we attempt to analyse the statement 'there is a ripe tomato before me' and consider the sort of sense-data statements one might think are part of the analysis of this statement. Some of these statements would be about what one is sensing at the moment, for example, a reddish, roundish sense-datum, others would be hypothetical statements about what one would be sensing if one were in different circumstances. These hypothetical statements would tell us what one would be sensing if one were in a different position, if the tomato were to be manipulated in a variety of ways, if the surrounding conditions were altered in a variety of ways and so forth.

Some of these hypothetical statements would have to be justified by evidence, if they are justified at all. Many of them would be contrary to fact, asserting what one would sense if certain facts were other than they are. One could be completely justified in believing such statements without evidence if they were not contrary to fact. Given that such a statement is contrary to fact, it is non-basic. Belief in the truth of a contrary to fact conditional, if it is justified at all, is justified on the basis of evidence. Therefore, the set of statements S_1, S_2, and so forth to S_n of any plausible phenomenalistic analysis cannot all be completely justified basic beliefs. Hence, such an analysis will not show how a set of basic beliefs about sense-data statements can guarantee the truth of a physical-object statement.

The upshot of this argument is that the sense-data statements S_1, S_2, and so forth to S_n of any plausible phenomenalistic analysis of physical-object statements cannot all be basic. If not all the sense-data statements are basic, then the analysis does not provide us with a set of basic statements that guarantee the truth of a non-basic statement.

Analytically Reductive Theories

The preceding argument can be extended to a variety of analytically reductive theories. Philosophers who have eschewed phenomenalism as unrealistic have often embraced some other analytically reductive theory to sustain their own version of a foundation theory. For example, some philosophers of science have regarded observation statements as basic and have proposed some reductive analysis of generalizations and theories in terms of observation statements. It was once argued, for instance, that generalizations of the form 'Any thing that is O_1 is O_2', where 'O_1' and 'O_2' are observation terms, may be analysed as a conjunctive statement: If x_1 is O_1 then x_1 is O_2 and if x_2 is O_1 then x_2 is O_2 and so forth. Here the difficulty mentioned above becomes obvious, since it is clear that not all the hypothetical statements are completely justified basic statements. If they are all completely justified, at least some of them must be completely justified as non-basic beliefs, that is, their justification must be based on evidence. The reason is that we shall not have observed every one of the objects x_1, x_2, and so forth, and, thus, even if we allow that beliefs in observation statements are self-justified, we shall not have observed enough to render all the hypothetical statements in the analysis of the generalization self-justified. Consequently, some of those beliefs will be non-basic. Hence, such a reductive analysis will not show how basic observation statements justify and guarantee the truth of non-basic generalizations.

Similar remarks apply to reductive analyses of theoretical statements in terms of observation statements. Moreover, other reductive analyses, such as behaviouristic analysis of psychological statements in terms of behavioural statements fail to support a foundation theory for the same general reasons. These reasons should be clear from the preceding arguments concerning phenomenalism. Suppose we analyse a psychological statement P as the conjunction of behavioural statements B_1, B_2, and so forth to B_n, where the latter are intended to be basic. The appeal of the idea is that the conjunction will be logically equivalent to P, and hence, P can be deduced from the set of the statements so conjoined. By deduction, then, the basic statements would guarantee the truth of the non-basic psychological statement.

In any plausible analysis of the kind in question, however, some of the conjuncts B_1, B_2, and so forth to B_n will be such that if we are completely justified in believing them, the justification will be based on evidence. The reason is that they will be contrary to fact conditionals concerning behaviour. Hence, some of the statements will turn out to be non-basic. Put in old-fashioned language, our justification for believing at least some of the statements must be *indirect*, and this suffices to ensure that they are not self-justified. Again, at least some statements in the reductive analysis are not basic. The best guarantee of truth which basic statements might provide for non-basic ones is unavailable. Analytically reductive theories provide a logical guarantee of truth, but they lead to incoherence when we attempt to combine them with a foundation theory. Statements we assume to be basic turn out to be non-basic. Hence, to sustain a foundation theory, basic statements must justify and guarantee the truth of non-basic statements in some other way.

Meaning and Inductive Justification

Another proposal is that statements completely justify non-basic statements by virtue of the meaning of words. A similar proposal was considered when we investigated the question of the justification of basic statements, and rejected because it rendered scepticism contradictory. The issue is slightly different here, however. First, even if the theory leads to the conclusion that scepticism concerning non-basic statements is contradictory, this conclusion is not as implausible as the assertion that universal scepticism is contradictory. Given basic statements, which are self-justified and guarantee their own truth, it could be contradictory to suppose that those statements do not completely justify or guarantee the truth of any other statements.

Moreover, a familiar problem of inductive inference suggests that the meaning of terms determines whether justificatory inference is legitimate. We have already noted that there are cases in which a conclusion is deducible from the premisses in which the deduction depends on the meaning of descriptive terms within those statements. One is the deduction from the statement 'The table is red' to the statement 'The table is coloured.' Another deduction we considered above is from the statement. 'John is taller than Bill' to the statement 'Bill is shorter than John.' In the former inference, the deduction depends on the meaning of the qualitative terms 'red' and 'coloured' and in the latter case on the meaning of the relational words 'taller' and 'shorter'. So deduction depends, in some cases, on the meaning of descriptive (non-logical) words in the statements. Here, meaning is what guarantees that the premisses deductively justify the conclusion.

There are also, however, cases where the inference is clearly non-deductive, let us say inductive for convenience, in which the justification of the conclusion by another statement also depends on the meaning of words. It is natural and traditional to suppose that inductive inference depends only on the form of statements. For example, suppose I observe that x_1 which is A is B, that x_2 which is A is B and so forth to observing that x_n which is A is B. Imagine that x_1 to x_n are all the things I have observed that are A. In that case, assuming that n is a large number, I might inductively infer that all things that are A are B. Moreover, one might, if one is embracing a foundation theory according to which the observation statements are basic, maintain that if n is large enough, then the observation of n things could completely justify the conclusion that all A is B. By holding this form of the foundation theory, one would be in a position to contend that particular basic statements could justify general non-basic statements, and, consequently, that the foundation theory is adequate to explain the justification of generalizations.

There are two problems with this line of thought, one of which stems from Nelson Goodman.[5] The problem stemming from Goodman rests on a familiar counterexample to the thesis. Suppose, Goodman says, we define a rather peculiar predicate 'grue' as follows; a thing is grue if and only if it is observed and green, or unobserved and blue. Now, it happens that we notice that things, say emeralds, are grue, because we observe that they are green and observed. Consider the emeralds we observe. We then observe that x_1 is an emerald and grue, that x_2 is an emerald and grue, and so forth to x_n. By the rule above, we conclude that all the emeralds in question are grue; by the same rule, we conclude that all emeralds are green. The statement that all emeralds are grue logically entails that all unobserved emeralds are blue, while the statements that all emeralds are green logically entails that all unobserved emeralds are green. Hence, the observation statements cannot completely

[5] See Nelson Goodman's *Fact, Fiction, and Forecast* (Bobbs-Merrill, Indianapolis, Ind., 1965), 72–83.

justify and guarantee the truth of both of these conclusions without entailing the undesired consequence that there are no unobserved emeralds.[6]

It might seem as though there is an obvious objection to this argument, namely, that 'grue' is defined and 'green' is not. As Goodman points out, however, we could define another term 'bleen' as follows: something is bleen if and only if it is observed and blue or unobserved and green. If we take 'grue' and 'bleen' as primitive, then we can define 'green' and 'blue'. The former is defined as follows: something is green if and only if it is observed and grue or unobserved and bleen. Since what is taken as defined or primitive in language is arbitrary, the Goodman example holds.[7] We cannot base justificatory inference on the form of the inference alone.

There are diverse morals to be drawn. John Pollock draws the conclusion that the justificatory inference depends on the meaning of terms, and his conclusion is justified.[8] Of course, to say that justification depends on the meaning of terms does not explain why the observation that emeralds are green justifies the projection that unobserved emeralds are green, while the observation that emeralds are grue does *not* justify the projection that unobserved emeralds are grue. None the less, the meaning of the terms 'grue' and 'green' in some way accounts for why we can project in the one case and not the other, even if one has not accounted for the way in which the meaning of the terms limits projection in one case and permits it in the other. If 'grue' meant what 'green' meant and vice versa then, no matter which term was primitive and which was defined, 'green' should be projected and 'grue' should not.

This leads Pollock to contend that justification conditions for the application of terms are constitutive of the meaning of those terms.[9] This contention is not established by the insight mentioned above. It may be a *necessary* condition of the application of a term being justified that the term means what it does, but it does not follow that the meaning of the term is a *sufficient* condition for the application of the term. Whether certain

[6] Goodman, op. cit. 74.   [7] Ibid. 79–80.
[8] John Pollock, unpublished manuscript.   [9] Ibid.

basic statements completely justify and guarantee the truth of
certain non-basic statements depends on the meaning of
descriptive terms. That terms mean what they do is a necessary
condition for the basic statements justifying the non-basic
statements, but it does not follow that it is sufficient.

Whether a statement is completely justified by basic statements depends on the meaning of the terms within the
statement. Still, this leaves open the question of when the
meaning of terms ensures that a non-basic statement is completely justified by a basic statement which does not logically
entail the non-basic statement. The example of 'grue' and
'green' is not such a case. There is no contradiction involved
in denying that the statement 'the next emerald to be observed
will be green' is completely justified by the statement 'all of
the numerous emeralds that have been observed are green.'
Indeed, there is no contradiction in denying that the latter
provides any justification for believing the former.

Of course, someone may choose to use the terms 'justify'
and 'completely justify' in such a way as to make it a consequence of the meaning of these terms that the justification
holds, but this manoeuvre comes closer to changing the subject
than to solving the problem. We shall simply have to find new
words for old questions. We may, in this situation, ask whether
'completely justified' beliefs are completely warranted, or,
more to the heart of the matter, whether there is any connection
between 'complete justification' and truth. Once this redefini-
tion of terms takes place, we shall have to re-establish that
complete justification guarantees the truth of the belief
justified. And that is precisely our original question in a new
guise.

We started by asking whether a certain form of reasoning
completely justified and guaranteed the truth of a non-basic
belief. We are told that such reasoning does completely justify
the non-basic belief as a consequence of the meaning of the
term 'completely justify'. Now, however, we must ask whether
reasoning which completely justifies a non-basic belief
guarantees the truth of the non-basic belief. Of course, someone
might reply that it is a consequence of the meaning of the
words 'guarantee the truth' that such completely justified
beliefs are ones whose truth is guaranteed. Then we come down

to the epistemic finishing line, and ask whether there is any connection between guaranteeing the truth of a belief and the belief being true. We arrive, finally at the question of whether those beliefs whose truth is 'guaranteed' are even likely to be true.

Probability and Justification

The preceding formulation of the problem takes us to the most fundamental issue, one concerning the probability of truth. For the foundation theory to succeed, the basic beliefs of the theory must at least render it highly probable that non-basic beliefs are true. If the evidence formulated in self-justified beliefs which guarantee their own truth is to completely justify and guarantee the truth of non-basic beliefs, then the truth of non-basic beliefs must be highly probable on the basis of the evidence of basic ones. We arrived at the basis for this conclusion in our earlier discussion of analytically reductive theories employed to support the foundation theory. We saw that the justification relation between basic statements and non-basic statements could not be confined to deduction. Such confinement yields the result that the statements assumed initially to be basic turn out to be non-basic. For the purposes of the foundation theory, basic statements must guarantee the truth of non-basic statements without entailing them. By considering the role of probability in the foundation theory we can bypass further discussion of whether basic beliefs completely justify non-basic ones by virtue of the meaning of words. The truth of non-basic beliefs are guaranteed in the requisite sense only if they are at least highly probable on the evidence of basic beliefs.[10]

Even if basic beliefs render non-basic beliefs highly probable, it remains an open question whether the former guarantee the truth of the latter. Basic beliefs might render non-basic beliefs highly probable, but fail to render them sufficiently probable to guarantee their truth. There remains the question of when a probability is high enough to completely justify and guarantee

[10] This thesis may be questioned by those who defend a non-probabilistic account of inductive support, for example, L. Jonathan Cohen in *Implications of Induction* (Methuen, London, 1970).

the truth of a belief. We shall return to this question after a brief consideration of the concept of probability.

Three Concepts of Probability

Philosophers and logicians have distinguished a number of different conceptions of probability.[11] Among these are the frequency concept, the logical concept, and the subjective concept. We shall consider them all and ask what application each concept has to the problem of the justification of non-basic beliefs. First, we consider the frequency concept. This conception of probability is based on a familiar feature of statistical inference. Sometimes we infer that a certain percentage of things of one class also belongs to a second class from our observation of a sample. The inferred statement is a probability statement. A frequency probability statement tells us the numerical frequency with which members of a class A are also members of class B. Or less specifically, the statement might tell us that the frequency falls within certain numerical limits. An example of that first kind of statement is one telling us that the frequency with which a coin falls heads when flipped is one out of two or $1/2$, while an example of the second kind of statement is one telling us that the frequency with which a person is born female is within the interval of $2/5$ to $3/5$. What exact interpretation is given to such statements is controversial. Some philosophers have interpreted such statements as expressing the limit of the relative frequency in an infinite series. Other philosophers have interpreted the frequency statement as expressing a propensity of members of one class to be members of a second class. However, the crucial feature of such statements for the purposes of our discussion is that all such statements turn out to be very general contingent statements about the world. Consequently, if such probability statements are to enter into the justification of non-basic beliefs on the basis of basic ones, the probability statement must itself be known or at least completely justified.

[11] The frequency concept is articulated by Hans Reichenbach in *Theory of Probability* (University of California Press, Berkeley, 1949), the logical concept is developed by Rudolf Carnap in *The Logical Foundations of Probability* (University of Chicago Press, Chicago, 1950), and the subjective concept is developed by Richard Jeffrey in *The Logic of Decision* (McGraw-Hill, New York, 1965).

Frequencies and Justification

In order to consider the application of this concept of probability to the foundation theory of justification, let us return to the special case of justifying physical-object statements on the basis of sense-data statements. There is a classical objection to the strategy of employing frequency probability statements to justify physical-object statements on the basis of sense-data statements. First, a probability statement must relate some class of true physical-object statements to a class of true sense-data statements. Thus, it must tell us that the frequency of statements being members of a class of a specified kind of true sense-data statements accompanied by statements being members of a class of true physical-object statements of a special variety is some very high number or is within an interval of very high numbers. To arrive at such a probability statement, it is objected, one would already have to know that a sample of true sense-data statements of the specified kind were accompanied by a high percentage of true physical-object statements of the special variety. To know this, however, one would have to know precisely what the frequency probability statement was supposed to enable us to know, namely, that the physical-object statements in question are true. The attempt to justify physical-object statements by appeal to frequency statements is, therefore, futile because it presupposes that we already know and are already justified in believing those statements that were supposed to get justified.

This argument is correct in some respects but inadequate in one important way. If we grant that the only method we have of knowing that a frequency statement is true is by inference from what we know in a sample, then the argument is decisive. Moreover, it is most natural to make just this assumption, for how else are we to know that the frequency statement is true? And if we do not know that it is true, how can we completely justify any belief by appeal to it? However, the assumption, though natural, is not forced. A philosopher might claim that at least some such frequency statements are basic statements, ones we are completely justified in believing without being justified by any other statements. This option has had some takers. It is tempting to suppose that we simply could not be mistaken in thinking that certain physical-object statements, for example, that I see my hand, are almost always true when certain sense-data statements are true, those characterizing the sort of sense-data I experience when I take it for granted that I am seeing my hand. A philosopher willing to defend the foundation theory by arguing that the frequency statements needed for basic statements to justify non-basic ones are themselves basic statements, may avoid the need to justify the frequency statements by appeal to knowledge of physical-object statements. By claiming the frequency statements are basic and self-justifying, he obviates the need to justify them by appeal to physical object statements. Being self-justified, the frequency statements can bridge the justificatory gap between basic sense-data statements and non-basic physical-object statements.

A sceptic might claim that such a foundation theory begs the question against scepticism. Moreover, some empiricists might protest that such a foundation theory abandons empiricism by supposing that *general* statements are justified without benefit of reports of particular observations. But these objections have no force against a foundation theorist who is willing to assume the inadequacy of scepticism and empiricism from the outset. We shall subsequently consider whether such an assumption would be warranted. We conclude, however, that there is no internal inconsistency or incoherence in the attempt to employ frequency-probability statements to explain how non-basic statements of a foundation theory are rendered highly probable by basic statements.

Logical Probabilities and Justification

The logical and subjective conceptions of probability fit even more readily into the foundation theory. According to the logical theory, probability is a logical relation, not between classes, but between individual sentences or propositions. An example of such a probability statement is the following: the probability that a coin will turn up heads on the evidence that it is fairly tossed is $1/2$. Such statements are said to be estimates of frequencies, but unlike frequency probability statements the logical probability statements are true by definition. Once the concept of probability is defined, then it is either true by definition or false by definition that a statement S is probable to degree m/n relative to statement E.

The statement that a hypothesis is probable to a specified degree relative to a second statement has two interpretations. One implies that the second statement is evidence we possess. The other affirms a relation between the two statements without any implication as to whether the second statement is evidence we possess. Of course, it is only on the latter interpretation that the probability statement is true, or false, by definition. Once the probability statement is interpreted as implying that something has the status of evidence, then the statement has the same semantic status as other evidential statements and may be contingent. (This would result if a relational probability statement were true by definition and was conjoined to a contingent evidence statement. The conjunction would then be contingent.)

If we suppose evidence statements are always basic, then the problem of explaining how basic statements render non-basic statements highly probable becomes a matter of drawing out the logical consequences of the definition of logical probability. Somewhat more formally, we define a probability relation between statements so that '$p(h, e)$' means 'the probability of h on (relative to) e'. The definition of the probability will enable us to determine the probability of any statement in a given language relative to any other statement. According to the logical conception of probability, to ascertain the truth of probability statements employed in the justification of non-basic statements, we need only know basic statements to be true and determine the consequences of the definition of probability.

Nevertheless, the encouragement offered by the logical conception of probability has a hidden defect. Since there is an infinite number of different ways in which we might define logical probability, all of which satisfy the general conditions we should wish to impose on the concept of probability, we face two problems. First, we must show that there is some connection between probability and truth. There may, after all, be none. Second, we must justify our choice of a single definition of probability out of a multiplicity of viable alternatives. Suppose we know certain basic statements to be true.

We might then appeal to a definition of probability, according to which a non-basic statement is highly probable on the basic statements we know, in order to justify believing the non-basic statement. Granting that our non-basic statement is highly probable relative to the basic statements we know, a detractor may query how the probability of the statement guarantees its truth. Indeed, how does it in any way justify us in believing the non-basic statement to be true when there are other ways of defining probability under which the same non-basic statement would be *improbable* relative to the same basic statements?

One reply to such a query is that the probability as defined is an *estimate* of truth frequency, but this reply, as it stands, is inadequate. The question remains whether it is a *good* estimate of truth frequency, or even a reasonable one. There are two lines of rejoinder for the defender of logical probability. First, he can maintain it as a basic, self-justified belief that certain logical probabilities are reasonable estimates of truth frequencies. Here we encounter a manoeuvre similar to the one employed in the defence of the use of frequency statements in the justification of non-basic statements by basic ones. We close a gap in the justification by filling it with a basic statement. In that context, the statement held to be basic was one to the effect that members of a class of non-basic statements are true with some specified frequency when basic statements of a certain kind are true. Here we have the same strategy used to defend the weaker claim that a logical probability statements are reasonable estimates of such truth frequencies. Again, our claim seems to depart from a strict empiricism. The contention that something is a reasonable estimate of truth frequency among two classes of empirical statements would, within a strictly empiricist tradition, be a thesis that would have to be justified by particular observations. It could not be justified without such confirmation. Nevertheless, there is nothing within the characterization of a foundation theory that would prohibit a departure from such empiricist requirements.

Subjective Probability and Justification

A second rejoinder in defence of the reasonableness of such estimates leads directly to the subjective interpretation of

probability. According to the subjective conception of probability, probabilities are degrees of belief representing rational
betting quotients. This idea may be elaborated as follows: the
subjective probabilities must be such that if they were taken as
betting odds, no one betting on the outcome of various events
at those odds would be *certain* of losing (or winning) no matter
what the outcome of the events. This idea of construing probabilities as rational if they are fair betting quotients in the
above sense allows great latitude in the choice of a probability
function. One could provide a set of betting quotients such that
no one could be certain of losing no matter what the outcome,
even though the betting odds were utterly unrealistic in terms
of the frequency probability of various outcomes. In short,
subjective probabilities which differ greatly from frequency
probabilities could be rational betting quotients in the required
sense.

Another way of thinking of subjective probabilities is as
functions of numerically assigned desirabilities or preferences.
Richard Jeffrey and others have shown how we can extra-
polate subjective probabilities from the preferences that a
person has.[12] The detailed elaboration of such a theory would
take us beyond the needs of the present study. For our purposes,
the important point is that the subjective theory enables us to
determine that an assignment of probabilities is rational. Your
assignment of probabilities can be said to be irrational if it is
possible to make book against you so that you cannot win no
matter what, and, correspondingly, an assignment is rational
if no one can make book against you in this way.

Though the subjective theory allows for shifting in the
assignment of probability in a way that the logical theory does
not, and though the logical theory places greater restraint on
the assignment of probability values than does the subjective
theory, they have similar problems from the standpoint of a
foundation theory of justification. First, some philosophers,
for example Putnam, have doubted that a justification relation
need be a probability in the sense of being a rational betting
quotient. Suppose one has some conception of justification
which does not depend on any conception of probability
interpreted as a rational betting quotient. What reason is there

[12] Jeffrey, op. cit.

to conclude that justification under such a conception would be any worse guarantee of truth than one based on high probabilities that were rational betting quotients? There does not seem to be any satisfactory reply to such a question from the premises of the foundation theory. A foundation theory requires that basic statements justify non-basic statements so as to guarantee their truth. That such and such is a rational betting quotient for betting on non-basic statements relative to basic ones, where all that is meant by a fair betting quotient is that book cannot be made against you, hardly shows that the basic statements guarantee the truth of non-basic statements or even that the basic statements provide us with any reason for believing the non-basic statement to be true.

We are back to where we stood when we considered the frequency conception of probability. There the problem was to explain how we are to ascertain that such frequency statements are true, for, if they are true, they establish a frequency relation between the truth of basic statements and the truth of non-basic statements. In the case of logical and subjective conceptions of probabilities, the problem of ascertaining probabilities is negligible. In the case of the logical conception, it is only a matter of drawing out the consequences of a definition of probability. In the case of the subjective conception, it is only a matter of extrapolating from the betting preferences of an agent. But though the problem of ascertaining probabilities is less, we are confronted with the problem of relevance. For here we must show that probability is relevant to truth, and, more specifically, to the frequency with which non-basic statements of a specified kind are true when basic statements of a certain sort are true. If there is no connection between the high logical or subjective probability of a non-basic statement relative to a basic statement and the truth of a non-basic statement relative to a basic statement, then such high probability is irrelevant for the purpose of justifying and guaranteeing the truth of non-basic statements relative to basic statements. Thus, in the case of both logical and subjective probability, we need an additional premiss before such probabilities can be relevantly employed in the justification of non-basic statements.

Probability, Truth, and General Statements

The logical and subjective conceptions of probabilities will necessitate the appeal to some basic statement of a very general sort, as did the frequency conception. Here the general statement is one affirming that a high logical or subjective probability is a guide to truth. We need to assume that if a non-basic statement is highly probable on the basis of basic statements, then we are completely justified in believing the non-basic statement to be true on the evidence of the truth of basic statements. This assumption, if we are justified in believing it at all, must surely be a basic belief. There is no other way of justifying it without already assuming that we know some of the non-basic statements to be true independently of the assumption, and the assumption is required for the justification of those non-basic statements. Ultimately, all conceptions of probability lead us to a similar problem. To employ probability statements in the justification of non-basic statements, we need to assume as basic some general statements about the relevance of the truth of basic statements to the truth of non-basic ones.

The foregoing consequence is a serious problem for the foundation theory even though it is not by itself decisive. It is, in fact, an exactly analogous problem to the one that arose concerning the justification of basic statements. The problem is that those general principles of justification, whether they concern the self-justification of basic statements or the justification of non-basic statements by basic statements, must be assumed to be basic statements, or else the foundation theory collapses. This means that our basic beliefs and non-basic beliefs are only justified if we take as basic some beliefs concerning the principles under which both kinds of beliefs are justified. This consideration is not intended to constitute any sort of refutation of the foundation theory; however, it does raise serious problems.

First, how are we to avoid the charge of being arbitrary in our choice of principles of justification? The foundation theory was to provide a safe and strict theory of justification where everything we claim to be justified was justified on the basis of a foundation of basic beliefs that guaranteed their own truth and the truth of all other justified belief. Now we see that in order to construct this edifice—indeed, in order to lay the first foundation stone, as well as to lay the second upon the first—we need to assume as basic a justificatory superstructure of general principles concerning the truth of basic and non-basic beliefs. The foundation, rather than consisting of particular beliefs that run a minimum risk or error, consists of general beliefs that suffer all the hazards of general conceptions. Second, it is difficult to understand why such general statements should not be justified by other statements. True, we cannot within a foundation theory justify these general principles of justification by appeal to particular beliefs without arguing in a circle. But we cannot justify particular beliefs by appeal to those general principles without arguing in a circle either. This suggests that the justification of both kinds of statements is reciprocal, that each justifies the other. To concede this, however, is to give up the foundation theory and embrace the coherence theory instead.

Justification and a Probability of One

The attempt to employ probability for guaranteeing the truth of non-basic beliefs reveals a crack in the structure of the foundation theory of justification that is quite beyond repair. Let us assume that the frequency probability statements are included among basic beliefs, and similarly that we include, among basic beliefs, assumptions to the effect that certain subjective and logical probability statements are reasonable estimates of frequencies. Such assumptions, rather than sustaining the foundation theory, provide for its destruction.

We assume probabilities are ascertained. We cannot, however, equate high probability with complete justification. The set of statements that are highly probable on the basis of an evidence statement will be logically inconsistent with the evidence statement, and we cannot be completely justified in believing each of a set of inconsistent statements. Consider any set of statements p_1, p_2, . . . and so forth to p_n, which describe outcomes of a lottery with one wininng ticket and n consecutively numbered tickets in all. Statement p_1 says the number one ticket will win in the drawing, p_2 says that the number two ticket will win in the drawing, and so forth. Moreover, evidence statement e says that the drawing has been held and the winning ticket is one of the tickets numbered 1, 2, and so forth to n. Now consider the hypotheses $\sim p1$, $\sim p2$, and so forth to $\sim pn$, denying that the number one ticket, the number two ticket, and so forth is the winner. The $p(\sim p1, e) = 1 - 1/n$. Indeed, for any pj, $p(\sim pj, e) = 1 - 1/n$. We can imagine $1 - 1/n$ to be as large a fraction less than 1 that we wish by imagining n to be sufficiently large. So if one allows high probability to be any probability less than 1, it follows that each of the hypotheses $\sim p1$, $\sim p2$, and so forth to $\sim pn$, is highly probable relative to e. The set of those hypotheses entails that none of the tickets numbered 1, 2, and so forth to n is a winner, in direct contradiction to the evidence which asserts that one of those tickets is the winner. Thus, if statements having a probability less than one can be considered highly probable, and if highly probable statements are ones we are completely justified in believing, then we will be completely justified in believing a set of statements that are contradictory, guaranteeing that not all of them are true.[13] This conclusion is entirely unacceptable.

The preceding argument shows that either we must deny that any statement with a probability of less than one is highly probable or we must deny that a highly probable statement is completely justified. It is a theorem in Carnap's theory of probability, and in that of Shimony and Kemeny as well, that in any finite language a hypothesis is probable to degree one on evidence only if the evidence logically entails the hypothesis. Moreover, in such systems, even in infinite languages, any non-general hypothesis, for example, that John has entered the room, is probable to degree one on any non-general evidence, for example, that I am having certain sensory experiences and remember certain particular facts about John and his appearance, only if the evidence logically entails the hypothesis. If a system of probability fails to yield these consequences then it is not strictly coherent.[14] Thus, for any statements in a finite

[13] The lottery paradox is due to H. E. Kyburg, Jr. in *Probability and the Logic of Rational Belief* (Wesleyan University Press, Middleton, Conn., 1961), 197.

[14] See Rudolf Carnap, 'A Basic System of Inductive Logic, Part I' in *Studies in Inductive Logic and Probability*, vol. i, ed. Rudolf Carnap and Richard Jeffrey (University of California, Los Angeles and Berkeley, 1971), 101 and 111-14. Also

language, or for any non-general statements in any language, we would, if our probability function is strictly coherent, be committed to the conclusion that such non-basic statements of the language are completely justified by basic ones only if the basic statements logically entail the non-basic ones.

The latter commitment is unacceptable because most of our non-basic beliefs whose justification is based on evidence are not logically entailed by the evidence. Such evidence statements as those concerning the appearance of a man entering a room and those formulating what one remembers about John, though they do not entail that John has entered the room, do completely justify us in believing that he has. Thus, if we deny that any statement can be completely justified by the evidence unless it has a probability of one on that evidence, we shall be committed to an excessively restrictive theory of justification.

Decision Theory and the Objective of Truth

The foregoing result leads to the ultimate destruction of the foundation theory. To understand why, it is useful to consider the issue in a somewhat different light. Suppose a man is considering whether or not to accept a statement on the basis of evidence and wants only to accept those statements whose truth is guaranteed by the evidence. Suppose, moreover, that he wishes to decide whether there is any evidence which justifies and guarantees the truth of the statement in question. He might approach the decision much as one approaches a practical decision. In a practical decision a reasonable man considers the alternatives before him, how probable various outcomes of the alternatives are, and the value he attaches to those outcomes. According to a current model, he then decides on that alternative which has the highest expected value. The expected value of an alternative is calculated mathematically by first multiplying the probabilities of each possible outcome times the value one attaches to that outcome and then adding up the results of products for that alternative. One then com-

---

see Carnap's *Logical Foundations of Probability*, 321; John G. Kemeny, 'Fair Bets and Inductive Probabilities', *Journal of Symbolic Logic*, xx (1955), 263–73, especially 264; and Abner Shimony, 'Coherence and the Axioms of Confirmation', ibid. 1–28, especially 7.

pares that sum to the sum of similar products for the other alternatives. The highest sum indicates the most reasonable alternative.

This model, known as Bayesian decision theory, is similar to traditional utilitarianism in ethics. According to the latter, the right action is the one yielding the greatest amount of intrinsic ethical value. When one is choosing between actions in a condition in which one is uncertain about the consequences of one's actions, one needs to take into consideration the probability of various consequences of the alternative actions one can perform, as well as the value of those consequences. Bayesian decision theory is a generalization of this model for rational action, in which all values, not simply ethical ones are considered, as well as the probabilities of consequences or outcomes of alternative actions.

The same model may be employed for deciding what action is justified, and, with some slight modification, what beliefs are justified.[15] In considering whether a belief is justified on this model, one considers both the consequences of the belief and the probability of those consequences. This is the point at which we require modification of the model to make it applicable to choosing what to accept or believe. In the case of belief, we may only be interested in a very limited variety of consequences. Indeed, when we are asking whether a belief is justified in the manner required by a foundation theory of knowledge, we are asking whether it is justified in such a way as to guarantee the truth of the belief. Hence, we need consider only two outcomes of the belief; true belief and false belief. One outcome of belief is that one believes what is true, and the other is that one believes what is false. These are the only outcomes of belief relevant to deciding what one would be

---

[15] The application of decision theory to epistemic issues is due initially to Carl G. Hempel in his article, 'Deductive—Nomological vs. Statistical Explanation', in *Minnesota Studies in the Philosophy of Science*, vol. iii, ed. Herbert Feigl and Grover Maxwell (University of Minnesota Press, Minneapolis, Minn., 1962), 98–169. Later developments in this same strategy are made by Jaakko Hintikka and J. Pietarinen in 'Semantic Information and Inductive Logic' in *Aspects of Inductive Logic*, ed. Jaakko Hintikka and Patrick Suppes (North-Holland Publishing Co., Amsterdam, 1966), 96–112; by Risto Hilpinen in *Rules of Acceptance and Inductive Logic* (North-Holland Publishing Co., Amsterdam, 1968); and by Isaac Levi in *Gambling with Truth: An Essay on Induction and the Aims of Science* (Knopf, New York, 1967).

justified in believing if the purpose of justification is to guarantee truth.

We now have a simplification of the problem. We consider ourselves faced with a choice between beliefs, that is, with a decision of what to believe, when the outcome of such belief is either truth or error. Moreover, we may suppose that there are certain basic beliefs constituting evidence on the basis of which we can calculate the probability of the truth and falsity of various statements under consideration. All we need to do in order to prepare ourselves for the decision of what to believe is assign values to the outcomes. Let us consider a particular non-basic belief that q when we have a basic belief that e as evidence. Moreover, let us suppose we can calculate the probability of being correct in believing that q on the basis of e as well as the probability of being incorrect. We say that $p(q,e) = n$ and $p(\sim q,e) = 1 - n$. The first probability is that of the belief being true, and the second is that of the belief being false. Hence, to calculate the expected value of believing that q, we need only assign some value to each of these outcomes. This might seem to be an insurmountable problem, but it is less difficult than it seems.

First recall that we are interested in the question of whether the truth of the belief is guaranteed, and, hence all that is relevant is whether the belief is true. Consequently, we can regard ourselves as obtaining maximum value if the belief based on that evidence turns out to be true, and we can consider ourselves to have suffered the loss of that value if our belief is false. It follows that if we assign a value of v to the outcomes of having a correct belief on the basis of the evidence, then we should assign a value of minus v to the outcome of having an incorrect belief on the basis of the evidence. The value v is the value of truth and minus that quantity is the disvalue of falsity. It now turns out that it does not matter what the value of v is taken to be so long as it is some positive number.

To see that this is so, consider briefly the formula for calculating the expected value of the belief that q. Letting '$E(q, e)$' mean 'the expected value of believing that q on the basis of e' and '$v(q, e)$' mean 'the value of being correct in believing q on the basis of e', we obtain the following formula:

$$E(q, e) = [p(q, e)v(q, e)] + [p(\sim q, e) \, (-v(q, e))].$$

Now let us assume that we assign the value 1 to $v(q, e)$ and, from the equation above, obtain the following:

$$E(q, e) = p(q, e)1 + p(\sim q, e)(-1)$$

Hence

$$E(q, e) = p(q, e) - p(\sim q, e).$$

It is perfectly obvious that $E(q, e)$ will be highest when $p(q, e)$ equals 1, and will be less when $p(q, e)$ is less than 1. Moreover, the same result would emerge if $v(q, e)$ were assigned any value greater than 0, provided it is the same for every q and e, which it must be if the purpose of justification is to guarantee truth.

For those who are adverse to mathematical formulas, the result amounts to saying that, if the purpose of justification is to guarantee truth, then the greater the probability of a statement on the basis of evidence, the greater the justification of the statement by the evidence. The consequence which follows is that evidence never *completely* justifies a belief in such a way as to guarantee the truth of the belief unless the probability of the statement on the basis of the evidence is equal to one. When a man considers what he is completely justified in believing on the basis of evidence and his purpose is to guarantee true belief, he is forced to conclude that he is not completely justified in believing anything with a probability of less than one on the evidence. The expected value of believing something, when what he values is true belief, is completely determined by the probability of what is believed on the evidence. The expected value is, therefore, highest only when the probability is highest. Since one can always choose to restrict his beliefs to those that have the highest expected value, and, since in terms of what he values, there would be no justification for believing anything of less than the highest expected value, it follows that no one is ever completely justified in believing anything with a probability of less than one on the basis of the evidence—if the purpose of justification is to guarantee truth.[16]

We have demonstrated that no non-basic belief is ever completely justified by a basic belief in such a way as to guarantee the truth of the non-basic belief unless the non-basic belief has a probability of one relative to the basic belief. As we

[16] Cf. Levi, op. cit. 6–7.

noted above, if the basic and non-basic statements are non-general or are expressed within the resources of a finite language, this has the consequence, for any strictly coherent probability function, that a non-basic statement is only completely justified by a basic statement which logically entails it. In general, no matter how we assign probabilities, if we restrict completely justified non-basic beliefs to those having a probability of one on the evidence of non-basic beliefs, we shall be committed to some form of scepticism.

Probability and Basic Beliefs

We have considered the question of how one belief justifies another by guaranteeing its truth. We have arrived at the conclusion that the probability of the belief justified in this way must be equal to one. If we now consider the question of how probable a belief must be in order to be self-justified, an analogous argument shows that the belief must have an initial probability of one. Again we consider ourselves faced with a choice among beliefs when the outcome of belief will be either true belief or a false belief. Here we consider the probability of what we believe and the value of the outcome of believing in the absence of evidence. The value of true and of false belief are as before. We thus have the following formula for expected value: letting '$E(q)$' mean 'the expected value of believing that q' and '$v(q)$' mean 'the value of being correct in believing q'

$$E(q) = [p(q)v(q)] + [p(\sim q)(-v(q))]$$

which when we assign the value 1 to $v(q)$ reduces to

$$E(q) = p(q) - p(\sim q).$$

The rule to maximize expected value again will lead us to the conclusion to believe those statements having a probability of one and no others. So basic beliefs must be limited to those having an initial probability of one in the absence of evidence.

Therefore, the foundation theory of justification yields the consequence that basic beliefs guaranteeing their own truth must be limited to those statements having an initial probability of one without evidence to support them. Completely justified non-basic beliefs whose truth is guaranteed by basic beliefs must be limited to those having a probability of one on basic beliefs. All lower probabilities become irrelevant to the justification of beliefs. For any strictly coherent probability function, no statement has an initial probability of one unless it is a logical truth, and in infinite languages no non-general statement has an initial probability of one unless it is a logical truth.[17] Hence, with the exception of certain general statements in infinite languages, completely justified basic beliefs would have to be restricted to logical truths, and completely justified non-basic beliefs would have to be restricted to logical consequences of completely justified basic beliefs. Thus, in the realm of non-general statements, completely justified beliefs would have to be restricted ultimately to logical truths. We would be locked out of the realm of the contingent, and scepticism would reign supreme there.

In the case of general statements in infinite languages, it would not be necessary to restrict statements having an initial probability of one to logical truths, nor, as Hintikka has ably demonstrated, would it be necessary to restrict statements having a probability of one on the evidence to those that are logical consequences of the evidence.[18] Nevertheless, for any strictly coherent probability function, restricting justification to a probability of one will lead us deeply into the den of scepticism. All of the contingent and non-general statements we naturally assume we know would turn out to be statements we are not completely justified in believing and could not possibly know.

Summary of the Argument Concerning the Foundation Theory

According to the foundation theory of justification, justification must provide a guarantee of truth. Basic beliefs must be self-justified, guarantee their own truth, and be incapable of justification by non-basic beliefs. On the other hand, non-basic beliefs must be justified by basic ones which thereby guarantee the truth of the non-basic beliefs so justified. The non-basic

---

[17] Carnap, *Studies*, 111–14.
[18] The latter is shown in a system of logical probability developed by Hintikka, Hilpinen, and Pietarinen. See Jaakko Hintikka and J. Pietarinen, 'Semantic Information and Inductive Logic', and Jaakko Hintikka and Risto Hilpinen, Know ledge, Acceptance, and Inductive Logic', 96–112 and 1–20, respectively, in *Aspects of Inductive Logic*, ed. Jaakko Hintikka and Patrick Suppes.

beliefs thus provide a completely justified and epistemically autonomous foundation for the justification of all other beliefs. Justification which guarantees the truth of a belief is the complete justification requisite to knowledge. Such a foundation theory is neutral between empiricistic and rationalistic epistemologies because the *source* of justification is left open. Nevertheless, whatever one considers the source of the truth guaranteeing justification to be, the foundation theory is untenable.

In the preceding chapter we considered the problem of basic beliefs which are supposed to guarantee their own truth without being justified by other beliefs. We noted that the strongest guarantee of truth, a logical guarantee, is not provided. If we were to restrict our basic beliefs to those that are logically incorrigible, we would find ourselves confined to an exceedingly small number of beliefs, indeed, almost none. Moreover, if we hoped that a complete justification and guarantee of truth might be provided by the meaning of words expressing those basic beliefs, we shall be disappointed. There is no such guarantee forthcoming from such semantic considerations. Finally, even if we abandon the quest for a logical or semantic guarantee of truth, we still cannot obtain a supply of completely justified basic beliefs. Any belief involves the application of terms or concepts, and to be completely justified in such application, one requires the information justifying one in concluding that the conditions are the kind in which such a term or concept is correctly applied. Hence, the only way to save the doctrine of basic beliefs is to allow that such additional information itself consists of basic beliefs. In short, one must add that it is a basic belief that certain beliefs are completely justified and guarantee their own truth. This manoeuvre, though logically consistent, opens the door to the most rampant forms of speculation. Anyone wishing to argue that he knows anything whatever can then claim that what he knows is a basic belief. When asked to defend this claim, he can again retort that it is a basic belief that this belief is basic, and so on.

The lesson to be drawn from that chapter is that if we try to find some guarantee of truth for basic beliefs outside of the basic beliefs themselves, we fall into the coal-pit of scepticism. If on the other hand, we allow basic beliefs themselves to be the source of the guarantee of truth basic beliefs are to have, we open the way to the ravishment of unrestrained speculation. Either way, we court epistemic disaster.

The didactic implications of the present chapter are no less dire. When we consider the question of how basic beliefs can justify and guarantee the truth of non-basic beliefs without being justified by the latter, we confront similar problems. Again, the attempt to find a logical or semantic guarantee leads to insuperable difficulties. It is doomed to failure unless it can be shown that the basic beliefs alleged to justify the non-basic ones at least render the latter highly probable. In considering how probable the non-basic beliefs would have to be in order for their truth to be guaranteed by basic beliefs, we concluded that the probability must be at least one. This consequence again leads to scepticism. There is the possibility of arguing, as in the case of basic beliefs, that it is a basic belief that certain non-basic beliefs are completely justified by basic beliefs which guarantee their truth. But, once again, to avoid the deprivation of scepticism in this way is to do so at the cost of opening the gates of speculation. The conclusion is inescapable. To avoid sanctioning either scepticism or speculation, we must abandon the foundation theory altogether.

7

Systematic Justification (I):
The Explanatory Coherence Theory

THE foundation theory of justification has been rejected. We shall now consider the opposite theory of justification, one denying that justification is a guarantee of truth conferred by a foundation of self-justified beliefs, and affirming instead that justification is a reciprocal relation of *coherence* among beliefs belonging to a system. According to a coherence theory, a belief is completely justified if and only if it coheres with a system of beliefs. Hence, to justify a belief or knowledge claim is to show that the belief coheres with other beliefs of a system.

A theory of justification is required within a theory of knowledge in order to explicate the condition:

> (iii) If S knows that p, then S is completely justified in believing that p.

The following is a schema for a coherence theory of justification:

> S is completely justified in believing that p if and only if the belief that p coheres with other beliefs belonging to a system of beliefs of kind k.

This schema raises one question immediately and a second is hardly concealed. The first is what kind of system is kind k? That is, what sort of system of beliefs makes a belief completely justified when the belief coheres with others in that system? The second question concerns the relation of coherence. What is coherence? In what way must a belief *cohere* with other beliefs belonging to a system of beliefs to be completely justified? Definite answers to these questions are needed to convert our schema into a substantitive theory.

Before attempting to answer these questions, however, an objection to any sort of coherence theory must be considered. It has been argued that no coherence theory is feasible. The argument purports to demonstrate the unavoidability of basic beliefs, and hence of a foundation theory, for an adequate theory of justification. The argument is at least as old as Aristotle. It affirms that unless some beliefs are basic, the justification of all beliefs must inevitably lead either to an infinite regress or to a circular argument. Its conclusion is that either consequence is epistemically intolerable. Thus, is it inferred that we must uphold the foundation theory.

This argument needs more precise articulation. We have noted in the preceding chapter that if a man is completely justified in a belief on the basis of evidence then appeal to that evidence would constitute a correct answer to the question 'How do you know?' Now suppose no beliefs are basic. Then every completely justified belief is so justified by appeal to evidence but evidence must itself be completely justified belief, and, therefore, it must also be justified by appeal to evidence. This means that every completely justified belief must be justified by some other, thus leading either to an infinite regress or to a justificatory circle. If both those alternatives are unacceptable, then there must be some basic beliefs.

This argument must be met, or the project of constructing a coherence theory will be doomed from the outset. Fortunately for the coherence theorist, the argument is defective despite its distinguished credentials. First of all, it does not follow from the assumption of there being no basic beliefs that there are no self-justified beliefs because basic beliefs have other features in addition to being self-justifying. Second, even if we took as our initial assumption the simpler thesis of there being no self-justified beliefs, the argument still fails. It does not follow from this assumption that all completely justified beliefs must be justified by appeal to evidence. Each completely justified belief *could be* justified by some other belief, we might aver, though not all beliefs are actually justified by appeal to other beliefs. We might be *able* to justify each belief by appeal to other beliefs in some system, and our being able to do so might suffice for the complete justification of those beliefs.

It may yet be objected that if a belief is completely justified when no belief is self-justified, then one must be able, at least in principle, to carry out the justification completely. That is, he must be able to justify the belief by appeal to evidence, and to justify his belief in that evidence by appeal to other evidence, and to justify his belief in that evidence by appeal to still other evidence, and so forth. One reply to this objection is that a man might in principle be able to carry out each step of this justification without being able to carry out the entire process. As an analogy a man might be able to add three to each number without being able to carry out the whole process. It would be mistaken to infer that there is some number to which a person is unable to add three from the fact that he is actually unable to carry out the infinite task of adding three to each number. Similarly, it would be a mistake to conclude that a man is not completely justified in any belief from the fact that he is unable to carry out the infinite task of justifying every belief by appeal to another. Hence, the regress argument fails.

Nevertheless, it is only fair to point out one further objection to the foregoing. Some beliefs surely appear to be such that, though they are completely justified, one cannot justify them by appeal to evidence. For example, a man might justify his belief that he sees an apple by appeal to the evidence that there is an object before him that looks red and apple-shaped, and he might justify his belief that the object before him looks this way by appeal to the evidence that he *thinks* that there is an object that looks this way, but; eventually, he must reach the point where no further evidence can be elicited. We would thus come to some completely justified belief which the man would be unable to justify by appeal to evidence. This objection takes us to the heart of the argument.

The reply to it is twofold. First, it must be noted that justification is ordinarily justification to someone else, and whether a justification given to someone suffices will depend on what that person is willing to grant. If he is willing to grant that the object in the distance is Argile Hill if it looks like the hill in a picture, one need only show him that the object looks like the one in the picture, to justify one's belief that the object is Argile Hill. If, on the other hand, he doubts that the object in the picture is Argile Hill, then justification will have to be extended. Hence, there is a pragmatic element in justification depending on the epistemic qualification of the person to whom the justification is directed.[1] If a man is asked 'How do you know?', his answer may satisfy one man and fail to satisfy another.

The second reply is more fundamental, however. Even if there are some cases in which a man is unable to provide a satisfactory answer to the question, 'How do you know?', he may be completely justified in his belief even though the belief is not self-justified. If that belief coheres with a system of appropriate beliefs and the other conditions of knowledge are met, that may suffice for his knowing. The justification of his belief may depend on relations to other beliefs which he is unable to articulate. This does not make the belief self-justified or irrefutable. Thus, for example, we may all take it for granted that a man is completely justified in thinking that there is something that looks red before him even when he is incapable of providing any argument in defence of his claim. As Reid once suggested, a man may be unable to provide any justificatory argument for a belief precisely because the belief is so certain he cannot find any more certain premiss to which he might appeal. Such beliefs, however, might not be justified in themselves. Instead, the justification may result from coherence between the belief in question and others. This coherence might be taken for granted by most normal men because of beliefs they hold in common.

The foregoing reflections show that a coherence theory is not impossible and a foundation theory not necessary. We have yet to explain what coherence is or what sort of a system a belief must cohere with to become justified. We now turn to answer these questions.

The Traditional Answer: Coherence as Entailment

Let us begin with the relation of coherence. Idealists who were defenders of the coherence theory conceived of the relationship of coherence as a relation of necessary connection.[2] Thus, a belief that p coheres with other beliefs of a system k

---

[1] Cf. Robert Fogelin, *Evidence and Meaning*, 94–8.

[2] They also conceive of coherence as truth. See Brand Blanshard's *The Nature of Thought* (Allen and Unwin, London, 1939), particularly vol. ii, chapters 26 and 27, pp. 250–331.

if and only if *p* either necessarily implies or is necessarily implied by every other belief in *k*. Suppose, however, that we have a system of beliefs that is logically consistent, contains some logically contingent statements, and is such that every statement in the system either necessarily implies or is necessarily implied by every other statement. We can easily form another system having these same characteristics by taking the contingent statements in *k*, negating them, and forming a new system containing the negations of the contingent statements in *k* together with whatever non-contingent statements may have been contained in *k*. This new system will be consistent if *k* was, and it will be such that every statement in the new system either necessarily implies or is necessarily implied by every other statement. The new system, though just as coherent as the old in terms of the necessary connections between statements, will tell us exactly the opposite about the world. Every contingent statement in one system is negated in the other. Thus, if we were to assume that such coherence was sufficient for complete justification, we should have to admit that any contingent statement a man is completely justified in believing is such that he is also completely justified in believing the denial of that statement.

Such logical coherence is not, moreover, necessary for complete justification. Take any two observation statements describing observations of different and unrelated objects. Neither of these necessarily implies the other, but we can be completely justified in believing both of them. Similarly, consider any two laws, one about stars and the other about mice. These may also be such that neither necessarily implies the other, but we may be completely justified in believing both of them. The two laws or the two observation statements may be related in some way: they may be consequences of some more general law, but they are not necessary consequences of each other.

These objections are decisive. The question is, how can a coherence theory avoid such difficulties? First, we must keep distinct the two questions raised above, namely, what is coherence? and, secondly, what kind of a system is required? We shall not obtain a satisfactory coherence theory of justification by answering only the first question. In defending a belief or knowledge claim by arguing that it coheres with certain other beliefs, we must be prepared to explain why coherence with those beliefs provides complete justification. Hence, to articulate a satisfactory coherence theory, we must answer the second question as well. We must say what kind of system provides complete justification for those beliefs that cohere with the system.

Coherence as Explanation

A coherence theory of justification may affirm that the kind of coherence required for justification is explanatory coherence. Wilfrid Sellars has propounded such a view, and Gilbert Harman has argued at some length that whether a belief is justified depends on the way in which it fits into the best overall explanatory account.[3] The question of whether a belief is justified cannot be decided, according to such a theory, in isolation from a system of beliefs. It is in relation to other beliefs belonging to a system of beliefs that the justification of a belief must be decided. Moreover, the system of beliefs determining justification must be one in which we explain as much as we can and leave as little unexplained as we must. A system having a maximum of explanatory coherence confers justification on beliefs within it.

If the kind of coherence required for justification is explanatory, then it is the function of a belief in explanation that justifies it. There are two ways in which a belief can so function. It can either explain or be part of what explains something, or it can be explained or be part of what is explained. To have explanatory coherence, one must both have something to explain and something to explain it.

Bertrand Russell once remarked that, though we do not know of the existence of physical objects, we may reasonably infer the existence of such objects because the hypothesis of their existence is the simplest and best explanation of why we experience the sense-data we do.[4] A defender of the explanatory

---

[3] See Wilfrid Sellars's article, 'Some Reflections on Language Games', in *Science, Perception, and Reality* (Routledge and Kegan Paul, London, 1963), 321–58; and Gilbert Harman's article, 'Induction', in *Induction, Acceptance, and Rational Belief*, ed. Marshall Swain (Reidel, Dordrecht-Holland, 1970), 83–99. The author defended a similar view in 'Justification, Explanation, and Induction', ibid. 100–33.

[4] Bertrand Russell, *The Problems of Philosophy*, 22–6.

coherence theory of justification could reply that Russell does not go as far as explanation would warrant. The hypothesis that physical objects exist is such a good explanation of our experience of the sense-data in question that we are completely justified in believing and claiming to know of the existence of such objects. The traditional problem of the justification of perceptual claims on the basis of sense-data statements appears solved by the explanatory coherence theory.

Moreover, the problem of the justification of our claims about the mental states of others seems amenable to comparable treatment. If I see a man behaving just as I would were I in a certain mental state, then, one could argue, the best explanation I have for why he behaves that way is that he is in that mental state. Suppose, for example, that I see an injured man before me writhing, moaning, and otherwise behaving as I know I would if I were experiencing intense pain. The best explanation for why he behaves as he does is that he is feeling pain. To see that this is so, consider the problems one encounters with any hypothesis denying that the man is in pain. First, I must explain why the man is behaving in this way if he does not feel pain. Even if, however, my hypothesis does explain this, to obtain a satisfactory over-all explanatory account, I must explain more. In explaining his behaviour in some alternative way, I shall either assume, that, though this man feels no pain, others in such circumstances would, in which case I must explain why this man does not feel pain when others would; or I shall assume that others generally fail to feel pain in such circumstances, in which case I must explain why I do feel pain when others do not. In either case, I am left with an unsolved explanatory problem that would be avoided by hypothesizing that others generally, the man in question included, feel pain as I do under these conditions. From the standpoint of over-all explanatory coherence, the latter hypothesis is obviously advantageous.[5]

As we proceed from perceptual claims and claims about the mental states of others to statements about distant times and places and, finally, to statements about theoretical states and objects, the appeal to explanation becomes more obvious and familiar. We might think it odd to justify the claim that we see our bodies or that our friends are suffering by arguing that it

[5] Cf. Paul Ziff, 'The Simplicity of Other Minds', in *New Readings*, 418–23.

is best from the standpoint of explanation to suppose that these things are so, but it is commonplace to argue that hypotheses about the past, the physically remote, and the theoretically unobservable are completely justified by the way they explain what we seek to understand.

On the Justification of What is Explained

The thesis that hypotheses are completely justified because of what they explain is most plausible, but how are we justified in believing those things that are explained? If we claim that what is explained consists of basic facts and beliefs we shall merely appeal to explanation to justify the inference from basic beliefs to non-basic ones. It is a more radical departure from the foundation theory we are now considering. According to the coherence theory under consideration, there are no basic beliefs. All beliefs are justified by their explanatory role. To explain, however, one must have something to explain as well as a hypothesis to explain it. What justifies those beliefs that provide the matter to explain?

The answer is that if some beliefs are justified because of what they explain, others are justified because they are explained. Moreover, it is plausible to suppose that some beliefs are justified because they are so well explained. Suppose I believe I see a certain mountain in the distance which looks strange, different in both shape and colour from when I have observed it in the past. If someone explains why I see what I do, perhaps by appeal to perspective, light reflection, and so forth, then I shall be completely justified in believing I see *the mountain* looking as it does. It is the explanation that justifies my belief. Again, suppose I look at a streak in a cloud chamber and conjecture that the streak is the path of an alpha particle. If I do not understand how an alpha particle could make such a streak, I may not be completely justified in my belief. Once it is explained to me how the alpha particle causes condensation, I may become completely justified in believing that the streak is the path of the particle. It is no rare event in science or everyday life to have some doubt concerning a fact removed by some explanation of it. Such explanations may change dubious beliefs into completely justified ones.

Moreover, a belief may be justified *both* because it explains *and* because it is explained. That a chair supports me may explain why, in my present posture, I do not fall to the floor; and that the chair supports me may be explained, given my position on it, by the rigidity, and so forth, of the chair. Similarly the path of the alpha particle may explain why we see what we do and may be explained within atomic theory. The same belief may be both explaining and explanatory, and it may derive justification from both roles. It is those beliefs that both explain and are explained whose justification seems most adequate. Indeed, explained unexplainers, such as sense-data statements, have been epistemically controversial, as have unexplained explainers, such as statements concerning the supernatural. Recently, philosophers of empiricist leanings tend to construe the fundamental empirical statements as perceptual claims concerning physical objects rather than reports concerning sense-data. The underlying reason for this tendency may be an unrecognized desire to settle on some empirical statements that are *both* explained and explanatory. Perceptual statements both explain sense experience and are explained by theories of perception.

Explanatory Coherence and Justification: An Analysis

The foregoing considerations substantiate the suggestion that completely justified beliefs are ones that explain or are explained, or both. Explanatory coherence thus appears to determine justification. We shall now attempt to offer a precise analysis of such justification. Let us reconsider the formula for coherence theories introduced earlier.

> S is completely justified in believing that *p* if and only if the belief that *p* coheres with other beliefs belonging to a system of beliefs of kind *k*.

To offer a coherence theory of justification, we must offer an account of coherence and of the kind of system with which a belief must cohere. Let us first consider the question of what kind of system of beliefs is required. Sellars suggests that our choice of a system should be one that yields a maximum of explanatory coherence, but a problem of interpretation arises immediately. A number of systems of beliefs compete for the status of having a maximum of explanatory coherence, and some of these systems might be ones that any given person could hardly conceive. Are we to require that for a man to be completely justified in what he believes, his belief must cohere with a system of beliefs of which he could not conceive?

One answer is that the required system be the one with a maximum of explanatory coherence of all of which S could conceive. The other alternative is to require that his belief must cohere with that system having a maximum of explanatory coherence whether he could conceive of it or not. Both answers present difficulties. One problem with the first answer is that a man might turn out to be completely justified in believing something because of his inability to conceive of a system having a maximum of explanatory coherence with which his belief fails to cohere. One drawback of the second answer is that according to it a man might be completely justified in believing something even though it fails to cohere with systems he understands: his belief may cohere with a system of beliefs having a maximum of explanatory coherence which he is unable to comprehend. Of the two difficulties, the latter appears the more severe. It is more acceptable to suppose that a man might be completely justified in believing something because it fits in with a system of beliefs which is the best he can understand even though there may be a better system with which his beliefs fails to cohere. The other alternative is to suppose that a man might be completely justified in believing something which fails to cohere with the best system he can understand because it fits in with a system beyond his comprehension. Hence, we shall suppose that the system of kind k is the one having a maximum of explanatory coherence among those systems of beliefs understood by S. We shall be able to elucidate further the concept of *maximal* explanatory coherence when we have clarified the notion of coherence.

Explanatory Coherence

Now let us consider the concept of coherence. One ingredient in coherence is consistency. A belief logically inconsistent with others fails to cohere with them, but consistency is not enough because the kind of coherence required is explanatory. To explicate this kind of coherence, we shall take the concepts of explanation and of *better* explanation as primitive. It is agreed, however, that these concepts are themselves in need of clarification. We shall consider the problems surrounding such clarification subsequently.

To cohere with the beliefs belonging to a system, a belief must fill an explanatory role, but what sort? It would be too restrictive to require that the belief explain or be explained by *all* beliefs belonging to the system. We may, however, require that it be an essential part of an explanation of some beliefs belonging to the system or be part of what is explained by such beliefs. We shall speak of beliefs that are explanatory in this way as explaining something relative to system k, and of beliefs explained in this way as something explained relative to system k. Can we say that a belief coheres with a system of beliefs if and only if it is consistent with the system and either explains or is explained in relation to the system? No. A general belief may explain some belief within a system of the required sort, but fail to be completely justified because some other general belief explains that belief better. Two contradictory general statements may each explain what is believed to be a fact, when one explains better than the other. Obviously, a person cannot be completely justified in believing both hypotheses. Some additional restriction is needed.

We must require that a belief cohering with a system either explain or be explained in relation to the system better than anything which contradicts it. Contradiction must be made relative to the system. Two mutually consistent statements may be such that a system of beliefs entails that they cannot both be true. We shall speak of such beliefs contradicting each other and thus employ a relativized concept of contradiction. With this stipulation, the preceding problem is easily solved. A belief coheres with a system of beliefs if and only if the belief is consistent with the system and either explains something in relation to the system not explained better by any belief which contradicts it, or the belief is better explained by something in relation to the system, and nothing which contradicts it is explained better.

We thus arrive at a coherence theory of justification that may be expressed as follows:

S is completely justified in believing that p if and only if the belief of S that p is consistent with that system C of beliefs having a maximum of explanatory coherence among those systems of beliefs understood by S, and the belief that p either explains something relative to C which is not explained better by anything with which contradicts p or the belief that p is explained by something relative to C and nothing which contradicts it is explained better relative to C.

Let us now reconsider the concept of a system having a maximum of explanatory coherence. The preceding discussion suggests the way to elucidate this concept. If the beliefs belonging to one system explain better and are better explained than the beliefs belonging to a second system, then the first system has greater explanatory coherence than the second. A system C_1 has greater explanatory coherence than C_2 if and only if C_1 is logically consistent and C_2 is not, or both are consistent but more is explained in C_1 than C_2, or both explain the same things but some things are explained better in C_1 than C_2. We then adopt the following analysis of maximal explanatory coherence:

A system C has a maximum of explanatory coherence among those systems of beliefs understood by S if and only if there is no system having greater explanatory coherence among those systems.

This condition together with the preceding one constitutes a theory of justification in terms of explanatory coherence in which we have taken for granted the concepts of explanation, better explanation, and the usual logical notions.

On Explanation

Little has been written on the question of what it means to say that E_1 is a better explanation than E_2 of F. Moreover, we shall not attempt to explicate that concept here. The hopelessness of obtaining any useful analysis militates against the attempt. The conception of explanation is so interwoven with epistemic notions that we could not expect to explicate the concept of one explanation being better than another without at least covertly appealing to some epistemic notion. For example, one explanation is often said to be better than another solely because the first is more likely to be true from what we *know* than the second. Such considerations lead us in a small circle.

This difficulty can best be elaborated if we consider the concept of explanation *simpliciter*. There is an immense literature on this topic, of considerable linguistic and formal sophistication. This literature illustrates most clearly the futility of hoping to find an explication of explanation to which we can fruitfully appeal in our articulation of the explanatory coherence theory. Consider first the deductive model of explanation admirably articulated by Carl Hempel.[6] With various refinements, this model of explanation tells us that F is explained by a statement of boundary conditions B and law L if and only if F is deducible from B and L in such a way that B and L are both essential to the deduction. Such analyses are wont to lead to absurd conclusions, most notably that almost any law can be used to explain almost any statement.[7] Moreover, the qualifications needed to eliminate such untoward consequences often appear to be entirely *ad hoc*. The more important objections to such analyses from the standpoint of the explanatory coherence theory rest on counterexamples.

Consider the following example which is a modification of one proposed by Sylvain Bromberger.[8] Imagine that I am standing with my toe next to a mouse that is three feet from a four-foot-high flagpole with an owl sitting on top. From this information concerning boundary conditions and the Pythagorean Theorem, which we here construe as empirical law, we can deduce the mouse is five feet from the owl. Moreover, all the premisses are essential to the derivation. Thus, in the proposed analysis, the boundary conditions together with the law explain why the mouse is five feet from the owl. None the less, this deduction does not explain why the mouse is at that distance from the owl at all. If you have any doubts about whether this is an explanation, imagine that you *know* that the distance from the top of the

[6] Carl G. Hempel, 'Studies in the Logic of Explanation', in *Aspects of Scientific Explanation*, 245–90.

[7] See R. Eberle, D. Kaplan, and R. Montague, 'Hempel and Oppenheim on Explanation,' in *Philosophy of Science*, xxviii (1961), 418–28.

[8] Sylvain Bromberger, 'Why-Questions', in *Mind and Cosmos*, ed. Robert Colodny (University of Pittsburgh Press, Pittsburgh, Pa., 1966), 105.

flagpole to where you stand is five feet and that you have asked why the mouse is five feet from the owl. An answer to this question based on the boundary conditions cited and the Pythagorean Theorem would not be explanatory. Receiving such an answer, you would, perhaps, apprehend how to deduce that the mouse is five feet from the owl from some premisses, but those premisses do not explain why the mouse is five feet from the owl. And, moreover, the matter requires explanation —owls eat mice!

An Epistemic Analysis of Explanation

The sort of amendment required, according to Bromberger, is epistemic. An explanation supplies the right answer to a question, when the person to whom the matter is explained does not know the answer, and, indeed, would rule out any answer he could think of on the basis of what he does know. Such a person lacks understanding, and the understanding lacking is supplied by the explanation. These considerations lead Bromberger to offer an analysis of explanation consisting of an explication of sentences of the form—$SEBW$—where S and B take expressions referring to persons as values, E takes some form of the verb 'to explain' and W takes some question.[9] Thus, one instance of the formula would be: Hempel explained to Lehrer why the mouse is five feet from the owl. One truth condition of this sentence is that Lehrer at first does not understand why the mouse is five feet from the owl, that is, Lehrer does not know why. A second truth condition is that what Hempel communicates to Lehrer gives Lehrer knowledge of why the mouse is five feet from the owl.

The sort of analysis of explanation that Bromberger offers, however plausible and significant it may be, cannot be exploited here without rendering the explanatory coherence analysis of knowledge immediately circular. Knowledge would be analysed in terms of explanatory coherence which would be analysed in terms of explanation which would be analysed in terms of knowledge. Moreover, if we assume that Bromberger is correct, or very nearly correct, in his analysis, then it seems

[9] Sylvain Bromberger, 'An Approach to Explanation', in *Analytical Philosophy*, ed. Ronald Butler, second series (Basil Blackwell, Oxford, 1965), 72–105.

reasonable to conclude that if an analysis of knowledge is based on the concept of explanation, the latter concept should be taken as primitive in our analysis. This is, I believe, the proper moral of the story.

Explanation as a Logical Relation

Hempel has a reply to the preceding objection which we shall consider briefly.[10] He argues that the conception of explanation appealed to above, being relative to a subject and what he knows, is not the one he was attempting to explicate. The conception of explanation Hempel claims to be explicating is an objective logical relation between the law and what is subsumed under it. The question is whether the objective logical relation between a law and what is subsumed under it is a relation of explanation. For the purpose of explicating the logical structure of scientific theories, laws, and singular statements subsumed under them, it may not matter whether or not the relation of subsumption is that of explanation. For our purposes, however, it is crucial. I find the sort of counter-example considered above conclusive here: the subsumption relation may fail to be explanatory.

If we think, moreover, of the objective logical relation in question as being one of deduction, then we encounter another difficulty relevant to our discussion. Every law is superfluous in an important way when any singular statement is deduced from the law in conjunction with boundary condition statements. Moreover, this consequence does not depend on any special feature of Hempel's explication of the objective relation in question. It depends only on an assumption that Hempel grants, namely, that logically equivalent statements are equally explanatory. This must be granted if explanation is an objective logical relation between statements.

The proof of the superfluity of laws in such deductions is as follows.[11] Let L be a law and C be a condition meeting any restriction you care to impose but such that E is deducible from

[10] Hempel, *Aspects of Scientific Explanation*, 425–8.

[11] This argument is adopted from one presented by David Kaplan when commenting on a paper by Hempel at the Pacific Coast meetings of the American Philosophical Association in Honolulu, August 1968. I do not know whether he would accept the present formulation or application of his remarks.

and explained by L and C but not deducible from C or L alone. Then L is logically equivalent to the following conjunction of disjunctions: $(C v L)$ & $(\sim E v L)$ & $(\sim C v E)$. This conjunction is logically equivalent to the conjunction of L and $(\sim C v E)$. If E is not deducible from L but is deducible from C and L, then L logically implies $(\sim C v E)$, hence, L is logically equivalent to the conjunction of $(\sim C v E)$ and L. The latter conjunction by logical implication is equivalent to the conjunction: $(C v L)$ & $(\sim E v L)$ & $(\sim C v E)$. The last conjunct, $(\sim C v E)$, together with C logically implies E, but does not contain L, while neither of the other conjuncts taken together with C logically implies E. The conjunction of the other two conjuncts, $(C v L)$ & $(\sim E v L)$, together with C still does not logically imply L. Thus, it is precisely the conjunct, $(\sim C v E)$, which together with C is necessary and sufficient for the deduction of E. This conjunct does not contain L nor is it a law. In this way the law turns out to be superfluous for the deduction of E.

This problem is a direct consequence of the attempt to construe explanation as a logical relation between statements and is not avoidable by any minor repairs. If the relation between E and the conjunction of C and L is one of deduction, then it immediately follows that a small part of the logical content of L is all that is involved in the deduction, and the remainder of the logical content of L is superfluous deductively. The logical content of L employed in deducing E from L is contained in the statement $(\sim C v E)$, which is neither a law nor a general statement. The generality of L is excess baggage in terms of the deductive relation between E and the conjunction of C and L. What is essential to the deduction, that is, $(\sim C v E)$, is not explanatory. The deductive relation is non-explanatory, and what is explanatory is not the deductive relation.

The preceding remarks are not offered as a refutation of what Hempel has claimed. They are, instead, a defence of our strategy of taking as primitive the conception of explanation, and of one explanation being better than another, in our discussion of the explanatory coherence theory. From the foregoing remarks I conclude that if we attempt to explicate the relation of explanation as an objective logical relation between statements, we shall find that the deductive relation between those statements fails to explicate why the premisses of the deduction explain the conclusion. As we noted in the example of the owl and the mouse, sometimes the deduction is non-explanatory, and, as we noted above, even when deduction is explanatory, it is not the deductive relation that is explanatory but something else. To distinguish adequately those deductions that are explanatory from those that are not, and to explicate what makes some deductions explanatory, we would have to appeal, as Bromberger contends, to epistemic considerations, to what we do and do not know. Since such an appeal would render the analysis of explanation circular and otiose in the context of formulating an analysis of knowledge, we take our explanatory conceptions as primitive and assume they are antecedently understood. We shall have to rely on such understanding when we turn to a critical appraisal of the explanatory coherence theory.

These considerations are all the elucidation of the concept of explanation we shall offer. No thoroughly satisfactory analysis of explanation has been proposed, and, consequently, our remarks concerning theories of justification based on the concept of explanatory coherence shall inevitably fall short of demonstration. Yet, we can find arguments against the explanatory form of coherence theory strong enough to warrant abandoning it. It is to these that we now turn.

Objections to Coherence as Explanation

The first problem raised by our explanatory theory of complete justification concerns comparing systems with respect to explanatory coherence. Our theory tells us that one system has greater explanatory coherence than a second if the first leaves less unexplained or explains better what it does explain than does the second. Even so, one system may leave less unexplained and explain better what it does explain by containing less to be explained. One system may admit statements of unexplained facts which the other excludes. To reduce what is unexplained, one may simply deny the truth of those statements that need explanation. Explanation involves those statements which do the explaining, on one hand, and those which describe what is to be explained, on the other. One can increase the explanatory coherence of a system either by adding statements that explain or by substracting statements to be explained.

The method of increasing the explanatory coherence of a system by decreasing what is to be explained must be limited. Otherwise we may obtain a maximum of coherence at the expense of a minimum of content.

The foregoing remarks may be illustrated with a very simple formal example. Compare any system of beliefs within science to the following. Take a language with one observation predicate 'Ox' and one theoretical predicate 'Tx'. Then adopt a system affirming that everything is T, that everything T is O, hence, that everything is O. Let the system contain only these sentences. We can now get a maximum of coherence by adding just those observation sentences to our system that fit with our one empirical law. More concretely, if we wish to have the law affirming that all dragons breath fire, we may then add the 'observation' sentences that object one is a fire-breathing dragon, object two is a fire-breathing object, and so forth. The coherence between the law and observation statement will be perfect, and the absurdity of the system will be manifest. To avoid this sort of implausibility, philosophers have imposed further limitations on what observation statements may belong to a justificatory system.

Explanatory Coherence and Observation Statements

Both Quine and Sellars suggest conditioned responses as one determinant of whether a statement is epistemically qualified.[12] Of course, this amounts to abandoning the theory of justification under consideration, for whether we are completely justified in believing some observation statement to be true will then depend not only on its explanatory coherence with other statements but also on the existence of certain patterns of conditioned response to sensory stimulus.

[12] See Wilfrid Sellars's remarks on language entry transitions in 'Reflections on Language Games' in *Science, Perception, and Reality*, 321–58. It should be noted that Sellars explicitly denies that such conditioned responses are sufficient for establishing the meaning or justification of observation statements. Nevertheless, they do play a role in such justification. See Quine's remarks on stimulus meaning in *Word and Object* (M.I.T. Press, Cambridge, Mass., 1960), chapters 1 and 2.

Both Quine and Sellars advance theories of meaning according to which the meaning of terms and statements depends on the relations of those terms and statements to others. Thus, neither would identify the meaning of an observation statement with the pattern of conditioned responses in terms of which one responds with such a statement to sensory stimuli. Nevertheless, both authors consider such patterns to constitute the link between language and sensory experience. Hence, whether we are completely justified in believing some observation statement to be true depends on how that statement is linked to sensory experience by such patterns. These patterns accordingly constitute some restraint on the way in which we may eliminate observation statements from the system to save ourselves explanatory labour.

Observation Statements and Conditioned Responses

Clearly some amendment of the explanatory coherence theory is needed to preserve an explanatory base. Let us consider whether the present modification yields a satisfactory theory of justification. The authors in question do not *explicitly* endorse a stimulus-response theory of the justification of observation statements, so the following remarks are criticism of a hypothetical extension of their views rather than what they have explicitly written. Consider the view that what makes a man completely justified in believing some observation statement to be true depends, at least in part, on certain patterns of conditioned response associated with the sentence. Of course, *action* and not *belief*, is usually required as a response in stimulus theory, but let us extend the notion of response to episodes of belief acquisition. There is a defect in this proposal that is easy to appreciate and which infects sophisticated modifications. It is that a man may be conditioned to respond with erroneous beliefs.

Experiments regarding perceptual beliefs concerning the size of coins show that a poor man will respond with erroneous beliefs much more frequently than one who is not. Let the experiment be one in which a person is shown a coin, then shown a disc, and is asked to report whether they are the same size, or whether one is larger than the other. The poor man will frequently judge the coin to be larger than it is. Is he completely justified in his belief? Of course not. What this shows is that conditioned responses can regularly produce erroneous as well as correct belief. Conditioning in and by itself is neutral with respect to truth and error.

The preceding remarks are not intended to refute the proposal that a man might be fortunate enough to be completely justified in believing some observation statement whenever his belief is a conditioned response to a certain kind of stimulus. It may be true, just as it may be true that he is completely justified in believing an observation statement whenever he is in a brain state of some special kind. But even if such beliefs happen to be completely justified, it is not the conditioning or the brain state that *makes* them completely justified. If people happen to be so conditioned that what they believe is completely justified, that is fortunate. Still, they could equally well have been so conditioned that what they believe would not be. It may be that I am conditioned to believe that an object is red when I am confronted with a red object in certain circumstances, but I could equally well have been conditioned to believe that such an object is yellow. The latter belief would not have been completely justified. What makes the belief justified is not the conditioning, even if the completely justified belief is a response to a conditioned stimulus.

The foregoing argument applies against any theory affirming that what makes a belief completely justified even depends on the belief being a conditioned response to a stimulus of a certain kind. What a man is conditioned to believe is one thing, and what he is completely justified in believing is another, even if the two happen to coincide. Of course, we condition a child to have beliefs which we think are completely justified and discourage beliefs we think are completely unjustified. Nevertheless, it is not his being so conditioned that makes his belief completely justified.

Observation and Natural Selection

Another way of saving observation statements, by appeal to the theory of natural selection, is equally faulty for similar reasons. To argue that beliefs about what we observe must be completely justified because they have survival value in the process of natural selection will leave one epistemically bankrupt. First, the form of survival theory that currently appears most tenable is one recognizing that many factors bear little weight in the struggle for survival, and, consequently, may be retained even though they have almost no survival value. Hence, one cannot argue directly from the existence of beliefs to their survival value. Second, and more important, even if this inference is allowed, the epistemic leap to the conclusion that such beliefs are completely justified is totally unwarranted. Beliefs that are neither true nor completely justified may have considerable survival value. Perhaps the truth would destroy us.

An Ethical Analogy

One final argument. Consider briefly the parallel between ethics and epistemology.[13] Chisholm, following Lewis, has argued that a theory of justification provides a criterion of evidence and justification just as a theory of ethics provides criteria of right and wrong. Imagine a man arguing that an action he performed was right because he was conditioned to perform that action or because the performance of such actions has not been extinguished through the process of natural selection. The latter contention is absurd on the face of it. The former is less clear.

If we believed that a man was conditioned to perform a certain action, we might conclude that he could not help but perform it, that he was responding to a kind of compulsion, and thus refuse to condemn him. However, if the action was one intentionally aimed at producing wanton pain and suffering in others, we would not condone the action as right. The action was not right even if the man could not help but perform it. The claim that a man is completely justified in his belief because it is a conditioned response to sensory stimulation is no better warranted than the claim that a man is right in performing an action because it is such a response. Conditioned responses fail to justify our beliefs. Justification must emanate from another source.

[13] See the introduction to C. I. Lewis's *Mind and the World Order* (Dover, New York, 1929), and R. M. Chisholm's *Perceiving: A Philosophical Study*, chapter 3, 'The Problem of "the Criterion" ', 30–9.

We conclude that the appeal to conditioned responses, however interesting psychologically, will not suffice as the basis of a supply of completely justified observation statements to be explained within an explanatory system. Moreover, as we noticed earlier, the appeal to conditioned responses amounts to introducing an additional factor into the explanatory coherence theory. Is there any way of preventing the wholesale depletion of observation statements from our system of beliefs without abandoning the theory of justification as explanatory coherence? In fact, there is a way.

Self-explanatory Beliefs

One could maintain that observation statements are self-explanatory and, hence, that a gain of explanatory coherence results from the inclusion of such statements within the system. Such self-explanation would thus provide a form of self-justification. Moreover, though this may remind one of the foundation theory, it need not lead to it. Such self-justification need not constitute a guarantee of truth as required by the foundation theory. Moreover, such statements may be refuted by other statements which are not self-justified.

How can a statement be self-explanatory? When the truth of *p* explains why the person believes that *p*. For example, suppose I believe I see blood on my shoe. Now the statement that I believe I see blood on my shoe describes something that requires explanation. How is it to be explained? One explanation is that I *do* see blood on my shoe. To the question of why I *believe* that I see blood on my shoe it may be replied that I *do* see blood on my shoe. This way of answering a why-question, according to Bromberger,[14] appeals to an *exceptive* principle. In this case, we could say that in answering the question of why I believe that I see blood on my shoe, we are presupposing a principle affirming that no one believes that he does see blood on his shoe *except* when he does see blood on his shoe, or when he incorrectly takes what is on his shoe for blood, or when he is hallucinating, and so forth. If I believe that none of the other alternatives is correct and such beliefs cohere with my system of beliefs, then the statement that I see blood on my shoe explains, at least in

[14] Sylvain Bromberger, 'Why-Questions', 96–102.

part, why I believe that I see blood on my shoe. It is, therefore, completely justified.

The preceding argument shows how a belief could be justified by being self-explanatory. If what is believed is true, then the truth of the belief explains, at least in part, the existence of the belief. Of course, a fuller explanation should be forthcoming, one explaining how I happen to see blood on my shoe, perhaps because my bruised skin is bleeding, and so forth. Though the explanation is incomplete, it is acceptable as far as it goes. Moreover, those beliefs most plausibly taken to be self-explanatory in this way coincide with perceptual beliefs. Hence, this sort of justification promises to provide a base of completely justified observation statements. Memory statements seem amenable to comparable treatment.

Before turning to a critical examination of this theory, it is useful to notice its virtues. It offers the possibility of providing self-justifying beliefs within the context of an explanatory coherence theory without dragging in some non-explanatory feature to justify perceptual beliefs. Such beliefs are self-justified because the truth of the belief explains the existence of the belief, that is, the statement that a man believes what he does is explained by the statement that what he believes is true. Moreover, this explanation depends on the *system* of beliefs a man has, and, consequently, may be refuted by other beliefs in that system. Hence, we obtain self-justified beliefs whose self-justification is derived from the explanatory coherence of such beliefs within a system. We obtain an explanatory coherence theory with a base of self-justified perceptual beliefs.

Self-explanation: An Evaluation

The proposal that justification can be obtained through self-explanation in a system of beliefs, though promising, evokes criticism appropriate to the explanatory coherence theory as a whole. It may be doubted whether the purported self-explanation is explanation at all, and may be affirmed that the justification obtained does not depend on explanation. We shall examine these objections as they apply to the theory of justification through self-explanation and then to the more general form of the theory of justification by explanation.

First, it might be objected that the general principles involved in self-explanation, *exceptive* principles, are trivially true and, consequently, no explanation can be based upon them. The principle that no one believes he sees something *except* when he does see it, or when he erroneously takes something else for it, or when he is hallucinating, and so forth, has the appearance of a tautology. It tells us no more than that no one believes that he sees something except when he sees it or when he erroneously believes that he sees it. And, this, it might be objected, is not a principle of explanation, but rather the barest of tautologies. Moreover, men sometimes see things they do not believe they see just as they sometimes believe they see things when they do not. If the spot on my shoe is nail polish, not blood, then I may not believe that I see a spot of nail polish on my shoe though I do, and I may believe that I see blood on my shoe though I do not. Thus we lack any explanatory law, exceptive or otherwise, to provide an explanatory link between what a man believes he sees and his seeing that object.

Second, it might be contended that if a man believes he sees something immediately before himself, the existence of this belief justifies us in believing that he sees it, at least when one has no reason to doubt that he sees what he believes he does. If a man tells us that he sees something directly in front of him, and we have no reason to doubt what he says, then we take his pronouncement as evidence that he sees what he believes he does. If his belief justifies *us* in concluding that he sees the object in question, then his belief must also justify him. Thus, the example illustrates a self-justified belief, but does not depend on explanatory considerations. That a man believes he sees something provides justification for concluding that he does see it without explaining or being explained by any other belief or statement. In short, it may be concluded, the complete justification of perceptual beliefs does not depend on the explanatory rule of such beliefs however useful such beliefs may be for purposes of systematic explanation.

One might defend the explanatory coherence theory against such objections either by rejecting the doctrine of self-explanatory beliefs or by maintaining that such explanation is genuine. We cannot offer any decisive argument against the possibility of sustaining these alternatives, but neither seems tenable. Of course, these remarks are no defence of a foundation theory against a coherence theory. The way in which perceptual beliefs cohere with a system of beliefs may render them completely justified even though the coherence is not explanatory. This would mean that coherence may be explicated in some novel manner. We now turn to other criticisms of the explanatory coherence theory which point in that direction.

Justification without Explanation: Some Examples

The first example of a completely justified belief whose justification does not depend on explanatory considerations was presented above. It is the example in which a man deduces from the Pythagorean Theorem and boundary conditions that the mouse is five feet from the owl even though he has no explanation of why the mouse is five feet from the owl. The conclusion may be explained in some other way. But the complete justification of the belief does not depend on such explanatory relations. It is enough that the man knows the Pythagorean Theorem, the distance to the pole, and the height of the pole, and deduces the conclusion. He is then completely justified in his belief that the mouse is five feet from the owl.

For a second example, suppose I see a dead man before me. If asked whether this man was once sexually conceived, I would, without hesitation, affirm that he was.[15] Furthermore, I would be completely justified in my belief because all who die were once conceived. Death, however, does not explain conception any more than conception explains death. It is simply an observed truth that men come to exist by being conceived, and those who are dead once came to exist. Perhaps some day men will come to exist by some artificial means, but, for the moment, I am completely justified in believing that any man, dead or alive, that I see before me, was once conceived. I may not be able to explain his conception any better than I can explain his death, but, from the latter unexplained fact, I am completely justified in my belief of the former.

These are two examples of completely justified beliefs whose justification does not depend on explanatory relations to other

15 This example was provided by Frederick Schick.

beliefs. They may be neither explained or explanatory, but are justified because they cohere, in a way quite independent of explanatory function, with the other beliefs within a system of beliefs. Because the conclusions that the mouse is five feet from the owl and that the dead man before me was once conceived cohere with beliefs from which they are inferred, they are completely justified, but the coherence is not explanatory.

A defender of the explanatory coherence theory could reply to these objections that we have ignored the way in which the conclusions and premises in question function in the over-all explanatory system. He might argue that those beliefs are only completely justified because of the explanatory relations of those beliefs within an over-all system having a maximum of explanatory coherence. He could also claim that the Pythagorean Theorem and the general principle concerning how men come to exist are themselves completely justified because of their systematic explanatory role. Finally, he could say that such general beliefs within an over-all system having a maximum of explanatory coherence are what make our conclusions justified.

It is difficult to comment on this reply without indulging in simple counter-assertion. However, with some imagination we may, I believe, fabricate something of an argument. Imagine a group of men who, perhaps because of their religious beliefs, meticulously avoid asking for explanations of what they observe. They ask not why or how things happen but are content to observe the way things happen and rely on such observations without seeking explanations. Surely, such people might arrive at the Pythagorean Theorem from observation. They may not inquire as to why it is true, and they may not have deduced it from more general axioms. None the less, they might be completely justified from observation in believing what they derive from it, for example, that the mouse is five feet from the owl, whether or not the theorem or the conclusion derived from it contribute to the explanatory coherence of some over-all system of beliefs. It would be most peculiar to affirm that what made them completely justified in believing what they did on these matters was the explanatory role of such beliefs within the system of their beliefs. They would be wholly oblivious to such explanatory virtues, and, indeed, would be indifferent or perhaps even hostile to receiving suggestions concerning the explanatory merits of what they believed. What makes them completely justified in believing what they do may have something to do with the way in which these beliefs cohere with a system of beliefs they have, but the coherence involved is not explanatory. Thus, explanatory coherence is not necessary for complete justification.

Some Final Objections: Weak Explanations and Competing Systems

There remain two related objections which shall be mentioned because they illustrate some problems to be solved by any satisfactory form of the coherence theory, explanatory or not. First, suppose that some hypothesis provides a better explanation of other beliefs within a system having a maximum of explanatory coherence, even though the explanation is not fully adequate. Imagine, for example, that a man has been shot, and that the maid is the prime suspect. Her fingerprints are on the gun and she admits the deed. Moreover, suppose she has a motive. Nevertheless, imagine that she has never fired a gun previously, the spot from which she would have had to fire the gun was a good distance from the victim, and moreover, there are footprints outside the window and in the room where the crime took place, made by boots which clearly were not worn by the maid. Even if the maid avows that she made the footprints with boots to turn suspicion away from herself and then destroyed the boots, we may have our doubts. The hypothesis that she shot the victim may be the best explanation because we can conceive of no better explanation. In this situation, we would not claim to know, there is too much in doubt for that, and, even if we do believe that the maid is the killer, we would not be completely justified in believing this. We would not think we were that well justified, nor would others.

Following the justificatory theory offered above, we would be completely justified in believing that the maid is the killer. This suggests that we must require that a hypothesis not only explain better than any alternative we can conceive but also be a comparatively good explanation, good enough so that we are completely justified in accepting it. More generally, beliefs must cohere in some comparatively *strong* way with other beliefs within a system for such coherence, however it is explicated, to yield complete justification.

Our final objection to the explanatory coherence theory is that it has a defect characteristic of coherence theories, to wit, inconsistent statements turn out to be completely justified. Two systems of beliefs may each have a maximum of explanatory coherence and yet be inconsistent with each other. There may be two or more systems of beliefs each having a maximum of explanatory coherence. Each may be such that no other consistent system of beliefs leaves less unexplained, and none explains what it does explain better. Consequently, a belief may cohere with one system of beliefs having a maximum of explanatory coherence while the contradictory of that belief coheres with another system of beliefs having a maximum of explanatory coherence. In the current account both beliefs would be completely justified.

One might attempt to meet this objection by (i) requiring that there be *one* system which is, from the standpoint of explanation, the best, or (ii) requiring that the concept of complete justification be made relative to a system. Both these manoeuvres fail. The first fails because we have no reason to believe that there is *one* best system from the standpoint of explanation. There are always conflicting theories concerning some aspect of experience that are equally satisfactory from the standpoint of explanation. Hence, if it is required that there be a best over-all system before any belief is completely justified, we shall never be completely justified.

As for the second suggestion that complete justification be made relative to a system of beliefs, there remain two objections. First, and perhaps most important, the question of whether a man is completely justified in believing that p is not answered by the announcement that he is completely justified in believing it relative to a system B. We must ask whether a man who is completely justified in his belief relative to system B is completely justified in his belief. In other words, is system B a system to which a man may appeal to completely justify his beliefs? If B is but one of a set of systems having maximal explanatory coherence which are inconsistent with each other, then we have no way of answering this question.

We are left with the problem of inconsistent *systems* of

beliefs having a maximum of explanatory coherence, and, consequently, inconsistent beliefs being completely justified by such systems. It is interesting to notice that the very defect of idealistic coherence theories, the inconsistency of equally coherent theories, is also a defect of the theory of explanatory coherence. Moreover, the difficulty is not hard to discern. No relation between statements suffices to guarantee complete justification. In addition to relations between statements, some other feature must be an ingredient of justification.

Simplicity and Conservation

Some philosophers, such as Sellars, Quine, and Harman, for example, have appealed to the simplicity of the over-all system to supply the needed additional ingredient.[16] Of two systems that both have a maximum of explanatory coherence, the simpler of the two systems is the one providing complete justification for beliefs within it. There are some objections to this strategy. First, simplicity is both obscure and complex. The complexity of simplicity results from the different ways in which one system can be simpler than another and from a certain stress between these modes of simplicity. One system may be simpler than another in terms of the postulates of the system; in terms of the basic concepts of the system; in terms of the ontology of the system. We have, at least, postulational, conceptual, and ontological simplicity to consider, and these modes of simplicity may conflict. We sometimes purchase conceptual simplicity at the cost of ontological profusion. Moreover, the notion of simplicity is hardly pellucid. It is difficult, even on intuitive grounds, to judge when one system is simpler than another. When a philosopher says his system is simpler than another, one may fairly suspect him of special pleading for the sort of system he prefers. Perhaps there is some common feature of such preferred systems. Or maybe such preferences are shaped by the cognitive fashions of the decade. But we may reasonably doubt whether there is any sufficiently articulate conception of simplicity to which impartial appeal could be made in choosing between explanatory systems.

[16] In articles and books cited above.

Even if we were to grant, however, that there is some service-able conception of simplicity, this would fail to resolve the problem before us. There may be two systems that are not only maximal with respect to explanatory coherence but are all also minimal with respect to complexity. If we have two systems that are equally coherent and equally simple, we shall have no way of deciding which system provides complete justification for the beliefs within it. Moreover, we actually complicate matters by introducing the concept of simplicity. Now we must balance simplicity against coherence when, for example, one system is slightly less coherent and leaves more unexplained, while the other is slightly simpler and presupposes a smaller ontology.

Finally, the appeal to simplicity exacerbates a problem we left unsolved above, namely, that we may justify beliefs by depleting a system of statements to be explained. By rejecting concepts and entities we can obtain a simpler system as well as a more coherent one. If we seek both simplicity and coherence, we shall have the very strongest motive for rejecting observa-tion statements for the purpose of reducing what needs to be explained thereby obtaining greater explanatory coherence and simplicity. We again confront the sterile simplicity of a system confined to one theory, one law, and one set of conforming singular statements. Everything else may be hygienically dis-posed of, to avoid explanatory untidiness, and thus keep the system clean and neat.

The authors cited appeal to a principle of conservation in an effort to escape the unwanted diminishment of the system. Sellars stresses the need to conserve observation statements.[17] Quine and Harman refer to a principle of conservativeness or laziness in the general retainment of beliefs.[18] If we apply their remarks to the problem before us, it is proposed that if two systems are equal in explanatory coherence and simplicity, and all others are less coherent and simple, then that system provides complete justification for beliefs within it which con-serve what we believe, at least among statements of a specified variety.

[17] Sellars, 'Some Reflections on Language Games', section 85, p. 356.
[18] Quine in *Word and Object*, chapter 1, pp. 20–1; and Harman in *Thought* (Princeton University Press, Princeton, N.J., 1973), 159.

The primary problem with this proposal is simply that it is a principle of epistemic conservatism, a precept to conserve accepted opinion. On some occasions, such a precept may provide good counsel, but often it will not. The overthrow of accepted opinion and the dictates of common sense are often essential to epistemic advance. Moreover, an epistemic adventurer may arrive at beliefs that are not only new and revelatory, but also better *justified* than those more comfortably held by others. The principle of the conservation of accepted opinion is a roadblock to inquiry, and, consequently, it must be removed.

The preceding remarks are less than argument. Moreover, this principle of conservation, though wide of the mark, embodies at least one important insight, to wit, that whether a man is completely justified in believing something depends on his other beliefs and upon the beliefs of other men. Indeed, I shall argue that the fact of belief itself, the subjective reality of conviction, provides the basis for a satisfactory coherence theory of justification. Such a coherence theory of justification based on the existence of belief and upon the comparative degree of such beliefs will find maxims of conservation and stability unnecessary and unwarranted. On the contrary, such a theory contains within it an explication of the way in which shifts and changes of belief, however radical, bring with them changes in what a man is completely justified in believing. Before turning to the development of these ideas, however, it will be useful to have a summary of the results of this chapter before us.

Summary

We have found three major reasons for rejecting the explanatory coherence theory of justification developed at the beginning of the chapter. We explicated the notion of the maximal explanatory coherence of a system by saying such a system is consistent, explains more, or explains better what it does explain, than any other system of beliefs understood by the person in question. We then said that a belief coheres with such a system if it either explains something in the system not explained better by anything that contradicts the belief or is explained by something within such a system and nothing that contradicts the belief is explained better. We then noted that the explanatory coherence of a system could be increased by decreasing what needs explanation. We thus reduce the problem of explanation by systematically denying the truth of those statements describing whatever is unexplained until we obtain a very simple system in which everything is perfectly explained because there is almost nothing to explain. No explanatory function or role of statements suffices to prevent this artificial manipulation of explanatory systems. Second, we found examples of statements and beliefs that were completely justified by general statements within a system, such as the conclusion derived from the Pythagorean Theorem, quite independently of any explanatory role or function of such statements. Finally, systems may tie for the award of being the system with a maximum of explanatory coherence. A statement completely justified with respect to one such system is not justified with respect to another. Indeed, some statement inconsistent with the first may be completely justified in another equally maximal system.

All these difficulties spring from the same source. Having abandoned a foundation theory in which justification is built upon self-justified basic beliefs, we are lead by the explanatory coherence theory to build justification on the explanatory relations between statements. But such explanatory relations will not suffice. Explanatory relations between statements fail to pick out a *unique* set of completely justified beliefs, because we may, with sufficient imagination, concoct a myriad of different systems of statements in which such explanatory relations hold. Explanatory relationships *can* yield complete justifications, in this the theory is correct, but there must also be some other ingredient determining what needs to be explained in the first place. Here one might be tempted to waiver and return to the foundation theory for a supply of basic beliefs in need of explanation. But that way is closed. We must proceed without a signpost guaranteeing the way to truth. There is nothing other than coherence among our beliefs on which to rely. The element needed to produce a sound coherence theory of justification has been constantly before us. We need not seek any guarantee for the truth of what we believe, nor need we appeal to explanatory relations among beliefs to provide a justification. Our set of beliefs can offer complete justification to deserving beliefs among its membership without any external support or sustenance. The beliefs a man has make up a self-sufficient epistemic community.

8

Systematic Justification (II): Truth and Coherence

We shall now construct a coherence theory of justification built upon the accumulated insights of our inquiry. From the preceding chapter we conclude that explanation, though apparently relevant to justification, is neither necessary nor sufficient. Coherence is not entirely a matter of explanation. It is time to reconsider truth. We concluded earlier that justification need not guarantee truth, but our examination of the explanatory coherence theory teaches us not to disdain it. Whatsoever objective we seek in justification, we must also seek truth. An explanation, that has no better chance of being true than some competing explanation, fails to yield complete justification. On the other hand, any belief we show to be true on the basis of what we already know is completely justified whether or not our reasoning is explanatory. How, then, can coherence within a system give us a good enough chance for truth to completely justify our beliefs?

As we noted in the preceding chapter, an adequate coherence theory must specify both a requisite system and a relation of coherence. So far we have attempted to find some objective property of beliefs in terms of explanatory excellence to supply this pair of specifications. The problems we have encountered are a direct consequence of our proclivity for the objective. We now abandon the search for some objective feature to justify our beliefs and frankly appeal to a subjective one instead.

The Circle of Belief

In whatever way a man might attempt to justify his beliefs, whether to himself or to another, he must always appeal to some belief. There is nothing other than one's belief to which one can appeal in the justification of belief. There is no exit from the circle of one's beliefs. This might not seem obvious. It might, for instance, seem that one can appeal directly to experience, or the testimony of others, to justify one's beliefs. But this is illusory. Sense experience, whether commonly casual or carefully controlled, always leaves open the question of what we are to believe. The prick of sense often elicits ready consent, but what we believe in the face of sensory stimulation depends on our antecedent convictions. For example, imagine we believe we see something red before us, and this belief arises so naturally and quickly that no other belief seems to be involved. But we are enmeshed in our beliefs. We believe our circumstances are those in which we may trust our senses and, consequently, that there is little chance of error. If we believed instead that the chance of error was great, we would resist responding with such perceptual belief. Thus the stimulation of the senses elicits belief through the mediation of a system of antecedent beliefs.

The example of perceptual belief reveals the system and relation required for our theory of justification. Such beliefs some philosophers consider self-justified. Chisholm, for instance, claims such beliefs are evident, or, in our terms, completely justified, whenever they arise, though he suggests such justification is defeasible.[1] In general, men think there is very little chance that such beliefs are erroneous. If I believe I see something red just before me, and have no reason to doubt this at all, then I shall believe there is so little chance I am in error that I readily repudiate any competing hypothesis and claim complete justification for my belief. This simple belief shows us the outline of a satisfactory theory of justification. It is the relation of this belief to others that yields justification. The belief does not depend on anything other than my beliefs for complete justification. Among these beliefs is a belief about the chances of error in such matters. I believe that there is comparatively little chance of such beliefs being in error. The chances of error are thought to be less than for any competing hypothesis. These features account for the complete justification of the belief. Indeed, they illustrate the system and relation required for the complete justification of any belief.

[1] R. M. Chisholm, *Theory of Knowledge*, 48.

The Doxastic System and Complete Justification

First, the system a man's beliefs must cohere with, in order to be completely justified, consists of a set of statements articulating what he believes. The system will consist, not of the statements believed, but statements saying that the man believes what he does. It is such a system that completely justifies a man's belief. An example may be helpful. A distinguished chemist who is a friend told me that isotopes differ in certain chemical properties from paradigm elements. He then went on to tell me about his research aimed at explaining these differences. Now I believe that I understood his words correctly and that he is altogether reliable in such matters. What he said is consistent with my understanding of chemistry. My believing these things, about chemistry, about a man and about what he has said, together with my belief that there is comparatively little chance of my believing these things and yet being incorrect in believing that some isotopes differ in chemical properties from paradigm elements, makes me completely justified in believing the latter. Thus, the system with which my belief must cohere is a system of statements to the effect that I believe these things: it is the justificatory system. I call such a system a *doxastic* system of a man. The doxastic system of a man, a set of subjective statements articulating what he believes, is what his beliefs must cohere with in order to be completely justified. It contains—not the statements believed by a man— but those statements to the effect that he believes what he does.

One additional qualification is required. If the doxastic system of a man is to completely justify a belief when truth is the objective of justification, then some beliefs must be purged from the doxastic system. A man may believe things because of the comfort it gives him, because of greed, because of hate, and so forth. Such beliefs may be totally irrelevant to the question of what the man is completely justified in believing. It is only those beliefs which he would retain in an impartial and disinterested search for truth that sustain justification aimed at veracity. Hence, for justification with truth as the objective, the doxastic system of a man must be suitably corrected.

Let us put the matter somewhat more precisely. The *doxastic* system of a person S, is a set of statements of the form, S believes that *p*, *S* believes that *q*, and so forth, which describes what *S* believes. The *corrected* doxastic system of *S* is that subset of the doxastic system resulting when every statement is deleted which describes *S* as believing something he would cease to believe as an impartial and disinterested truth-seeker. I shall hereafter refer to such impartial and disinterested truth-seekers as *veracious* inquirers.

It may be wondered how a man decides what statements are contained in his corrected doxastic system. How, that is, may a man decide what he would believe as an impartial and disinterested seeker after truth? We shall soon lay down some general criteria appropriate to an effective hunt for the verific, but an informal reply may be offered. The way for a man to find out what he would believe as a veracious inquirer is for him to strive for that ideal and see what he believes. In short, the test is in the trial.

Coherence and the Chance of Truth

Let us now turn to the matter of coherence. Suppose we agree that a corrected doxastic system of a man is the one with which a statement must cohere for him to be completely justified in believing it to be true. What does it mean to say that a statement *coheres* with such a system? The answer was suggested above. A statement coheres with a corrected doxastic system of a man if and only if the statement is believed within the system to have a good chance of being true. But how good is good enough for complete justification?

Earlier we noted that if any probability less than one is taken to completely justify believing a statement on the basis of some evidence, then, by appeal to lotteries, we can show that a man would be completely justified in believing a set of statements inconsistent with the evidence in question. A theory of probability is a theory of chance. Hence, if we suppose that a man is completely justified in believing some statement whenever the statement is believed to have a chance of being true less than one but of at least some fixed value, then, chances being probabilities, we would be led to the lottery paradox.[2] For example,

---

[2] See H. E. Kyburg Jr., *Probability and the Logic of Rational Belief*, 197. A solution along somewhat different lines from those suggested here was proposed by the author in 'Induction, Reason, and Consistency', in the *British Journal of the Philosophy of Science*, xxi (1970), 103–14.

if the fixed value in question was m/n, where m is less than n and both are integers, each ticket in a n ticket fair lottery with a single winner would have a chance of at least m/n of not being picked, and hence, if we know this much about the lottery, we would be completely justified in believing that each of the tickets is not the winner. From the completely justified conclusion that each ticket will not win it follows that lottery lacks a winning ticket. This conclusion is, of course, inconsistent with what we know. Therefore, we cannot claim that any fixed level of probability less than one is good enough for complete justification.

We shall offer a quite different theory of complete justification in terms of the chance of truth. First, we shall not assume a a *quantitative* measure of the chance of truth a man believes a statement to possess. A man may believe that one statement has a better chance of being true than another without believing either statement to have any precise numerical chance of being true. In our explication of complete justification we shall only presuppose comparisons and not quantities. Recent work in the theory of subjective probability suggests that under certain conditions we may derive a quantitative measure of subjective probability from the comparative beliefs, but our coherence theory of justification will assume no more than comparisons.[3] We shall assume that for any two statements a person believes to be relevant to each other in a way to be specified, one is believed to have a better chance of being true than the other or neither is believed to have a better chance of being true than the other, within the person's corrected doxastic system.

Problems concerning the ascertainment and justification of probability statements do not arise in the present context. One reason is that we shall not assume any quantitative measure of probability. The most important reason is that we do not require the comparisons in question to guarantee truth. If we claim that our believing one statement to have a better chance of being true than others *guaranteed* the truth of the former, we would require some justification for our beliefs about the comparative chances. Of course, if we explicated justified belief in terms of beliefs about the comparative chances of a statement being true, and then went on to require the latter to be antecedently

---

[3] See, for example, Richard Jeffrey's *The Logic of Decision*, 100–16.

justified, our project would become strikingly unilluminating. This is not our approach. Unlike defenders of the foundation theory, we do not suppose that we have any guarantees of truth. Our justification has truth as an objective, but rather than demanding some external guarantee of success, we construct our theory on the subjective integrity of a veracious inquirer and the internal relations among his beliefs. The belief that one statement has a better chance of being true than another need only belong to the corrected doxastic system of a man to provide justification in the quest for truth. We do not assume there to be any guarantee of the truth of these beliefs or those they serve to justify.

Justification and Competition

We shall now answer the central question before us. For a man to be completely justified in believing a statement to be true, the statement must be believed to have a better chance of being true than certain others within the corrected doxastic system of the man in question. Our problem is to designate those other statements. To rephrase our solution, a man is completely justified in believing a statement to be true when, within his corrected doxastic system, he believes the statement to have a better chance of being true than any statement with which it competes for that status. We conceive of a statement competing with others for the epistemic status of the completely justified and winning the competition by being believed to have a better chance of being true than its competitors. Putting the matter this way, we only need a method for determining the competitors of a statement to complete our analysis.

The lottery paradox illustrates the need to construe broadly the relation of competition. Each hypothesis to the effect that a certain ticket is a loser has a high probability, higher than its denial for example. Yet the total set of such statements taken in conjunction with the statement that the lottery has one winning ticket, is a logically inconsistent set of statements. The members of the set are related to each other in a very important way. Each statement is negatively relevant to each other. One statement is negatively relevant to a second if and only if the second statement has a lower chance of being true on the assumption that the first is true than otherwise. To illustrate, suppose there is some fixed number of tickets in the fair lottery, consecutively numbered, one of which is the winner. The hypothesis that the number two ticket is a loser is negatively relevant to the hypothesis that the number one ticket is a loser, because, assuming the truth of the latter statement, the former has less chance of being true than otherwise. If there are one thousand tickets in the lottery, the chances are 999/1,000 that the number one ticket is a loser. However, on the assumption that the number two ticket is a loser, the chances of the number one ticket being a loser are reduced to 998/999.

The foregoing suggests an explication of competition. A statement competes with all those statements believed to be negatively relevant to it within the corrected doxastic system of the man in question.[4] This proposal, however, requires modification. Suppose that there is some statement r which is negatively relevant to a statement p. Suppose that q is a statement that is quite irrelevant to p, that is, the chances of p being true are no better or worse on the assumption that q is true than otherwise. Nevertheless, the inclusive disjunction (r or q) may be negatively relevant to p simply because r is negatively relevant to p. The chances of that disjunction being true are at least as good as the chances of q being true, because the disjunction is true if q is true. Hence, by the suggested explication, a man is completely justified in believing that p only if he believes that there is a better chance that p is true than that q is true even though q is quite irrelevant to p. In short, if we so explicate competition that a statement competes with all those statements negatively relevant to it, we would obtain the result that a statement competes with many irrelevant statements. This is clearly unsatisfactory.

We must restrict the conception of competition to some stronger form of negative relevance. Consider again the disjunction (r or q) in which r is negatively relevant to p and q is irrelevant to p. It is tempting simply to exclude all such

[4] Construing competition as negative relevance was proposed to me by Marshall Swain a number of years ago but was rejected because of the difficulty mentioned below. Interpreting competition in this way yields very similar results to the way in which the author interpreted that notion in 'Induction and Conceptual Change', *Synthese*, xxiii (1971), 206–25, and in 'Evidence and Conceptual Change', *Philosophia*, ii (1972), 273–81.

disjunctions as competitors of p. However, every statement that is negatively relevant to r is logically equivalent to some disjunction which has a disjunct that is irrelevant to p. Most simply, consider the disjunction of r and any contradictory statement c. Such a disjunction is logically equivalent to r, and, presumably, the contradictory disjunct, c, is irrelevant to p. Moreover, unless r logically entails the falsity of p, we can find a disjunction logically equivalent to r with a disjunct that is relevant to p and non-contradictory. If r does not logically entail the falsity of p, then there will be some statement, s, such that the conjunction (r and s), is irrelevant to p because s offsets the negative relevance of r. But r is logically equivalent to the disjunction of that conjunction and the conjunction of r and $\sim s$, that is, to ((r and s) or (r and $\sim s$)). Hence we cannot rule out a statement as a competitor of p just because it is a disjunction or is logically equivalent to a disjunction which contains a disjunct irrelevant to p. Honest competitors of p are going to be logically equivalent to such disjunctions.

The solution to the problem is to find one disjunctive form of a statement that is suitable for evaluating the relevance of it to other statements. In Carnap's system, a disjunction of the state descriptions in the range of a statement provides such a disjunctive form.[5] However, the analysis of statements in terms of state descriptions rests on assumptions concerning logical theory that remain controversial. For our purposes what is important about state descriptions is that they constitute a partition, that is, a set of statements which are logically inconsistent in pairs and such that it is logically impossible for all of the statements in the set to be false. From any set of statements, $s1$, $s2$, and so forth to sn, we can readily construct a partition. The partition consists of the conjunction of this set of statements in numerical order and all other conjunctions formed by replacing one or more statements in that conjunction by its negation. These conjunctions will be logically inconsistent in pairs, and it will be logically impossible for all of the conjunctions to be false. The resulting partition may be inflated by conjunctions that are internally inconsistent. These are disregarded. Each of the original statements is logically equivalent to some disjunction of members of the resulting partition.

[5] Carnap, *Foundations*, 70-80.

We may employ these logical considerations to construct a stronger conception of negative relevance appropriate to our theory of justification. Note that it is somewhat unrealistic to expect even the best-intentioned pursuer of truth to reflect on *every* other statement to decide whether it competes with a statement whose epistemic status is under scrutiny. Surely he is going to restrict his consideration to some set of statements which he, as a veracious man, believes to be germane to the statement in question. We shall speak of such a set as an *epistemic field*. For example, in considering whether a given ticket is the winner in a lottery, an appropriate field of statements would be those that concern the outcome of the lottery and not ones about planets, rulers, and pure mathematics. A man may change his mind about such matters. What a man deems epistemically pertinent at one time, he may not at another. Of course, if a man is veracious, his choice of an epistemic field will not be capricious or arbitrary but will conform to the interests of truth.

Once we elicit a set of statements constituting the epistemic field of a statement for a man, we obtain a partition by the method of forming conjunctions cited above. The members of the partition will be conjunctions. Using this partition, we can construct a standard disjunctive form for each statement in the epistemic field of a statement. Each statement in the epistemic field will be logically equivalent to a member, or to a disjunction in numerical order of all those members of the partition consistent with it. We may then require that a competitor of a statement, in addition to being negatively relevant to it, be one whose standard disjunctive form does not contain any disjunction irrelevant to the statement. Thus, if r is logically equivalent to a disjunction (m_1 or m_2 or m_3 or m_6 or m_9) of members of the partition formed from the epistemic field of p for a person S, then, even if r is negatively relevant to p, r would not compete with p if the disjunction (m_2 or m_9) was irrelevant to p.

Let us call the partition formed from the epistemic field of a statement for a person the *epistemic partition* of that statement. Then we may define *strong* negative relevance. A statement r is strongly negatively relevant to p for S if and only if (i) r is negatively relevant to p and (ii) the disjunction of members in numerical order of the epistemic partition of p for S that is logically equivalent to r, is such that no disjunction of those members is irrelevant to p. In the lottery example, statements describing the possible winners of the lottery (or conjunctions equivalent to those statements) may be thought of as forming the epistemic partition for statements concerning winners and losers. The statement that the number one ticket is the loser is equivalent to a disjunction stating that either the number two ticket is the winner, or the number three ticket is the winner and so forth. None of those disjuncts or any disjunction of them is irrelevant to the statement that the number two ticket is a loser. Hence the statement that the number one ticket is a loser is strongly negatively relevant to the statement that the number two ticket is a loser.

Other gambling situations provide further illustration. Suppose you have drawn a marble from an urn you know to contain 60 per cent black marbles but have not looked at the colour. Consider the statement that the marble drawn is black. The statement that the marble is not black is strongly negatively relevant to this statement, and so is the statement that there are non-black marbles in the urn. If the statement that there are non-black marbles in the urn has a better chance of being true than the statement that the drawn marble is black, then the man is not completely justified in believing or claiming to know that the marble he has drawn is black. Thus, it is a consequence of the theory here espoused, that a man is not completely justified in believing that a randomly selected member of a class has a certain attribute unless it is more probable that the member in question has that attribute than that there are members of the class not having that attribute.

It may be useful to consider a non-mathematical example. Consider a perceptual belief, my belief that I see a red apple before me. Now not only do I believe this, I also believe that there is comparatively little chance that I am in error, that is, when I compare the statement that I see an apple with those with which it competes. For example, I believe that the statement has a better chance of being true than the statement that present circumstances or my own condition have somehow conspired to deceive me about the existence or the character of the object I believe I see before me. More particularly, I believe that there is a better chance that I see a red apple before me than that I see only a wax imitation of an apple, or that I see only a painting of an apple, and so forth. These statements are not only strongly negatively relevant to the statement that I see a red apple, they logically imply that I do not.

Other statements, for example, that I am hallucinating in such a way that I would not be able to tell whether or not I am seeing a red apple, or that there are such perfect wax imitations of red apples placed about in my vicinity that no one can tell them from the real thing by sight, do not logically imply that I do not see a red apple. But they too have strong negative relevance to the statement, and, therefore, I must believe that there is a better chance that I see a red apple than that each of these statements is true in order to be completely justified in believing I see a red apple before me. I do believe these things, and these are beliefs I would retain if I were interested in nothing but the truth in these matters and were not in any way swayed by hunger or apple lust. In short, I believe that there is a better chance that I see a red apple than that any statement is true which, if pressed by another as an objection to my claim to complete justification, would constitute a serious objection to my contention.

By contrast general statements such as that people sometimes mistake one object for another, or that people sometimes have red apple hallucinations, are not competitors of the statement that I see a red apple. Such general statements are not serious objections to my contention. They are not strongly relevant either. In my corrected doxastic system such statements may be simply irrelevant to my perceptual belief. If they are negatively relevant, some disjunction of disjuncts in the standard disjunctive form of such statements may be irrelevant, for example, statements about the perceptual errors and hallucinations of people entirely unlike myself.

An Analysis of Complete Justification

The conception of strong relevance supplies the needed ingredient for our definition of competition. A statement competes with a second within the doxastic system of a man if and only if the first statement is believed to have strong negative

relevance to the other within that system. With this definition
we proceed directly to an analysis of complete justification. It
is as follows:

> (cj) *S* is completely justified in believing that *p* if and only
> if, within the corrected doxastic system of *S*, *p* is
> believed to have a better chance of being true than the
> denial of *p* or any other statement that competes with
> *p*.

The account of complete justification is a coherence theory in
which the relation of coherence is explicated in terms of a statement being believed to have a better chance of truth than its
competitors within a system of a specified sort. The system is a
set of statements describing the beliefs a man would retain
were he to purge his beliefs to bring them in line with an impartial and disinterested search for truth, that is, the beliefs he
would retain as a veracious man.

We have not imposed any restrictions on how a man should
go about the search for truth. He might, in seeking truth, be
guided by experimental study or theoretical speculation, by the
authority of others or the light of his reasoning, by considerations of explanatory coherence or predictive fecundity, and so
forth. The diverse ways in which scientists and plain men have
pursued the truth with integrity and success belies the idea that
there is a single way with truth. Our epistemology, being doxastic, is at the same time pluralistic. It assumes the competence
of man in his quest for truth.

Comparison with the Foundation Theory

The preceding analysis allows us to account for the observations of earlier chapters within a doxastic framework. In the
chapters on the foundation theory, we examined the feasibility
of arguing that some logical or semantic feature provided a
guarantee of truth for what we are completely justified in
believing. When logic and semantics fail to provide us with an
adequate theory of justification, other forms of objective sustenance may be sought. Chisholm, in his early book, argues that
principles of justification are synthetic *a priori* principles. An
example of such a principle would be—if a man believes that

he sees something to be *F*, where to be *F* is to have some sensible characteristic like being red, then he has adequate evidence that something is *F*. Chisholm argues that such principles are neither analytic nor empirically justified and thus concludes they are synthetic *a priori*.[6] To thus sustain an epistemology is unnecessary and dialectically ineffective. It is ineffective when confronted with one who rejects the principle. Announce to such a person that the principle is a synthetic *a priori* truth, and he will rightly consider such a reply to be simple dogmatism. When you claim the principle is a synthetic *a priori* truth, you but mask the subjectivity of your contention. And that is why the claim to synthetic *a priori* truth is unnecessary. The subjectivity of belief is adequate to provide complete justification without appeal to the synthetic *a priori*. In brief, we can show how a man may be completely justified in what he believes, in terms of his corrected doxastic system, and at the same time dispense with all appeals to objective first principles binding on all men and all epistemology. We require no objective guarantees, whether of logic, semantics, or the *a priori*. We rely on nothing more than a man and his beliefs as they are shaped by an honest quest for the truth.

The justification of perceptual beliefs arises within a nexus of cohering beliefs. It is not the simple belief that I see something red, but that belief together with other beliefs about myself, my abilities, and my circumstances, on which justification depends. That is not all. My beliefs about others, about what they see and believe, may also be relevant. Doubts I have may be erased by the testimony of others which brings me to believe that they share my beliefs about what is before me. My beliefs concerning general theories, scientific or otherwise, contribute to justification. I may believe some theory according to which my perceptual apparatus is especially dependable in what I believe to be my present circumstances. The general theory may be a scientific theory about the psychology and physiology of perception. The complete justification of our perceptual beliefs depends on a myriad of other beliefs, about ourselves, about others, about experience, and about the entire universe. Coherence with other beliefs in a corrected doxastic system completely justifies a perceptual belief. The latter is believed,

[6] Chisholm, *Perceiving*, 109–12.

within such a system, to have a better chance of being true than those with which it competes.

This is not a refutation of empiricism. Empiricism, and rationalism as well, can be given expression within our framework. An empiricist is one who believes that certain perceptual beliefs have the best chance of being true. A rationalist, by contrast, believes that beliefs arrived at through certain processes of reasoning have the best chance of being true. And one may be more or less of an empiricist, more or less of a rationalist, depending on how good a chance one believes statements of a certain kind have of being true. Empiricists and rationalists of varying extremities simply have different corrected doxastic systems.

The Explanation Theory

In the preceding chapter, we considered the role of explanation in justification. That role, somewhat downgraded, can be accommodated within our theory. In the search for truth, statements that explain or are explained, or both, are believed by many to have a good chance of being true. As we understand it, this is a doxastic fact. Similarly, simpler theories are believed to have a better chance of being true than those that are more complex. Comprehensiveness, completeness, and elegance also shape our doxastic commitments.

In principle, there is no limit to what may alter our beliefs, and by so doing change what we are completely justified in believing. This remark will seem epistemically promiscuous to many. They will claim that what we are justified in believing must be faithfully limited in some objective manner by sense experience or scientific method. Such admonition is useless rhetoric. Sense experience is by itself mute. The question of what we are to believe when our senses are pricked has no answer in the prick of sense. What we are justified in believing in the confrontation with experience must be decided by what we already believe. If we go to experience empty-headed we shall return in no better epistemic state. Similarly, we may believe that if we follow some scientific methodology, we shall have a better chance of arriving at the truth. But these beliefs, about how good a chance we shall have of reaching the truth if we follow one method rather than another, are the subjectivity on which all justification depends. They are not an objective guarantee of truth. They are not a foundation. They are a subjective commitment that constantly changes in the uncertain search for truth. They are the shifting sand.

The Rationality of Completely Justified Belief

It is time to turn from rhetoric to demonstration. We shall prove that it is reasonable for a man seeking truth to believe a statement if and only if he is completely justified in believing the statement in the sense explicated above. Our proof will be decision-theoretic, that is, it will be formulated in terms of the concept of expected value restricted to the values of a veracious man. To obtain such a proof, we shall initially assume a quantitative measure of the chance a man believes a statement to have of being true. We shall subsequently dispense with this assumption.

We shall let '$p(h)$' mean 'the chance S believes h to have of being true within his corrected doxastic system', and '$p(h,e)$' mean 'the chance S believes h to have of being true within his corrected doxastic system on the assumption that e is true'. We can then define the notions we introduced earlier as follows.

(i) r has strong negative relevance to h within the corrected doxastic system of S if and only if $p(h,r)$ is less than $p(h)$ and the disjunction d which is logically equivalent to h and contains as disjuncts members $m1$, $m2$, and so forth of the epistemic partition of h for S in numerical order, is such that no disjunction d' of any of those members can be formed where $p(h,d')$ $= p(h)$.

(ii) r competes with h for S if and only if r has strong negative relevance to h within the corrected doxastic system of S.

(iii) S is completely justified in believing that h if and only if $p(h)$ is greater than $p(\sim h)$ and for any r, if r competes with h for S, then $p(h)$ is greater than $p(r)$.

With this somewhat more formal statement of our analysis, we can proceed to our decision-theoretic defence. We argued in an

earlier chapter that if one seeks a guarantee of truth from justification, the expected value of believing some statement is at a
maximum only if the probability of the statement is one. That
result we said leads to scepticism. Now we are concerned with a
man who without demanding any guarantee is nevertheless
seeking truth in his beliefs.

A man may seek truth in two senses. First, he may seek truth
in the sense that he seeks to believe *only* what is true. Second, he
may seek truth in the sense that he seeks to believe *all* that is
true. These two objectives are quite distinct. The first, believing
only what is true, may be achieved most effectively by extreme
circumspection, by believing almost nothing. The less one
believes the less one is apt to believe what is not true. The
second objective may be achieved most effectively by extreme
boldness, by believing almost everything, because the more one
believes the less apt one is to miss believing what is true. Thus,
a veracious man who aims at *both* believing only what is true,
and at believing all that is true, has some difficult choices to
make. In order to obtain both, he must not be so circumspect
as to believe nothing and thus forego the chance to believe
anything true, nor so bold as to believe everything and thus
fall into error.

Consistency

The foregoing suggests a consistency restriction on corrected
doxastic systems. If a man believes a set of statements that are
inconsistent, then not all statements of those beliefs should be
included in his doxastic system. If a man believes p, believes q,
and so forth, when the statements p, q, and so forth are inconsistent, the statements affirming that he believes each of
these things will be consistent. No statements accurately describing the beliefs of a man can be inconsistent even if the
statements he believes are inconsistent. Within a corrected
doxastic system, we shall require that the set of statements a man
is described as believing be consistent as well as the set of
statements describing those beliefs. Hence a doxastic system
must be shorn of some statements, when the beliefs it describes
are inconsistent, to correct it so that it describes the beliefs of a
veracious man.

Suppose, unrealistically, that a man believes only three contingent statements, p, q, and r, all of which are logically independent of each other. If the man adds the belief that at least one of these three statements is false to his doxastic system, his beliefs would become inconsistent. It is also the case that he would be certain of having at least one true belief. Believing the first three statements alone, he might be entirely in error, that is, all three statements might be false. If he adds to his beliefs the belief that at least one of the first three statements is false, then if the other beliefs are false, this one will be true. He will be certain to bag at least one truth. A man interested in believing what is true may gain something by adding a belief that makes his beliefs inconsistent.

However, the addition of such a belief is not worth the loss measured in terms of the objective of believing *only* what is true. By believing at least one of the three statements is false a man makes certain that at least one of the things he believes is erroneous. If the first three statements are all true, then the added belief will not be true. He has purchased the certainty of having one true belief at the price of ensuring that he has one false belief. The price is even more dear. By adding the belief that renders his beliefs inconsistent he automatically foregoes the chance of optimum success in the search for truth, that is, believing truths and only truths. Hence we impose the requirement of consistency of belief on corrected doxastic systems.

To ensure consistency among those statements a man is completely justified in believing the different epistemic partitions used by a veracious man must be independent of each other. Otherwise, inconsistency may result. For example, suppose a man used as an epistemic partition the two statements, 'the number one ticket is the winner', and 'the number one ticket is a loser'. On the basis of this epistemic partition, the second statement would only have to compete with the first for the status of being completely justified and would thus achieve that status. If the man proceeded to form such two-membered partitions for each of the statements describing a ticket as a winner or loser, he would be completely justified in believing that the number one ticket is a loser, the number two ticket is a loser, and so forth. We would thereby again obtain the lottery inconsistency.

Of course, we intended to block such a selection of epistemic partitions by requiring that the selection of an epistemic partition by a veracious man not be arbitrary or capricious. However, it is useful to specify a condition for the selection of epistemic partitions that will guarantee the consistency of the set of statements a man is completely justified in believing. We therefore impose the condition that the total set of epistemic partitions a veracious man uses at any one time should be such that we obtain a consistent set of statements by taking any single member from each of the epistemic partitions.

Since every statement we are completely justified in believing is logically equivalent to some member of an epistemic partition or some disjunction of such members, this condition provides consistency. Members of an epistemic partition logically entail all disjunctions of such members. Therefore, if any set of members drawn singly from those epistemic partitions is logically consistent, so are the entailed disjunctions of members of those epistemic partitions. The consistency condition is a condition requiring that epistemic partitions be strongly independent of each other. This means that the epistemic partitions a man uses must be broad enough to cover an entire field or subject-matter in sufficient detail so that no other epistemic partition encroaching on the area is needed to formulate the competitors for other statements.

Expected Utility

What would it be reasonable for a man to believe to obtain a maximum of expected value in the search for truth? As we noted in an earlier chapter, expected value is based on quantitative probabilities. We shall initially assume quantitative probabilities, and, subsequently in the argument, explain how our justification rests only on comparative probabilities. We have already discussed subjective probabilities. The theory of probability is the theory of chance. We assumed that within the corrected doxastic system of a man there are beliefs concerning the chances of statements being true. We also assumed that this set of beliefs is consistent. The theory of probability partially defines, at least implicity, chances or probabilities. Therefore beliefs about the chances of statements being true must be consistent with the theory of probability. Hence beliefs about the chances of statements being true contained within in a corrected doxastic system may be construed as subjective probabilities.

Assuming quantitative subjective probabilities, we can offer a decision-theoretic defence of our theory of justification.[7] In the decision-theoretic model, reasonableness is determined by two factors. One is the value assigned to certain outcomes in terms of how they contribute to the attainment of ones objectives, and the other is the probability of those outcomes. Once the values are assigned and probabilities ascertained, we can calculate what is reasonable by applying the formula for expected value.

When a man seeks to believe all that is true and only what is true, we need only consider two outcomes of belief. If I believe that p, and have truth as my objective, then there are two relevant outcomes; namely, that I believe that p and am correct, and that I believe that p and am in error. Symbolically, then, we let '$vt(h)$' mean 'the value for S of believing that h when it is true that h', '$vf(h)$' mean 'the value for S of believing that h when it is false that h', and '$e(h)$' means 'the expected value for S of believing that h'. The formula for the calculation of expected value is:

$$e(h) = p(h)vt(h) + p(\sim h)vf(h).$$

This formula tells us that expected value is the sum of value of true belief times the probability of that outcome, plus the value of erroneous belief times the probability of that outcome. We have suppressed, for typographical simplicity, reference to time and subject. But the values and subjective probabilities are those of a person at a given time.

---

[7] The application of decision theory to epistemic problems was proposed by Hempel, and developed by Pietarinen, Hintikka, Levi, and Hilpinen in works cited in chapter 6, footnote 15. The present work is greatly indebted to the results obtained by these authors. Application to the selection of evidence was proposed by the author in 'Evidence and Conceptual Change', and more elaborately in 'Evidence, Meaning, and Conceptual Change: A Subjective Approach', in a volume on conceptual change forthcoming from Reidel. The earlier articles were concerned with the application of decision theory to the acceptance of statements by inductive inference. The latter two articles are the first attempt to apply such theories to the problem of the selection of statement of evidence.

The Value of Truth and Error

Assuming subjective probabilities are given, we need only specify the values of outcomes to calculate expected value. Let us consider the value of erroneously believing some statement to be true. Erroneous belief is what we seek to avoid in seeking truth. Hence error has negative value, that is, it constitutes an epistemic loss. We can measure this loss in terms of the probability of a strongest competitor of the statement in question. We discussed the concept of competition above. A strongest competitor of a statement, h, is a statement, $h*$, which has as high a probability as any competitor of h. Formally, this gives us the equality.

$$vf(h) = - p(h*).$$

Intuitively, what this says is that the loss resulting from erroneously believing h to be true is equal to the highest chance any competitor of h has of being true. In believing h to be true, we pass up the opportunity to believe any competitor of h, and hence our loss is equal to the greatest chance for truth we passed up in believing what we did.

Specifying the value of erroneous belief in this way, the value of correct belief is readily derived. Since we are equating gains and losses with probabilities, the maximum gain is unity. The gain resulting from correctly believing h to be true is equal to the maximum gain, less the loss that would have resulted from erroneously believing it. Formally, we obtain the equality

$$vt(h) = 1 - p(h*).$$

From the foregoing equalities together with the theorem

$$p(\sim h) = 1 - p(h)$$

we obtain by substitution in the equation for expected value

$$e(h) = p(h)(1 - p(h*)) + (1 - p(h))(- p(h*))$$

which by algebraic manipulation reduces to

$$e(h) = p(h) - p(h*).[8]$$

[8] These results were obtained by the author in the two articles cited in the previous footnote.

The latter formula tells us that the expected value for a man of believing h to be true is positive if and only if the chance he believes h to have of being true within his corrected doxastic system is better than the chance he believes the strongest competitor of h to have of being true.

Complete Justification and Positive Value

We relate this result to the explication of complete justification formulated as (i), (ii), and (iii) above by the addition of the following principle:

(iv) h^* is a strongest competitor of h for S if and only if h^* competes with h for S and, for any k, if k competes with h for S, then $p(h^*)$ is at least as great as $p(k)$.

It follows from (iv) that $p(h)$ is greater than $p(h^*)$ if and only if, for any r that competes with h for S, the $p(h)$ is greater than $p(r)$. Thus we obtain the following final result:

(v) S is completely justified in believing that h if and only if $e(h)$ is positive, that is, $p(h)$ is greater than $p(h^*)$.

Hence we have obtained the conclusion that a man is completely justified in believing a statement if and only if the expected value for him of believing the statement is positive.

This conclusion shows us how we may dispense with the assumption of a quantitative measure of subjective probability employed in the argument from expected value. Complete justification presupposes no more than comparisons of the chances we believe statements to have of being true. The equivalence of complete justification and positive expected utility shows that the comparison of the chances statements are believed to have of being true suffices for the determination of positive expected value. For our purposes, the assumption that there is a single correct quantitative measure of the chances we believe statements to have of being true is no more than a convenient fiction. Any arbitrarily selected quantitative measure compatible with the comparative chances is equally satisfactory for obtaining the decision-theoretic demonstration of rationality articulated above.

To complete our decision-theoretic demonstration of the rationality of believing exactly those statements one is completely justified in believing according to our analysis, we must argue for the rationality of believing exactly those statements having a positive expected value. The standard account of rationality in decision theory tells us that only an alternative having a *maximal* expected value is rational. Decision theory finds primary application in the case of action where the alternatives are logically disjoint, that is, where it is logically impossible to adopt more than one alternative. The rational course is to obtain as much expected value as you can, and therefore we have the rule to adopt an alternative having a maximum of expected value. However, in the present application, the alternatives are not disjoint. A man may believe all those statements whose expected value is positive; he is not logically limited to a single alternative. Hence, on the principle of obtaining as much expected value as one can, the rational course is to believe every statement when we obtain a gain in expected value by so doing. Seeking truth, it is rational to believe a statement just in case the expected utility of doing so is positive. This means that, as we have specified the values of truth and error, it is rational, on decision-theoretic grounds, for a person to believe a statement if and only if he is completely justified in believing it in terms of our analyses. This completes our demonstration of the rationality of our results.

Objections and Replies

There are a number of objections that might be raised to the foregoing theory of justification. Rather than leave the reader to conjecture what the reply of the author might be, we shall attempt to anticipate those objections here and formulate our reply. By so doing, we shall be able to explain further what we mean by some of our conceptions.

FIRST OBJECTION. A man might be completely justified in believing something on our account as a result of believing little. For example, imagine a man, seeking to have a completely justified belief that God exists, bringing himself to a state of mind in which he believes that God exists, believes that this statement has a better chance of being true than its denial, and believes nothing else. On the proposed analysis he would be completely justified in believing that God exists.

REPLY. A veracious man would not believe only those things. A person who seeks after truth in a disinterested and impartial manner would not arbitrarily restrict his beliefs in this way. Hence, for the man in question the beliefs of his doxastic system would not be beliefs of his *corrected* doxastic system. Consequently the man would not be completely justified in his belief.

SECOND OBJECTION. A veracious man could be completely justified in believing statements to be true without being able to give any reasons for believing them to be true. For example, a detective might believe a certain statement to the effect that a suspect committed a crime, and believe that statement to have a better chance of being true than any of its competitors, without being able to offer any reason for his belief. Even if the detective is correct in all that he believes, his inability to offer any line of reasoning in defence of his conviction shows that he is not completely justified in his belief.

REPLY. The reply to this objection depends partly on recalling what was said in chapter 3 on the belief condition. There we interpreted belief in such a way that a man who believes that p must be convinced that p and ready to affirm that p in the appropriate circumstances, for example, to defend his belief that p. Furthermore, a veracious man, one who seeks truth, must be ready to supply reasoning where it is called for and to defend his affirmations. It would be too much to require that before a man can be completely justified in his belief he must be able to justify that belief to the satisfaction of anyone who asks. It would be too little to require only that he be able to justify his belief to the satisfaction of those with the same beliefs. It is appropriate to require that he be able to justify his belief to the satisfaction of one who is seeking the truth in an impartial and disinterested way, to another veracious man. To say that a man is able to justify his belief to the satisfaction of such a person is not to say that the reasoning need elicit consent. It is to say rather that the veracious questioner must be satisfied that the man who offers the reasoning is completely justified in his belief, whether or not the interlocutor is himself convinced.

THIRD OBJECTION. The theory fails to preserve the distinction between inferential and non-inferential knowledge. Some statements, that a man knows to be true, he knows by inference, for example, theorems or other consequences derived from antecendent knowledge. Other statements, that a man knows to be true, he knows without inference, for example, observation statements or other initially evident statements. On the theory in question, this distinction is lost entirely. All that matters according to the theory espoused is whether a statement believed coheres with a corrected doxastic system. The distinction between the inferential and non-inferential should be maintained in any adequate theory of justification, that is, such a theory should distinguish between those beliefs that are completely justified inferentially and those that are justified non-inferentially.

REPLY. This question was partially answered in chapter 4. There we pointed out that a man who comes to believe something by fallacious inference may, nevertheless, have knowledge if he is able to provide adequate justificatory reasoning on request. Thus, how a man comes to know something is, more often than epistemologists have noted, quite a separate matter from the question of how he knows it to be true once he does know. Moreover, the appeal to observation statements and the initially evident assumes the doctrine of basic statements we have already refuted.

The most critical reply, however, is that our theory of justification in no way precludes the possibility that a man might come to be completely justified in believing something as a result of inference or that he might be completely justified in believing other things without inferring them from anything else. On the theory of justification articulated, there is always the *possibility* of offering some defence of any belief, if only by explaining that the belief has a better chance of being true than its competitors. This does not imply, however, that the person having the beliefs has consciously reasoned in this way. It is quite possible that he has become completely justified in the belief without any engaging in reasoning on the matter. In short, there is nothing in our theory to prejudge how a person might come to be completely justified.

Moreover, a theory of justification should not prejudge the question of how a person can come to know. It seems theoretically possible that a person, or some being like a person, might come to know things in a manner that would seem altogether strange to us. There is the theological notion of omniscience attributed to God. This knowledge is, presumably, non-inferential. Those who prefer science fiction to theology might reflect on the possibility of a group of extraterrestrial beings who inherit knowledge by means of a genetic mechanism that does not operate in people. Or perhaps we shall one day understand the human brain well enough to implant knowledge by electrochemical means. Men might then know non-inferentially what we know by inference. An acceptable theory of knowledge and justification should not exclude these possibilities. The current theory leaves the question of the etiology of completely justified beliefs entirely open.

FOURTH OBJECTION. Beliefs about what we observe, formulated in observation statements, are completely justified because of the sensory experiences that *cause* these beliefs to arise. It is the way these beliefs are caused that makes them completely justified rather than their relations to other beliefs.

REPLY. We have argued above that what a man believes in the causal confrontation with the world depends, not only on the sensory stimulus, but also on the nexus of beliefs with which a man confronts experience. In response to sense experience, men have believed every manner of absurdity because of illusion, hallucination, and prejudice. There is nothing whatever in the causal process of sensory stimulation to ensure that a belief will be completely justified—even within the corrected doxastic system of the percipient.

Causal history may be relevant to a question of whether we know that a statement is true, especially some perceptual statements, simply because the statement is a causal description. For example, if I believe that some object before me is causing me to have a visual experience of something red, then the occurrence of that causal process is a necessary condition of the truth of my belief. However, my belief that I am having the experience need not be caused by my having it. I may not notice that I am having the experience—it may be called to my attention by someone else. In this case, his remarks cause the belief to arise. Thus the fact that certain causal processes are necessary conditions for the truth of beliefs concerning those processes should not confuse us into concluding that a completely justified belief in those processes must be caused by them.

Once again, it is not the etiology of the beliefs that makes them completely justified. If we were caused to believe what we now believe in some novel way by some mechanism directly influencing our brains, we might be completely justified in believing what we are now completely justified in believing. We might have the same corrected doxastic systems, even though the etiology of our beliefs was altogether different. It is the strongest advantage of our theory that it allows for a multiplicity of ways in which men, or other creatures, might come to know the universe.

Summary

We shall now review our progress and then articulate one remaining problem to be solved in the next chapter. We have formulated a theory based on the beliefs of a man and coherence within the system of his beliefs. As a coherence theory, our theory affirms that a man is completely justified in believing that p if and only if the statement that p coheres with a system of kind k. The system of kind k is a system of beliefs. It contains statements describing the beliefs of S which we call a doxastic system of S. Because the justification requisite for knowledge must aim at truth, the doxastic system must be corrected. To obtain the corrected doxastic system of S, all those statements must be deleted from the doxastic system of S which S would not retain as an impartial and disinterested truth-seeker. We have called such a man veracious. A veracious man seeks to believe only what is true and all that is true. A corrected doxastic system of a veracious man must describe a consistent set of beliefs to make it logically possible for him to avoid erroneous belief.

Our analysis of coherence, like our specification of the requisite system, is based on the beliefs of a veracious man. A statement coheres with the corrected doxastic system of S if and only if the statement is believed within the corrected doxastic system of S to have a better chance of being true than those with which it competes for S. A statement competes for S with those statements that are believed within the corrected doxastic system of S to have strong negative relevance to it.

Moreover, a statement coheres with the corrected doxastic system of man, and thus he is completely justified in believing it, if and only if, in terms of the value of true belief and the disvalue of erroneous belief, the expected value for S of believing the statement is positive. Thus, a man seeking an ultimate gain of expected value in what he believes will believe exactly those statements that cohere with the appropriate system and therefore are ones he is completely justified in believing.

It is a salient feature of our account that the beliefs of a veracious man, about the chances statements have of being true, for example, are subject to a myriad of influences. Perceptual experience, the testimony of others, our recollection of the past, our methodological and theoretical commitments, may all guide us toward the belief that a statement is true or at least has a better chance of being true than some other. As truth-seekers, we are apt to be most influenced by our desire for explanation and prediction that is simple, coherent, and complete. In the quest for truth, however, any method of a veracious man may lead him to a justified belief. We make no effort to mandate the methods by which a man may arrive at true beliefs and eschew false ones. Variety is the salt of inquiry.

The Problem of Truth

It may be objected to this account that by defining complete justification in terms of the doxastic system of a veracious man we allow for the possibility that a man could be completely justified in believing statements because they cohere with false beliefs. A veracious man, though meaning to serve truth well, could have entirely erroneous beliefs about the world. This is at least a logical possibility on the account we have offered. To seek truth in a disinterested and impartial way is one thing, to obtain the truth is yet another. In fact, we are convinced that a veracious man will get a firm handle on the truth, that the power of the human intellect suffices for us to escape from deception and error, at least for the most part. However, there is no guarantee that this is so, and therefore the possibility must be admitted. In terms of our analyses, it remains a logical possiblity that the beliefs of a man about the world described within his corrected doxastic system could be entirely erroneous.

Moreover, such a man could still be completely justified in believing certain statements to be true. This would result when in his corrected doxastic system a statement is believed to have a better chance of being true than any competitor. Thus, the man would be completely justified in believing a statement to be true because of the relations of that statement to false beliefs within his corrected doxastic system. The statements that make the man completely justified are statements describing his erroneous beliefs.

A man who is completely justified in believing a statement in this way surely does not know the statement to be true. His justification depends essentially on false beliefs. We do not claim that completely justified true belief is knowledge. We shall, in the next chapter, formulate a fourth condition of knowledge to exclude instances in which justification depends essentially on false beliefs. We do affirm that beliefs may be completely justified even though beliefs essential to the justification are false. When a man is veracious, when he is a hunter after truth, we allow that he is completely justified in believing that he killed his prey, even if, as luck would have it, his best shot has missed the mark. What a man is completely justified in believing depends only on what he would believe as a veracious man, on what is contained in his corrected doxastic system. What he knows depends, in addition, on whether his hunt is successful, on whether what is contained in that system describes true beliefs.

Those who remain unconvinced, and protest that a man cannot be completely justified in believing something on the basis of false beliefs, may be accommodated within our epistemology by some verbal modification. Such a critic may call the justification we have articulated *subjective* justification, and reserve the name, *complete* justification, for what is to come later. This is a mere verbal difference we would happily countenance. If our disputant will but concede that a man may achieve some justification, if only subjective, from beliefs representing his impartial and disinterested effort to reach the truth, we can appease him. With a simple qualification for the sake of veracity, such justification, despite the subjective spring from which it runs, may be purified to yield the sweet taste of knowledge.

9

Systematic Justification (III):
The Fourth Condition of Knowledge

In our first chapter, we noted that completely justified true belief may fall short of knowledge, since a justification, though complete, may depend on some erroneous statement or belief. Our theory of justification yields the same result. We are now in a position to apply our theory of justification to explicate the following fourth condition of knowledge:

> (iv) If S knows that p, then S is completely justified in believing that p in some way that does not depend on any false statement.

This condition may be formulated in terms of defeasibility as follows:

> (iv') If S knows that p, then S is completely justified in believing that p in some way that is not defeated by any false statement.[1]

The problem, of course, is to give some adequate account of the notions of dependency or defeasibility embedded in these conditions. To understand what is required, we shall review some examples employed to show that completely justified true belief is not equivalent to knowledge.

The Gettier Example

The simplest example appeals to the logical principle of addition, affirming that if p is true, then the truth-functional

[1] This formulation was proposed by Keith Lehrer and Thomas Paxson, Jr. in 'Knowledge: Undefeated Justified True Belief', *Journal of Philosophy*, lxvi (1969), 225–37. The article was discussed critically by Ernest Sosa in 'Two Conceptions of Knowledge', ibid. lxvii (1970), 59–66.

disjunction of p and q is also true whatever q may happen to be. By a truth-functional disjunction of p and q we mean, of course, a disjunctive statement that is true if and only if p and q are not both false. Taking an illustration from Gettier,[2] suppose that I am completely justified in believing that Smith owns a Ford, in terms of my beliefs about Smith, and, being something of a logician, notice it follows from

(s) Smith owns a Ford

by the principle of addition that

(d) Smith owns a Ford or Brown is in Barcelona.

This inference does not rest on any assumption about the ordinary meaning of the word 'or'. Using that term as a logician does, the deduction of (d) from (s) is valid.

Of course, I may well deduce (d) from (s) even though I have no beliefs one way or the other concerning whether Brown is in Barcelona. Nevertheless, Gettier argues, if I am completely justified in believing (s), and thus deduce (d) from (s), I must also be completely justified in believing (d). He does not formulate any argument in defence of this assumption. Assuming that the object of justification is to reach the truth, Gettier could defend it on the grounds that the truth of (s) guarantees the truth of (d). No doubt his underlying presupposition is that if we are completely justified in believing (s) in our quest for truth, and the truth of (d) follows from the truth of (s), then we must also be completely justified in believing (d) in that quest.

However, this assumption has been controverted,[3] and it is not sustained by our theory of justification. What has strong relevance to (d) might not have strong relevance to (s), and,

---

[2] Edmund Gettier, Jr., 'Is Justified True Belief Knowledge?' in *Analysis*, xxiii (1963), 121–3, and reprinted in *Knowing*, ed. Roth and Galis, 35–8, and in *New Readings*, 317–19. Also see other articles on the Gettier problem in *Knowing*. The problem originates from Bertrand Russell in *Problems of Philosophy*, 132ff.

[3] Irving Thalberg rejects the principle in 'In Defense of Justified True Belief', *Journal of Philosophy*, lxvi (1969), 794–803, and Joseph Margolis does the same in 'The Problem of Justified Belief', *Philosophical Studies*, xxiii (1972), 405–9, as does Charles Pailthorp in 'Knowledge as Justified True Belief', *Review of Metaphysics*, xxiii (1969), 25–47. The latter article was discussed critically by Keith Lehrer in 'The Fourth Condition of Knowledge: A Defense', ibid. xxiv (1970), 122–8.

therefore, (d) might fail to compete favourably where (s) succeeds. Consider the statement

(nb) Brown is not in Barcelona.

That statement is irrelevant to (s) as we have imagined the case, but it is negatively relevant to (d), it entails the falsity of one disjunct, and the negative relevance is strong. Thus, in my corrected doxastic system, (d) competes with (nb) while (s) does not. Therefore, (d) must be believed to have a better chance of being true than (nb) before I am completely justified in believing it, but (s) need not be. Hence, even if I understand the deductive relationship between (s) and (d) and come to believe (d) because I have deduced it from (s), it remains possible that I am not completely justified in believing (d). Though I am completely justified in believing (s), (d) may fail to compete favourably with (nb) while (s) does not compete with (nb) at all.

Technically, we could avoid the Gettier example by rejecting the principle of justification on which his argument rests. This escape-route is superficial. It is perfectly easy to imagine that (d) does compete favourably with (nb), simply because we have no more reason to believe (nb) than to believe Brown is in Barcelona. What the deduction of (d) from (s) guarantees is that, within my corrected doxastic system, I believe (d) has at least as good a chance of being true as (s), and that may be enough, as it is in the imagined example, to ensure that I believe (d) has a better chance of being true than its competitors. Thus, being completely justified in believing (s), I may, as a result, be completely justified in believing (d), though my beliefs are irrelevant to the added disjunct.

A problem arises if (s) happens to be false but (d) true because Smith does not own a Ford and Brown is in Barcelona. My belief in (d) is correct and completely justified, but I do not know (d) because the truth of (d) is entirely a consequence of the truth of the statement that Brown is in Barcelona which I am not completely justified in believing. Indeed, I have no reason whatever to believe it. Hence my being correct in believing (d) is, in this instance, totally a result of my good fortune in happening to pick the statement I did to disjoin to (s).

To make the argument more compelling, imagine that,

being logically clever, I had, in addition to deducing (d) from (s), also deduced

(dnb) Smith owns a Ford or Brown is not in Barcelona.

I was thus completely justified in believing (dnb) in the same way as (d). I might have reasoned that by deducing each of these statements, and believing each disjunction, I would certainly wind up being correct in one of my beliefs. When (s) does turn out to be false, however, I have no idea which of the two statements (d) and (dnb) is in fact true. I can hardly, therefore, know that either of them is true.

Some Inadequate Solutions

Solutions to the problem tend to be superficial and *ad hoc*. For example, some philosophers aver that the problem is solved by requiring that for a man to know, his justification must not involve deduction from a false premiss.[4] As the problem was formulated, a deduction from a false premiss is involved. It need not be. A man might be completely justified in believing that (d), not because he has deduced it from (s), but because (d) is believed to have a better chance of being true than its competitors. This may result from believing (s) to have almost no chance of being false. Consequently, because (s) logically implies (d), (d) has almost no chance of being false. The actual deduction of (d) from (s) is then inessential to the justification of (d) and yet we have a counterexample none the less. To be sure, it is the falsity of (s) that defeats the conclusion that I know (d), but I need not deduce (d) from (s). My inference to (d) may be a non-deductive inference from perfectly true beliefs that completely justify me in believing (s).

A Non-inferential Example

Moreover, the complete justification a man has for believing a true statement may be non-inferential when the conclusion that he knows is defeated by some false statement. An example from Chisholm, which we have already considered in another

---

[4] Thalberg and Margolis, in the works cited above, seem to think that is all there is to the problem.

context, illustrates this quite clearly.[5] Suppose I see an object
in a field that looks exactly like a sheep and I, in fact, take it
for a sheep. If I have considerable experience with sheep, I
may be completely justified in believing that I see a sheep.
Imagine that I also see another object at the same time which
does not look like a sheep and which I do not take for one. If
the object I thus take to be a sheep is not one, then I do not
know that I see a sheep, even though I am completely justified
in believing, and do believe, that I see one. Imagine, finally,
that the second object I see actually is a sheep. Then it is true
that I see a sheep. I have a completely justified true belief, but I
do not know that I see a sheep because what I take for a sheep
is not a sheep, and the sheep I see I do not take to be one. Here
we do not have a inference in the example at all. It is a simple
case of mistaking one thing for another. It is an example of
non-inferential perceptual error.

In all these cases a false belief is critically involved. In the
first case it is the belief that Smith owns a Ford, and in the
second it is the belief that what I take to be a sheep is one. This
observation leads philosophers to demand that what completely
justifies a man in believing something must not completely
justify him in believing any false statement at all. But it may
well be that whatever completely justifies us in believing anything also completely justifies us in believing at least some
false statements. Other philosophers have suggested that for a
man to know something, he must not only be completely
justified in believing it, his justification must not contain any
false statements or beliefs. This suggestion, similar to condition
(iv), we must briefly investigate.

A Harmless Error

Let us consider a modification of the Gettier example.
Suppose there are two men, Mr. Nogot and Mr. Havit, each of
whom I see before me with others in the room. Imagine that,
from what I believe about Mr. Nogot, I am completely justified
in believing that he owns a Ford. Moreover, imagine that
because of this, in response to the question of whether I know
whether anyone in the room owns a Ford, I reply that I know

[5] R. M. Chisholm, *Theory of Knowledge*, 23, footnote 22.

at least one person owns a Ford. Again, it seems that, if Mr.
Nogot does not own a Ford but someone else in the room does,
though I would have a completely justified true belief that at
least one person in the room owns a Ford, I would not know
this to be true. What justifies me in believing this is my false
belief that Mr. Nogot owns a Ford. Suppose, however, I am
completely justified on independent grounds in believing that
Mr. Havit owns a Ford, and, indeed, Mr. Havit does own a
Ford. In this case, though part of what justifies me in believing
that at least one person in the room owns a Ford is my false
belief that Mr. Nogot owns a Ford, I have a justification that
does not depend on this false belief. It is based on my completely justified and correct belief that Mr. Havit owns a Ford.[6]

The Knowledge of Falsity

The foregoing illustrates why we have formulated condition
(iv) so as to require only that S has *some* justification that does
not depend on any false belief. We have yet to explain what it
means to say that a justification depends on a statement or
belief. A proposal advanced independently by Klein and
Hilpinen is relevant to the explication of dependency.[7] In our
terminology, they propose that the complete justification that
a man has for believing that p depends on the false statement q
if and only if S would not be completely justified in believing
that p if S knew q to be false. If I knew it to be false that Smith
owns a Ford, then I would not be completely justified in
believing that Smith owns a Ford or Brown is in Barcelona. If I
knew it to be false that what I take to be a sheep is a sheep,
then I would not be completely justified in believing that I see
a sheep. On the other hand, in the last case considered, if I
knew it to be false that Mr. Nogot owns a Ford, I would remain
completely justified in believing that at least one person in the
room owns a Ford because I am completely justified in believing that Mr. Havit owns one.

[6] This argument appeared originally in the author's 'Knowledge, Truth, and
evidence', *Analysis*, xxv (1965), 168–75, and reprinted in *Knowing*, eds. Roth and
Galis, 55–66.

[7] Peter Klein, 'A Proposed Definition of Propositional Knowledge', *Journal of
Philosophy*, lxviii (1971), 471–82; and Risto Hilpinen, 'Knowledge and Justification',
Ajatus, xxxiii (1971), 7–39.

The Grabit Example

Nevertheless, the proposal remains *ad hoc*. In these cases, there is some false statement which misleads one, and knowing the statement to be false would clarify matters. This is a special feature of these examples. There are situations in which knowing some statement to be false would be misleading rather than clarifying. Another example from the literature illustrates this.[8] Suppose I see a man, Tom Grabit, with whom I am acquainted and have seen often before, standing a few yards from me in the library. I observe him take a book off the shelf and leave the library. I am completely justified in believing that Tom Grabit took a book, and, assuming he did take it, I know that he did. Imagine, however, that Tom Grabit's father has, quite unknown to me, told someone that Tom was not in town today, but his identical twin brother, John, who he himself often confuses with Tom, is in town at the library getting a book. Had I known that Tom's father said this, I would not have been completely justified in believing I saw Tom Grabit take the book, for if Mr. Grabit confuses Tom for John, as he says, then I might surely have done so too. Under the Klein and Hilpinen proposal, I do not know that Tom Grabit took the book.

Imagine further that John Grabit is nothing more than a figment of the demented imagination of Mr. Grabit who had a neurotic desire to have twin sons because his older brother has twin sons. Moreover, imagine that, but for this peculiar quirk of telling tales about his non-existent son John, Mr. Grabit is a quite reliable and truthful man, indeed, more so than the rest of us. Thus, it is true not only that Tom's father said what he did about John Grabit, it is also true that Mr. Grabit is a generally reliable and truthful man. Surely, if I had known just the latter truths about Mr. Grabit, I would not, within my corrected doxastic system, believe that there is a better chance that Tom Grabit took the book than that John Grabit took it. On the present account of condition (iv), I would fail to know that Tom Grabit took the book.

But do I lack knowledge? Notice that I originally have no reason to believe that Mr. Grabit said what he did, I might not

---

[8] Lehrer and Paxson, 'Knowledge: Undefeated Justified True Belief', 228–9.

have any beliefs whatever concerning him. Moreover, I did see
Tom Grabit take the book. Mr. Grabit's remarks, of which I am
totally ignorant, are completely misleading. We should, therefore, not deny that I know that Tom Grabit took the book
because of the prevarications of his father of which I am
fortunately ignorant. I know Tom Grabit took the book just as I
know other people do the things I see them do. Moreover, and
most important, the reason that I know is not merely my good
fortune at missing out on the speech of Mr. Grabit; it is the
consequence of two other important features. First, if I knew not
only Mr. Grabit's words but also the truth about those words,
to wit, they are neurotic lies, I would remain completely
justified in believing that Tom Grabit took the book. Second,
the beliefs within my corrected doxastic system that make me
completely justified in believing that Tom Grabit took the book
do not include any beliefs about Tom's father and what he
might or might not have said. Given these two features, I may
be said to know that Tom Grabit took the book despite the
fact that, had I known what his father said without knowing
about his quirk, I would not know whether it was Tom who
took it.

The Newspaper Example

The Tom Grabit example is to be distinguished from one
suggested by Harman to illustrate how a man may lack
knowledge even though his belief is justified entirely by true
statements.[9] Suppose a man reads in a newspaper that a civil-
rights leader has been assassinated. The story is written by a
dependable reporter who in fact witnessed and accurately
reported the event. The reader of the story believes this and is
completely justified in believing that the civil-rights leader was
assassinated. However, for the sake of avoiding a racial explo-
sion, all other eye-witnesses of the event have agreed to deny
the assassination occurred and affirm that the civil-rights
leader is in good health. Imagine, finally, that all who surround
the man in question have, in addition to reading the story,
heard the repeated denials of the assassination and thus do not

[9] Gilbert Harman, 'Knowledge, Inference, and Explanation', reprinted in
New Readings, 357–68.

know what to believe. Could we say that the one man who, by accident, has not heard the denials, knows that the civil-rights leader was assassinated? The answer appears to be that he does not know.

If we agree to this, the obvious problem is to explain the difference between this case and the case of Tom Grabit. In both cases, there is some misleading information which, were it possessed, the man in question would not know. In the newspaper case, when a man lacks this information, we still deny that he knows the civil-rights leader was assassinated, while in the case of Tom Grabit, we affirm that the man knows that Tom Grabit took the book. What is the difference? In the Grabit example, no beliefs of mine concerning Tom's father or what he might have said serve to justify me in believing that Tom took the book. In the newspaper example, though this is unstated, part of what justifies the man in believing that the civil-rights leader has been assassinated is his belief that the newspaper story is generally considered to be a reliable source of information. The man's justification for believing that the civil-rights leader has been assassinated depends on his false belief that others believe the story, but my belief that Tom Grabit took the book does not depend on any false belief about what Tom's father did or did not say. One who doubts this should reflect on how the newspaper case is altered if it occurs to the reader that other eyewitnesses might deny the success of the assassination, and, because he completely trusts the reporter, resolves not to let the doubts of others shake this confidence. With this modification, I suggest that we would say that the man does know that the civil-rights leader was assassinated. He has placed his confidence in the right place.

A Solution: Verific Alternatives

The foregoing remarks all lead to one conclusion. The justification a man has for believing that p depends on a false statement q if and only if an alteration of his beliefs making them all true would result in his no longer being completely justified in believing that p. To put the matter the other way round, a man is completely justified in believing that p in a way that does not depend on any false statement if and only if he would be completely justified in believing that p when his beliefs were changed to make them all true.

This requires more formal articulation. Let D be the corrected doxastic system of S. Every statement in D is of the form: S believes that p. Form a set V from D by retaining all such statements of D in V when it is true that p, and when it is false that p substitute in V the statement that S believes the denial of p. We shall call V the *verific alternative* to D. The verific alternative to a doxastic system is one in which each belief of a true statement is retained and each belief of a false statement is replaced with the belief of the denial of that false statement.[10] With this conception of a verific alternative, we obtain the following explication of condition (iv):

> S is completely justified in believing that p in a way that does not depend on any false statement if and only if S is completely justified in believing that p in the verific alternative to the corrected doxastic system of S.

The application of this explication to most of the examples is obvious. If, as would be the case in the verific alternative, Smith is believed not to own a Ford, the object taken to be a sheep is believed not to be a sheep, and the readers of the story are believed not to consider it reliable, then the men in question will lack knowledge.

In all these examples in which a man is completely justified in believing some true statement but fails to know, the belief that the statement is true will be retained in the verific alternative. In the sheep example, to take the most difficult case, the statement that the man believes that he sees a sheep in the field will be retained in the verific alternative. However, the statement that the man believes the object he takes to be a sheep is not a sheep will also be included in the verific alternative because of his erroneous belief that what he takes to be a sheep is a sheep. Since the statement that he believes the object he takes to be a sheep is not a sheep is in the verific alternative, his belief that he sees a sheep, though true and retained in the verific alternative, is not completely justified. The belief that what he takes to be a sheep is not a sheep undermines his

---

[10] This proposal concerning verific alternatives is similar to one made by Marshall Swain in 'An Alternative Analysis of Knowing', *Synthese*, xxiii (1971–2), 423–42.

justification for his belief that he sees a sheep. In those examples in which some false statement is employed as a premiss for deducing a true statement, the belief of the denial of the false statement contained in the verific alternative would undermine the original justification. Hence the man would not be completely justified in believing the true statement that was the conclusion of the original deduction in the verific alternative.

Application to the case of Grabit might seem less obvious. The conclusion that I do know that Tom took the book results from the fact that no belief about Tom's father is in the verific alternative to my corrected doxastic system. The reason is that no belief about what Tom's father said is contained in my corrected doxastic system. I have no beliefs about what he said. In the newspaper case, by contrast, I do believe others believed the story, and that belief is within my corrected doxastic system. Consequently, the belief that they do not believe the story is contained within the verific alternative. This dissident belief within that system would suffice, as we originally imagined the case, to keep the man from being completely justified in his belief that the civil-rights leader was assassinated within the verific alternative.

In dealing with these examples, and others as well, it is critically important that *not every* true statement is said to be believed by S in the verific alternative to his doxastic system. If belief in every true statement were attributed to S in his verific alternative, then, in the newspaper example as well as most of the original counterexamples, S would be completely justified in believing those statements in the verific alternative whose original justification depended on some false belief. If the verific alternative were construed in that manner, the notion would be entirely useless for dealing with problems under discussion. To obtain satisfactory results, the statements of what S believes contained in the verific alternative must be limited to the original true beliefs of S and the denials of the original false beliefs of S as described in his corrected doxastic system.

Our explication meets the objection raised at the end of the preceding chapter. As we explicated complete justification in that chapter, a man may be completely justified in believing some statements because of false beliefs which he has. This does not undermine our analysis of knowledge. A man must have more than completely justified true belief in order to know that p. He must also be so justified that he would remain completely justified if all his false beliefs were replaced with true ones, namely, with beliefs in the denials of what he erroneously believes. His being completely justified must not depend on any false belief.

Perception and Inference

We have now to deal with some traditional epistemological questions in terms of our theory. First, we shall consider the role of perception and inference in the complete justification of belief. There is an epistemic use of the term 'perceive' and of the term 'inferred'. If I say that a man perceives that the cat is on the dog what I have said entails that he is completely justified in believing, and, indeed, knows that the cat is on the dog. Similarly, if I say that the man inferred that the cat is on the dog, what I have said entails that he is completely justified and knows that this is so. Indeed, S perceives that p if and only if S knows that p by perception, and S infers that p if and only if S knows that p by inference. There is also a non-epistemic use of the terms 'perceive' and 'infer'. This becomes apparent when we speak of *incorrect* perception and inference. The non-epistemic use of these terms does not entail knowledge. Misperception and fallacious inference do not constitute knowledge. Thus, we may speak of a man perceiving or inferring something without this entailing that he knows what he perceives or infers.

When we consider perception and inference epistemically, that is, as knowledge by perception or inference, this knowledge results from the influence on belief of perception and inference considered non-epistemically. Less technically, our perceptual and inferential beliefs shape our doxastic systems in a manner that explains the complete justification with which we believe various statements. These beliefs are not unique in the formation of a doxastic system. They are a salient influence in the formation of the doxastic systems of people doxastically responsive to sense experience and ratiocination.

We confront again the fundamental subjectivity of justification. Consequently, we reject the assumption, made by many

philosophers, that some principles of justification are universally valid. Consider the principle that if S is completely
justified in believing that p, and believes q because he deduces
q from p, then S is completely justified in believing that q. It is
not universally valid, as Harman has illustrated.[11] A man may
have beliefs which completely justify him in believing that p,
he may believe that q as a result of deducing p from q, but, at the
same time, come to have doubts about the beliefs that completely justified him in believing that p in the first place. For
example, I might be completely justified in believing Mr.
Nogot who is in the room owns a Ford and deduce that at least
one person in the room owns a Ford; but at the same time it
may occur to me that Mr. Havit who is not in the room might
own the Ford instead of Nogot. The inference thus reminds me
of a possibility that had not occurred to me previously. Once it
does occur to me, I may have some doubts about what completely justified me in believing that p, and, when I come to
believe that q by deduction from p, I am no longer completely
justified in believing either p or q. In short, inference, by calling
up a variety of new considerations, can change beliefs in a
myriad of ways. What a man is completely justified in believing
depends on what he believes, and what a man may come to
believe as a result of inference, deductive or otherwise, is not
constrained by any universally valid principle of justification.

Similar remarks apply to perception. Perceptual beliefs may
fail to be completely justified. One may come to have such a
belief and, at the same time, have other beliefs that render the
perceptual belief less than completely justified. Moreover, in
both the case of perceptual and inferential beliefs, even if they
are true and completely justified, it by no means follows that
they therefore constitute knowledge. Complete justification of
the perceptual belief may depend on some other false belief
which, when extirpated from one's corrected doxastic system,
leaves the perceptual belief less than completely justified. It may
be believed in the verific alternative to have no better chance
of being true than some competitors.

Thus, it is unwarranted to lay down any general principles

---

[11] This claim is implicit in Harman's discussion of inference that involves the
rejection of previously held beliefs in 'Induction', in *Induction, Acceptance, and
Rational Belief*, ed. Marshall Swain, 91.

of justification, whether pertaining to perceptual belief as Chisholm does, or to inferential belief as Gettier does.[12] It is no universal *a priori* truth that if a man believes that he sees something red, then he is completely justified in believing this. He may not be completely justified because of other beliefs he has which render his perceptual belief less than completely justified. It is no universal *a priori* truth that if a man is completely justified in believing that *p* and believes that *q* as a result of validly inferring *q*, whether deductively or inductively, that he is completely justified in believing that *q*. He may not be completely justified because of other beliefs for the reason we have noted. If any such principles as these were universally true, they would be factual truths about how human beings shape their beliefs in an effort to arrive at truth. They would not be *a priori* necessary principles.

In none of this do we intend to deprecate scientific methodology, perceptual test or cogent reasoning. Far from it. It is our fundamental conviction that cogent reasoning and experimental inquiry have the best chance of reaching the truth. But we steadfastly refuse to confuse our personal convictions and those of our associates with *a priori* first principles of human knowledge. Our convictions about the proper methods to inquire after truth, no matter how confident we may be in them, remain simply our convictions. They may be correct convictions, and we may know they are. Nevertheless, that people will arrive at the truth by one method rather than another is a contingent and factual truth. Knowledge in such matters, if we possess it, is *factual* knowledge beyond the scope and limits of *a priori* demonstration.

Knowing that We Know

These remarks raise one final and fundamental question which we shall now answer and then conclude our chapter. The question is whether we ever know that we know.[13] To clarify

[12] In works cited above.

[13] For some important articles on this topic see E. J. Lemmon, 'If I Know, Do I Know That I Know?' and Arthur C. Danto, 'On Knowing that We Know', both in *Epistemology: New Essays in the Theory of Knowledge*, ed. A. Stroll, 54–82 and 32–53, respectively; and Carl Ginet, 'What Must Be Added to Knowing to Obtain Knowing That One Knows', and Risto Hilpinen, 'Knowing That One Knows and the Classical Definition of Knowledge', both in *Synthese*, xxi (1970),

the question, it is useful to notice that on our analysis the four conditions of knowledge turn out to be logically independent. The independence of truth and belief were discussed earlier. What is important to notice here is the independence of belief from complete justification, and the independence of the latter from the fourth condition. I may obviously believe something I am not completely justified in believing and vice versa. Moreover, I may be completely justified in believing something I am not completely justified in believing within a verific alternative, and I may not be completely justified in believing something I am completely justified in believing in a verific alternative. The latter could result, for example, when substituting some true belief for a false one in my corrected doxastic system would make me completely justified in that belief.

For S to know that S knows that p, S must know that the four conditions for knowing that p are all satisfied. To answer the question of whether S knows that S knows that p, we shall assume that S knows that p. We shall later consider the merits of this assumption. On the assumption that S knows that p, S knows that the first condition is met, that is, he knows that p. Presumably there is no difficulty about S knowing that he believes that p. The next two conditions become more problematic. Since S must know that he is completely justified in believing that p, he must be completely justified in believing that he is completely justified in believing that p. This is less of a problem than might appear given one doxastic principle, to wit, that if, within the corrected doxastic system of S, S believes that p, then within that system S believes that he believes that p. Given this doxastic iteration principle, it follows that for every statement in the corrected doxastic system of S, the statement he believes that statement is also in the corrected doxastic system. From the doxastic iteration principle, we obtain an iteration principle of complete justification, to wit, if S is completely justified in believing that p, then he is completely justified in believing he is completely justified. If S believes that p has a better chance of being true than its competitors within

163–86 and 109–32, respectively. See also the discussion by Jaakko Hintikka in *Knowledge and Belief* (Cornell University Press, Ithaca, N.Y., 1962), 103–25, and Chisholm's analysis of Hintikka's position in 'The Logic of Knowing', reprinted in *Knowing*, ed. Michael Roth and Leon Galis, 189–219.

his corrected doxastic system, he also believes that this belief has a better chance of being true than its competitors within that system. This is a corollary of the doxastic iteration principle when we treat beliefs about chances as comparative degrees of belief.

The doxastic iteration principle does not lie beyond the threshold of philosophical controversy. Our discussion of belief in the third chapter may be referred to for defence. It would be pedantry to repeat those arguments here in the slightly modified form needed to defend the iteration principle. It will suffice, therefore, to note that the usual objections to that principle depend on construing belief in two quite different senses. If we stick to one sense, in which for a person to believe that p he must be convinced that p and ready to affirm that p in the appropriate circumstances, then, if a man seeking truth believes that p, he also believes that he believes that p. A man who is convinced that something is so and is ready to affirm this in appropriate circumstances is also convinced that he thus believes it and is ready to affirm that in the appropriate circumstances. This is all we assume. We do not deny that there might be some weak sense in which a person believes something but does not, perhaps in a stronger sense, *believe* that he believes it. Such senses of the term, whether common or technical, are not ones that concern us here.

A last problem remains in defence of our principle of epistemic iteration, and, of course, it is the most difficult. Chisholm noted that adding a fourth condition to the analysis of knowledge is perilous for those who wish to claim that anyone ever knows that he knows anything.[14] However, the perils vanish immediately. For, if a man knows that p, then he is completely justified in believing that p in the verific alternative to his corrected doxastic system. Moreover, by the argument for the iteration of complete justification, it follows that if a man is completely justified in believing that p, then he is completely justified in believing that he is so justified. Hence, if a man is completely justified in believing that p, then he is completely justified in believing that he would remain completely justified in believing that p in the verific alternative.

We have now shown that if a man knows that p, then the

14 Chisholm .*Theory of Knowledge*, 23, footnote 22.

first three conditions of his knowing that he knows that p are satisfied. Is the fourth condition of his knowing that he knows satisfied? Given the iteration principles mentioned above, if a man would remain completely justified in believing that p in the verific alternative, then the statement that S believes that p has a better chance of being true than its competitors is in the verific alternative. If that statement is in the verific alternative, then by the doxastic iteration principle, so is the statement that S believes that statement and believes it to have a better chance of being true than its competitors. Hence if S is completely justified in believing that p in the verific alternative, then S is completely justified in believing in the verific alternative that S is completely justified in believing that p in the verific alternative. Thus, if S knows that p, then all four conditions of his knowing this to be so are satisfied. If a man knows, then he knows that he knows.

The foregoing argument illustrates the advantages of our doxastic approach to knowledge and complete justification. The principle of the iteration of knowledge becomes a consequence of the principle of the iteration of belief within corrected doxastic systems. By explicating complete justification in terms of what beliefs a man would retain as a veracious man, we escape problems arising for accounts of complete justification in terms of alleged universal *a priori* principles of justification. A man who happens to satisfy such principles may be quite unaware of their existence. If he knows something because his belief is justified by such principles, he does not know that he knows because he does not know his belief is justified by those principles.

Moreover, the principle that if a man knows, then he knows that he knows, is a principle that simplifies epistemology. Since it follows that if a man knows that he knows, then he knows, we obtain the result in our epistemology that knowing is equivalent to knowing that one knows. The equivalence principle that S knows that p if and only if S knows that S knows that p enables us to reduce all iterated claims to know, such as the claim that S knows that S knows that S knows that p to the simple claim that S knows that p. Hence all knowledge claims, however iterated, can be evaluated in terms of the four conditions of knowledge in our analysis. Any analysis of knowledge lacking the equivalence principles precludes reducing iterated knowledge claims and thereby complicates the procedure of evaluation. Thus, the equivalence principle is of fundamental theoretical importance. Indeed, if one highly values theoretical simplicity, it is doubtful that one should accept any theory of knowledge in which the equivalence principle fails. The potential complications of such theories are as unlimited as the iterations we can construct.

The Conditionality of Chance

The foregoing shows that if we know, then we know that we know. This leaves us with an unaffirmed antecedent. We shall turn to an examination of scepticism in our next and final chapter. A preliminary issue demands attention here. We have been concerned with verific alternatives to doxastic systems containing statements saying a man believes one statement has a better chance of being true than another. Such statements will be contained in the verific alternative only if the one statement has a better chance of being true than another. But, it may be queried, under what conditions does one statement have a better chance of being true than another? The interpretation of statements of chance or probability, whether quantitative or comparative, is a subject fit for a treatise, and so our remarks must be summary.

Beliefs about chances may be construed as subjective probability statements. We indicated this earlier. None the less, if the beliefs are subjective, what those beliefs are about, the chances of truth, need not be. If there are more green marbles in an urn than black ones and they are consecutively numbered by a random procedure, there is a better chance that the nth number marble is green rather than black. This is not a statement about what anyone believes but one about an objective feature of the world. The chance set up makes it easy enough to ascertain the statement of chance in question. Philosophers and mathematicians have attempted to explicate this objective feature in terms of frequencies, the limits of frequencies, and propensities to yield frequencies.[15] We shall not attempt to

---

[15] This interpretation of probability is advocated by Karl R. Popper in 'The Propensity Interpretation of Probability', *British Journal for the Philosophy of Science*, x (1959–60), 25–42.

adjudicate between such analyses here. Nevertheless, beliefs about chances, however subjective in themselves, are beliefs or estimates concerning such objective features of the world.

When it is believed within a corrected doxastic system that one statement has a better chance of being true than another, such beliefs must be construed as *conditional* on the other statements in the system. When we believe that one statement has a better chance of being true than another we believe this, not in a doxastic vacuum, but in the context of our other beliefs. The example we just cited, if formulated precisely, should also be conditional. That the nth ball is green has a better chance of being true than that the nth ball is black on the condition or assumption that more marbles in the urn are green than black.

We speak of a man believing within his corrected doxastic system that one statement has a better chance of being true than another, but this should be construed as elliptical. When the belief is spelled out, what is believed is that one statement has a better chance of being true than the other on the condition that the other statements in the system are true. Those statements are ones describing the beliefs of the man in question. Thus, statements describing his beliefs are true whether or not the beliefs themselves are true. For purposes of the last chapter, the conditional character of statements of chance was of little consequence.

On the other hand, for the purpose of understanding the conditions under which statements of chance are true, their conditional character must not be overlooked. Assuming that D is my corrected doxastic system, my believing within it that p has a better chance of being true than q is equivalent to my believing that p has a better chance of being true than q on the condition that the other statements of D are true. Similar remarks pertain to the verific alternative to my doxastic system. This is important for understanding what the statement believed tells us about the world. It tells us that p has a better condition of being true than q on the condition that I have certain beliefs, namely, those described within the system in question. That is a very different statement from the unconditional statement that p has a better chance of being true than q.

The preceding remarks may be clarified with an example.

Suppose I believe that the statement that what I see before me is a table has a better chance of being true than the statement that what I see before me is a chair. If we ignore the covertly conditional character of the statement believed, it would tell us that it is an objective feature of the world that there is a better chance that what I see is a table rather than a chair. In this unconditional form, the statement would, presumably, be true only if I see tables more frequently than chairs, and I do not. Of course, that is not what is meant. What is meant is that having the beliefs I now do, for example, beliefs concerning my ability to distinguish tables from chairs in the present setting, there is a better chance that what I see is a table rather than a chair. Even if I and others more often see chairs than tables, it is presumably more often true that what one sees is a table rather than a chair when one has the sort of beliefs I now do. People having such beliefs more frequently see a table, as they believe, and not a chair.

Hence, within a corrected doxastic system, a belief that one statement has a better chance of being true than another is conditional on the other statements in that system. Such a belief is contained in a verific alternative if and only if it is true that the one statement has a better chance of being true than the second on the condition of the truth of the other statements in the corrected doxastic system. As we noted before, even if some of the statements in my corrected doxastic system describe false beliefs, they are true statements describing my beliefs. Thus, a belief that is conditional on the truth of such statements is one whose truth may be ascertained on the basis of factual information about human beliefs.

Summary

We conclude that a man knows that p only if he is completely justified in believing that p in the verific alternative to his corrected doxastic system. The verific alternative to a corrected doxastic system is one in which all statements describing false beliefs in the corrected doxastic alternative are replaced with statements describing true beliefs. If the statement that S believes that p is in the corrected doxastic system of S, and it is false that p, then in the verific alternative this statement is replaced with the statement that S believes that it is not the case that p. The verific alternative is, therefore, a description of what S would believe were he to replace each erroneous belief with the contradictory of what he actually believes. If a man is completely justified in believing that p in his corrected doxastic system and he is also completely justified in believing that p in the verific alternative of that system, then his being completely justified does not depend on, nor is it defeated by, any false statement or belief.

Hence, the objection of the preceding chapter that a man may be completely justified in believing that p because of false beliefs in his corrected doxastic system, and, as a result, know that p on the basis of error, is overcome by adding the fourth condition. A man only knows something when his complete justification for believing it does not depend on false beliefs. Moreover, our theory of complete justification within corrected doxastic systems and verific alternatives yields the principle of the iteration of knowledge, to wit, that if a man knows that p, then he knows that he knows that p. This results from our doxastic explication of justification, given the principle of the iteration of belief, to wit, that if a man believes that p, then he believes that he believes that p, and the corollary that if a man believes that p has a better chance of being true than its competitors, then he also believes that this belief has a better chance of being true than its competitors. Thus, if we know anything, we know that we know it. The only question that remains is whether we do, in fact, know anything. With our analyses and explications laid before us, we shall advance upon the sceptic and test his mettle.

10

Metaphysical Speculations:
Scepticism and Materialism

WE say we know, but do we? Sceptics have denied it, and at
least one form of materialism entails such a denial. We shall,
in the light of our doxastic epistemology, assess the merits of
these sceptical and metaphysical claims. Let us first turn to
scepticism.

Scepticism and Agnoiology

Scepticism comes in different depths. Shallow forms deny
that we know a few things we claim to, and the deepest form
denies that we know anything at all.[1] Deeper forms of scepticism
are based on the ubiquitous chance for error. Plain men, who
comfort themselves in the snug foothills of accepted opinion,
overlook the possibilities for error residing in our most familiar
beliefs. In the minds of the dogmatic, what is familiar comes,
through long acquaintance, to appear completely dependable
and wins unquestioning confidence. The philosophical sceptic,
inclined to question when others are drawn to dogmatic
tranquillity, discovers the risk of error in our most trusted
convictions. On this discovery, he constructs an *agnoiology*, a
theory of ignorance.

Of course, sceptics who have denied we know what we say
we do have frequently been moved by more than a passion for
the study of agnoiology. Often, they espouse some theory that
conflicts with common opinion. Scepticism is defended to

---

[1] The author defended the deepest scepticism in 'Why Not Scepticism?',
Philosophical Forum, ii (1971), 283–98, and Peter Unger defended a very deep, if
not the deepest, form in 'A Defense of Scepticism', *Philosophical Review*, lxxx (1971),
198–219.

win consideration for their own theories. In reply, common-sense philosophers, like Reid and Moore, have rejected such speculative theories on the sole grounds that they conflict with common sense.[2] The beliefs of common sense are innocent, they say, until proven guilty, and constitute knowledge unless they are shown not to. Sceptics have been accused of semantic deviation, logical absurdity, and triviality. In an earlier chapter, we argued that what the sceptic says is semantically acceptable, logically consistent, and highly contentious. Rather than attempting to dismiss him abruptly, by some superficial artifice, let us consider what sustains his argument.

There are a number of classical sceptical arguments appealing to dreams and hallucinations purporting to show that, whatever we take to be true, there remains some chance of error.[3] However, sceptical argumentation does not depend on these appeals to dreams and hallucinations. They are simply familiar ways of explaining how men err. It matters little what the source of error might be. What is critical is most simple. Men often believe what is false, and, when what they believe happens to be true, there was some chance that they might have erred. This is the fundamental sceptical premiss.

Conception and the Chance of Error

There are a variety of ways in which a sceptic may press this premiss. Such arguments have the merit of calling our attention to some possibility of error we overlook. For example, a sceptic may base his argument on the nature of human conception. Experience by itself, as we have noted, tells us nothing. Knowledge and belief require the application of concepts to experience. The best entrenched concept remains constantly subject to total rejection. In the pursuit of truth, we may discard any concept as lacking a denotation. Any concept may be thrown onto the junk-heap of repudiated concepts along with demons, entelechies, and the like. Moreover, any discarded

[2] Thomas Reid, *The Philosophical Works of Thomas Reid*, ed. Sir William Hamilton, 234, and G. E. Moore in 'A Defense of Common Sense' in *Contemporary British Philosophy*, second series, ed. J. H. Muirhead (Macmillan, London, 1925), 193–223.
[3] The most famous, of course, is René Descartes in *Meditations*, I.

concept can be refurbished. The concepts we reject may be better than the ones that supplant them. We may have to recycle what we discard. No concept or belief is sacrosanct in the quest for truth. There is always some chance that any one may be cast off as misleading and erroneous.

The foregoing remarks describe more than a mere logical possibility. It is not only logically possible that any belief is in error, there is some genuine chance that it is so. The beliefs that have been most cherished and in which men have placed their greatest confidence, for example, the belief in the human spirit, have been demoted from literal truths to figures of speech. Strictly speaking, there is no such thing as a spirit at all. The concept of spirit, aside from use as a figure of speech, is a relic of religious conceptualization which, however comforting it may have been, is no longer tenable in an impartial and disinterested search for truth. This merely illustrates how, in the flux of conceptual change and innovation, any concept may be rejected for sake of conceptual improvement and increased veracity.

We must note in passing that the concept of belief, indeed, even the concept of a concept, is no more secure than others. Some materialists have said that belief is mental, and, consequently, there is no such thing as belief. We shall consider such materialism and the implications of it for our theory of knowledge below. Such materialism would require that if we have referred to anything real in the world when speaking incorrectly of belief, what is real may be correctly described within a materialistic vocabulary.

The sceptic is correct, we concede, in affirming the chance of error is always genuine. We grant the sceptical premise that if S believes that p, then there is some chance that S is incorrect in his belief.

A Refutation of Scepticism

To sustain scepticism, a sceptic must go on to argue that if there is some chance that S is incorrect in his belief that p, then S does not know that p. On the analysis of knowledge we have articulated, this premise is unavailable. It does not follow from the premise that there is some chance that S is incorrect in his belief that p, that p is not true, or that S does not believe that p, or that S is not completely justified in believing that p, or that S is not completely justified in believing that p in his verific alternative. Even if S believes in his corrected doxastic system and verific alternative that there is some chance that he is incorrect in believing that p, he may, none the less, believe that there is a better chance that p is true than that its competitors are. He may thus know that p, and, by the argument of the last chapter, know that he knows, even though there is some chance that p is false, and S believes this to be so. Hence we may accept the premiss of the sceptic concerning conceptual change and the universal chance of error implicit therein without accepting the deep sceptical conclusion of universal ignorance.

With this reply to scepticism set forth, we hasten to note that in some ways our position is very close to that of the sceptic. For very often when men claim to know something, they claim to know for certain. If they do know for certain, then there must be no chance that they are in error. When there is some chance that a man is in error, that his belief is incorrect, then there is some uncertainty, however slight, and he does not know for certain that what he claims is true. Hence, in agreeing that there is always some chance of error, we are agreeing with the sceptic that nobody ever knows for certain that anything is true. Joining hands with the sceptic in this way will win us little applause from those dogmatists who never doubt that people know for certain many of the things they claim to know.

Thus, our theory of knowledge is a theory of knowledge without certainty. We agree with the sceptic that if a man claims to know for certain, he does not know whereof he speaks. However, when we claim to know, we make no claim to certainty. We conjecture that to speak in this way is a departure from the most customary use of the word 'know'. Commonly, when men say they know, they mean they know for certain, and they assume there is no chance of being in error. This assumption enables them to lay aside theoretical doubts and to pretend they proceed on certain grounds. Such a pretence offers comfort and security in practical affairs and often in scientific investigation as well. None the less, it is a pretence exposed by the sceptic and repudiated by those who seek the truth. We, like the sceptic, deny that our beliefs have any guarantee of truth. We, like the sceptic, admit there to be a genuine chance that any of our beliefs may be false. We, like the sceptic, acknowledge that there is some chance, however small and remote, that the hypotheses are true which sceptics have conceived to call our dogmatic assumptions into doubt, and these cannot be ruled out by semantic shenanigans or appeal to the fiat of common sense. Our only reply to the sceptic is that even if there is some chance that any of our beliefs may be in error, and even if, therefore, we do not know for certain that any of them are true, still some of our beliefs have a better chance of being true than those with which they compete, including his hypotheses, and, if this is so, then there are things we know. This knowledge to which we lay claim is nothing certain or without risk of error. Nevertheless, if we are correct in what we believe in these matters, then we may know what we think we do despite the risk of error we confront.

The Merits of Scepticism

Before celebrating victory over the sceptic, however, it should be carefully noted that the agnoiology of some sceptics is closer to the truth than the epistemology of many dogmatists. We offer no proof that the sceptic is wrong. A sceptic, reflecting on the harrowing vicissitudes of human conception, may come to believe within his corrected doxastic system that one belief has as good a chance of being true as another, or, more moderately, that any belief has at least one equal competitor, that is, one whose chance for truth is no worse than the belief in question. Such a sceptic will not be completely justified in anything he believes, and therefore on our theory will not know that any statement is true. Even if he is incorrect in denying *we* have knowledge, he will be correct in denying this in his own case. He will know as little as he says he does. Finally, there remains the chance, that the corrected doxastic system of the sceptic may be verific, that is, the beliefs of that system may be true. If they are true, the beliefs in our corrected doxastic systems, which completely justify us in believing various statements, may be erroneous. Consequently, in the verific alternatives of our corrected doxastic systems, we would not be completely justified in believing any statements to be true. In that case, the sceptic would be right.

Thus, on our theory of knowledge, whether we or the sceptic win the day depends entirely on whether our beliefs are correct about the comparative chances of truth among statements. Here we may reach a basic subjective difference between men in search for the truth. We can not refute the sceptic by appeal to *a priori* demonstration. We argue against him from our system of belief which is precisely what he brings into question. We may know that he is wrong. Assuming that our complete justification for some of the things we believe is sustained within the verific alternative of our corrected doxastic system, we know those things to be true, and, indeed, we know that we know. If we do know that we know, then, of course, we know that the sceptic is mistaken in denying we know.

We avoid scepticism by constructing a theory of justification without a guarantee of truth. On our theory, if men know anything at all, this is because veracious men in quest for truth come to hold correct beliefs about their world and about the chances their beliefs have of being true. In this quest, we may become confident of some modest success and communicate our confidence to others by affirming that we know. We may then proceed to justify that claim to other veracious inquirers. We thus elicit their rejoinders and sometimes change our own beliefs as a result. By so doing, we hope to correct our beliefs and come to know our world. It is the purpose of our theory of knowledge and justification to explicate the uncertain epistemic adventure of man. One necessary step in this explication has been to repudiate the dogmatic prejudice of the vulgar that we often proceed without any chance of error. Our epistemology closely approaches the agnoiology of scepticism. We affirm that there is no security against failure or guarantee of success in our search for truth.

Materialism and Belief: The Identity Theory

We have one final and most speculative issue with which to deal before we bring this treatise to a close. The mere negative doctrine of universal ignorance, though it has fascinated philosophers, has often been backed by fanciful inventions rather than plausible theories. There is, however, at least one theory of some credibility that may support scepticism. It is the doctrine of materialism. Most simply stated, this is the doctrine that all that exists are physical particles and energy levels in space–time.[4] Assuming that human beings are no more than this, the question arises as to whether there are any such things as mental states. More specifically for our purposes, if materialism is true, are there any such things as beliefs? If the answer to this question were negative, then materialism would yield scepticism as a consequence. It would imply that there are no beliefs, hence no doxastic systems, and, therefore, no knowledge.

There are many refinements of materialism. Moreover, some formulations of materialism are compatible with our epistemology. For example, one familiar formulation maintains that, although everything is physical, mental states, such as believing, are identical to physical states.[5] As a result of being identical to physical states, beliefs attain materialistic respectability and ontological acceptability. If such a thesis is tenable, then materialism creates no problem for our theories of knowledge and justification. It is by no means obvious, however, that we may sustain such a moderate materialism, and, therefore, if we are to become materialists, our epistemology may be threatened.

How are we to interpret the claim that mental states are identical to physical states? According to one form of moderate materialism, this identity is an identity of properties.[6] Believing that there is a table before me is a property ascribed to a person,

---

[4] See J. J. C. Smart's 'Sensations and Brain Processes' and 'Man as a Physical Mechanism' in *Modern Materialism: Readings on Mind-Body Identity*, ed. John O'Connor (Harcourt, Brace and World, New York, 1969), 32–47 and 48–71, respectively.

[5] See the articles by Smart mentioned in the previous footnote, as well as the following articles which are also in the O'Connor volume: Paul Feyerband, 'Materialism and the Mind–Body Problem', 82–98; Norman Malcolm, 'Scientific Materialism and the Identity Theory', 72–81; Thomas Nagel, 'Physicalism', 99–116; and U. T. Place, 'Is Consciousness a Brain Process?', 21–31.

[6] Richard Brandt and Jaegwon Kim advance this thesis in 'The Logic of the Identity Theory' in the O'Connor volume, 212–37, as does David Armstrong in *A Materialist Theory of the Mind* (Routledge and Kegan Paul, London, 1968). Also see Herbert Feigl's 'The "Mental" and the "Physical"', in *Minnesota Studies in the Philosophy of Science*, vol. ii, ed. Herbert Feigl, Grover Maxwell, and Michael Scriven (University of Minnesota Press, Minneapolis, Minn., 1958), pp. 370–497, and James Cornman's *Materialism and Sensations* (Yale University Press, New Haven, Conn., 1971), particularly 265–81.

and, this property, given the identity thesis, is identical to some physical property. Two questions are immediately evoked. First, how are we to decide whether or not a predicate describes a property? Second, how are we to decide whether or not two predicates describe the same property? These questions are tightly connected. We cannot suppose that every predicate describes a property. Consider the predicate 'is a property that is not a property of itself'. If that predicate describes a property, it is property of itself if and only if it is not a property of itself. That predicate does not describe a property. We lack any simple criterion for determining whether or not a predicate describes a property.

The problem of deciding when two predicates describe the same property is not simple either. First, it is said that predicates having the same extension need not describe the same property, for example, 'is an angel' and 'is a devil' do describe the same property though, presumably, both have the same null extension. Second, it is said that two predicates may describe the same property even though they do not have the same meaning or intension, for example, 'is male' and 'is the sex of the child of my parents' have a different intension but, so it is claimed, describe the same property. How are we to tell whether or not this claim is correct?

Such unanswered questions do not constitute a refutation. However, though coextension of two predicates is not a sufficient condition for concluding that the predicates describe the same property, it is a necessary condition. Is there reason to suppose that a predicate like 'believes that he is seeing a yellow dragon' is coextensive with any predicate drawn from physical science describing particles and energy levels in space-time? Clearly not. Scientific language, as Körner and Ziff have argued, is exact in a way that ordinary speech is not, and, consequently, predicates from these two areas of discourse turn out not to be coextensive.[7] We have tried to render the concept of belief rather more precise than it is in ordinary use, but there is little reason to imagine that even this improved use of the term is coextensive with any expression drawn from mathematical physics, or, for that matter, neurophysiology. The tenacious

---

[7] Stephan Körner in *Experience and Theory*, Parts II and III, and Paul Ziff in 'The Simplicity of Other Minds' in *New Readings*, 418–24.

conviction that scientific language and ordinary language must always fit together extensionally rests on a misunderstanding of scientific innovation and conceptual change. It is one purpose of scientific theory and language to describe the world in a fundamentally different way that supplants our previous ways of describing the world. If there was exact coincidence of extension, the antecedently used predicates would suffice, and nothing would be gained by the change.

The way in which different schemes may be used to describe the same phenomena may be illustrated at the common-sense level. Suppose that we have two cultures of people who divide up the colour spectrum differently in terms of basic colour-predicates as indicated in the diagram.

In this diagram the lines represent the visible colour spectrum. The predicates P_1–P_5 of society A are atomic and apply to things in the marked area of the spectrum while predicates Q_1–Q_6 of society B are atomic and apply in the same way. No P_i is extensionally equivalent to any Q_i.

No atomic colour-predicate of one society has the same extension as any colour-predicate, atomic or compound, of the other society. If two sets of colour terms may fail to yield coextensional predicates, what reason is there to think that two sets of terms as different as those with which we describe our beliefs and those with which we describe particles and energy levels in space-time must yield coextensional predicates? There is no reason. The proposal is only barely intelligible and not at all plausible.

We conclude that a moderate materialism affirming that belief is identical to something described within the language of physical science has very little to recommend it. Even so, we cannot yet rule out moderate materialism. Moderate materialism may be formulated so that the thesis of identity is not one of the identity properties. One may argue that my believing that I see a yellow dragon is a concrete event that is identical to a concrete event that could be described in the language of physical or neurophysiological science. To sustain this thesis without falling back on the identity of properties, we require a criterion of identity. The most natural proposal is to say that an event $e1$ is identical to $e2$ if and only if every predicate that truly applies to $e1$ also truly applies to $e2$ and vice versa. However, this proposal is problematic. Suppose that you know the event of my believing to see a yellow dragon has occurred, but you do not know of any neurophysiological event that has occurred. You might be very ignorant of neurophysiology. In that case, the predicate 'known by you to have occurred' applies to my believing but not to any neurophysiological event. It would be preposterous, of course, to conclude from this that the event of my believing is not identical to any neurophysiological event. To avoid this consequence the criterion of identity must be restricted in terms of the class of predicates which must truly apply to identical events.

It would be unacceptable in this context, however, to exclude predicates describing what a person believes or knows as irrelevant to the identity of events, even though they are precisely the predicates that make the criterion ineffective. The reason we cannot exclude those predicates is that we are concerned here with the identity of believing and knowing, and such predicates are an essential part of the description of such events. We have argued that belief is iterative. Hence, if I believe I see a yellow dragon, I must also believe that I believe it. The iterated application of the predicate truly applies and is an essential part of the description of my believing. To speak of corrected doxastic systems, if that predicate did not truly apply to the event of my believing in some doxastic system, then the event of my believing could not exist in that system, for, in any doxastic system, to believe is to believe that one believes. Hence, the criterion for the identity of events cited above is beyond repair for the purposes of the present discussion.

Fortunately, there is another proposal. Davidson has proposed that an event $e1$ is identical to $e2$ if and only if every event that causes $e1$ causes $e2$ and vice versa and every event that $e1$ causes is caused by $e2$ and vice versa.[8] This amounts to the criterion that no two distinct events stand in the same causal relationship to all other events. The concept of causality raises

[8] Donald Davidson, 'The Individuation of Events', in *Essays in Honor of Carl G. Hempel*, ed. Nicholas Rescher (D. Reidel, Dordrecht-Holland, 1970), 216–34.

problems. In view of the difficulties we have uncovered in the consideration of other criteria, however, Davidson's proposal is relatively unproblematic. We find no compelling argument against the identity thesis articulated in the present manner.

Extreme Materialism

The identity theory as thus articulated is not yet a statement of materialism. From the identity thesis, one could go on to aver that all events are really physical; but one could just as well affirm that they are mental, or that they are neutral, that is, neither physical nor mental. Materialism adds another thesis, to wit, that the events described in ordinary parlance as belief and knowledge are really physical events. This additional thesis amounts to assigning ontological priority to the physical descriptions of science. If we so favour this way of describing the world, we commit ourselves to repudiating other descriptions as failing to tell us what there really is in the world. We might concede the utility of ordinary discourse for practical affairs but must deny the ontological veracity of such talk. When we describe a man as believing or knowing, our speech is ontologically antiquated. There really is no such thing as believing or knowing. When we describe the world in such terms, we are inaccurately describing what is correctly described in the terms of physical science.

Moderate materialists reject this extreme materialism. They wish to claim both forms of description are correct. They argue that since the language of epistemology and the language oι physical science describe the same events, therefore, both are correct. But the consequence does not follow. That an event may be described in two different ways does not imply that both descriptions are correct. Events once described as demonic possession might later be described as hysteria and may subsequently be described in neurophysiological terms. Describing events as demonic possession was incorrect. There really is no such thing as demonic possession. We reject such description as inaccurate in favour of scientific discourse. To say that all events are really physical commits one to a physicalistic description of the world. It would be incoherent to maintain also that non-physicalistic ways of describing the world are also correct.

For if non-physicalistic ways of describing the world are also correct then some events are non-physical. Unless one is willing to accept physicalistic description as the ultimate ontological word, one is not entitled to the claim that all events are really physical.

The Scientific Rejection of Materialism

If we are to favour physicalistic description of the universe, we must become extreme materialists and boldly repudiate the ontological claims of other descriptive modes.[9] Is there any reason for favouring such description? The most usual reason is that such language is scientific, and, science being the guide to truth, the language of the best of science tells us what there really is. Though we accept this scientific prescription for ontological veracity, the conclusion of extreme materialism is not sustained by it. Philosophers tend to focus all attention on physical science, but this is a myopic view. It comes from thinking of physics as *the* science. There are others. For example, in the social sciences, some of the best explanatory theories employ the language of decision theory. That is why we have adapted such methods in our epistemology. Decision-theoretic language contains expressions describing values and subjective probabilities. It is not physicalistic. Moreover, there is no reason to suppose that this branch of what is currently the best of science is about to be supplanted by or reduced to the science of neurophysiology or any other physical science. Thus, endorsing the scientific outlook, and enthusiastically following the dictum that what the best of science tells us is what it is most reasonable to believe, we reject materialism. The language of the best of science is not thoroughly materialistic.

Metaphysical Speculations

Having subscribed to the language of the best of science as dictating ontology, we shall, in conclusion, consider what we would say if some thoroughly physicalistic science were to emerge as the best for the purpose of describing, predicting, and

---

[9] Richard Rorty defends such materialism in 'Mind–Body Identity, Privacy, and Categories' in the O'Connor volume, 145–74.

explaining all aspects of our universe. At the moment, there is no such monophysicalistic theory of science. What if there were? In that case we would maintain that all events are physical and deny that there really are states of belief or knowledge. Our justification is simple enough. For a veracious man, the methods and conclusions of science are the ones to adopt. This is fundamentally a subjective commitment. Here the author must speak in the first person to speak most clearly.

I believe that scientific theories and descriptions that are simple, precise, comprehensive, coherent, and predictively fecund have a better chance of being true than those that are prescientific and lack these virtues. This statement is simply an articulation of my own corrected doxastic system. It is nothing that I could prove or argue for without appeal to that very system. Hence, I admit, indeed, I insist, that this confidence in science as the best fact eater of them all, is subjective and personal. If some equally veracious man believes that theological theory and description is best in the quest for truth, and that is an equally fundamental commitment of his, I shall not pretend to lift a premiss against him. Here we arrrive, not at rock bottom, but at the bottom rock of subjectivity on which all else rests.

There are at least two objections to this subjectivism. The first says that science, unlike theology, has empirical evidence to back it. This begs the subjective question. What we are completely justified in believing we see before us, what counts as empirical evidence for us, depends on what we believe as veracious men. My theological counterpart may, believing in demons and spirits, believe that he sees that the man before him is demonically possessed. He may believe that this perceptual claim has a better chance of being true than those with which it competes. He would be completely justified in believing that he sees what he believes he does. Of course, I believe that he is mistaken, and if my corrected doxastic system is closer to the truth than his, then his justification will be defeated and mine sustained in our verific alternatives. I am convinced I know that he is mistaken, but my conviction rests entirely on the bottom rock of the subjectivity of my corrected doxastic system.

The second objection is based on intersubjective agreement rather than an appeal to empirical evidence. Again, the precept to believe what most reasonable men believe, if it is relevant at all, rests on the belief in a corrected doxastic system that what most men believe has a better chance of being true than that with which it competes. Here I demur. In fact, I do not believe that accepted opinion is so likely to be correct or that agreement gives us so good a guide to truth. If you believe what others do, you will be thought a wise man by those with whom you agree, and that will provide you with some gratification. But there is historical precedent to suggest that by fitting your opinion to those of others in this way, you will forego the benefits of innovative and creative quests for truth. Indeed, if one were to formulate a precept for innovation and creativity, it might be: question what all reasonable men accept. The rejection of some sacrosanct assumption of the day is the touchstone of progress. Until one learns to reject the opinions of one's peers, including the most respectable among them, one lacks the spark of intellectual iconoclasm.

Now we must meet the most fundamental issue materialism thrusts before us. If materialism were to lead us to the conclusion that all is physical and that there really is no such thing as belief and knowledge, we would be led by our beliefs to the conclusion that there is no such thing as belief. It would be a consequence of our corrected doxastic system that there are no doxastic systems. Of course, we would expect there to be something in the physical world, in our bodies, that was in some ways like what we now describe as believing and knowing. There is comfort in that reflection. At the moment, however, we have no consistent way of saying what we would believe if we embraced extreme materialism. Were I such a materialist, which I happily am not, I would mimic what Wittgenstein once said about what he said. Once you have understood what I have said, you can use it to climb to the metaphysical rung on which I stand. What I say is strictly speaking nonsense.[10] Science being what it is, we may hope for a better way of saying it. In the meantime, whereof one cannot speak, thereof one can do metaphysics.

[10] Ludwig Wittgenstein, *Tractus Logico-Philosophicus*, trans. D. F. Pears and B. F. McGuinness (Routledge and Kegan Paul, London, 1961), 151.

Index

Ackerman, Terence, viii
Agnoiology, 236, 241. *See also* Scepticism
Analysis, of knowledge, 3ff.; of the meaning of words, 4–5; philosophical a. and meaning contrasted, 5–7; of complete justification, 162–5, 197–8; of explanation, 167–8; of not depending on falsity, 224
Analytically reductive theories, and non-basic beliefs, 126–31; phenomenalism characteristic of, 127–129; support of foundation theory, 128–31; lead to incoherence, 131
Analyticity, 81
Annis, David, 69, 70, 71
Anscombe, G. E. M., 109n
A priori, principles of justification, 198–200, 227–8
Aristotle, 15n, 155
Armstrong, D. M., 54, 73, 91, 92, 242n
Austin, J. L., 52, 53, 54, 55
Ayer, A. J., 5n, 12n, 13n, 18n, 79n, 127n

Basic beliefs, conditions of, 76; self-justified and irrefutable, 76ff.; foundation of justification, 77; and empiricism, 77; and sense experience, 77; and rationalism, 77–8; guarantee truth, 78ff.; as incorrigible, 80ff.; and independent information, 101ff.; corrigible, 101ff.; and right of ancient possession, 102; frequently perceptual, 103ff.; epistemic principles as, 122; probability statements and, 138, 140, 143; and probability of one, 150–1; unavoidability of, 155–7. *See also* Belief; Perceptual belief; Justification
Belief, as a condition of knowledge, 12–13, 49–74; and conviction, 63–74; basic and self-justified, 76ff.; incorrigible, 80ff.; corrigible, 101ff.; perceptual, 101ff.; innocent until proven guilty, 104–5; any contingent b. needs independent information, 107; and semantic information, 110–11; may be both explained and explanatory, 161–2; explanatory systems of, 163; no exit from circle of, 188; and complete justification, 188ff.; doxastic systems of, 189ff.; any b. may be false, 237ff.; and scientific terms, 243. *See also* Perceptual belief; Justification
Blanshard, Brand, 157n
Borderline cases, 61–3; and inexact terms, 62; of knowledge, 61–72. *See also* Inexact terms
Brandt, Richard, 242n
Butchvarov, Panayot, 79
Butler, Ronald, 39n, 167n

Carnap, Rudolf, 24n, 30n, 136n 145, 151n, 194
Cartwright, Richard, 39, 98
Causal theory, of justification, 122–126, 211–12
Chisholm, R. M., vii, 13n, 18n, 20n, 53, 79n, 103n, 108, 109, 110, 112, 127n, 174, 188, 198, 199, 218, 219n, 228, 229n, 230
Church, Alonzo, 30n
Circularity argument, 15–16, 155–7
Coder, David, 19n